Missions USA

Missions USA

by

Earl Parvin

MOODY PRESS

Chicago

© 1985 by
THE MOODY BIBLE INSTITUTE
OF CHICAGO

Parvin, Earl, 1930-
  Missions U.S.A.

  Bibliography: p.
  Includes index.
  1. Missions—United States.   2. Missions, Home.
I. Title.   II. Title: Missions USA.
BV2765.P37 1984   266'.022'0973   84-20643
ISBN 0-8024-5975-7

    1 2 3 4 5 6 7 Printing/RR/Year 90 89 88 87 86 85

         Printed in the United States of America

Contents

Preface

This study presents the thesis that, contrary to popular opinion, within the United States are people groups beyond the sound of the gospel. The United States is therefore a bona fide mission field that will only be evangelized with the help of mission organizations. The study provides a rationale for considering these Americans as a mission field, a history of missions in the fifty states, an analysis of forty-five unchurched people groups, and the results of a survey of mission boards ministering to these peoples.

America is a mission field even though 20 percent of its populace are evangelicals. This is a fact because the evangelicals are not distributed among the unchurched people groups. Although the gospel is presented twenty-four hours daily via mass media, it is not meaningful to the great majority of peoples in our pluralistic society.

The study reveals that some people groups are totally unevangelized, such as 27 million cultists, 3 million Muslims, or 2.4 million Hindus. Others essentially bypassed by the gospel are 35 million handicapped (80 percent), 10 million alcoholics (90 percent), 6 million Jews (95.5 percent), 4 million inmates (98 percent), 1.4 million native Americans (95 percent), 2.5 million French-speakers, and emigres in varying numbers from every nation in the world (95 percent).

American Christians are unaware that 26 million black Americans are only 30 percent evangelized, whereas black Africans are 50 percent evangelized. Nor do they know that while Christianity explodes in Latin America, 27 million Hispanics here are virtually untouched by the gospel. Or that nearly a million American Chinese remain almost as pagan as those living in China.

Although 60 percent of Americans claim church membership, in Alaska the percentage is 10 percent and in Hawaii it is 30 percent. America remains one of the larger mission fields with 181 million persons needing the gospel.

The home missionary movement is a relatively recent but growing phenomenon. Since 1930 more than two dozen missions have been established each decade. During the 1970s three missions per year were founded.

The analysis of the different people groups is divided into eighteen chapters. In each, evidence is marshaled to show that the group is essentially unchurched. Statistics are presented to indicate the relative size of the missionary opportunity. Historical background is given to help determine why the group is gospel-neglected or gospel-resistant.

The religious heritage of the people group is traced and their exposure to Christianity is noted. A list of mission organizations that service the group is appended for ready reference.

A list of 380 mission organizations ministering in the United States was compiled, and the first survey of home missions was conducted. Two mailings yielded a 60-percent return and provided the information given in Appendix 4, which includes the address, year of founding, field of ministry and number of missionaries. Included are forty-four foreign mission boards that have missionaries serving in the United States. This is the only list of home missions available.

The reporting missions in the survey revealed that 12,000 missionaries serve under 228 mission boards. The total number of missionaries could be 20,000 if all mission personnel were included. This figure does not include 1,000 staff serving with 250 missions listed in the International Union of Gospel Missions Directory, nor does it include 4,000 staff members listed in the Directory of Christian Camping International. Finally, the survey does not include denominational missions such as 2,800 missionaries serving under the Home Mission Board of the Southern Baptist Convention.

We conclude that this study substantiates the thesis that not only is America a mission field, but also a growing mission field. Peoples from most of the mission fields of the world are coming to the United States in unprecedented numbers and remain nearly as unevangelized here as they were in their native country. Also, Dr.

David Barratt suggests in his book *World Christian Encyclopedia* that Protestantism is shrinking from a two-third's proportion of the populace in 1900 to a projected one-third of the whole by the end of the century.

Part 1

Introductory Matters

Introduction

A biblical precedent for home missions can be found in the account recorded in John 4, where Jesus began to evangelize Samaria. He and His disciples were returning to Galilee, north of Judea. Between those two provinces of Palestine were couched the Samaritans, who for historic reasons had been refused the gospel.

They had intermarried with non-Jews;[1] therefore, they were deemed unworthy of the promises of Israel, and the Jews would have nothing to do with them (John 4:9). In the language of the missiologist, they became a "Hidden People"[2]—hidden from the truth and in need of evangelization. To the north and south were those who could have reached them with the truth—but who refused to do so. Jesus, aware of their need and the malignant neglect of His disciples to break from the traditional refusal of the Jewish people to "see the spiritual plight of the Samaritans in their midst," decided to set a good example. He and His disciples went to Samaria, where He evangelized the Samaritan woman who in turn brought her village to hear also (John 4:29-30).

Why is this home missions and not just evangelism? Although

1. James Orr, ed., *International Standard Bible Encyclopedia*, 5 vols. (Grand Rapids: Eerdmans, 1939), 4:2673-74.
2. C. Peter Wagner and Ed R. Dayton, ed., *Unreached Peoples '81* (Elgin, Ill.: David C. Cook, 1981), p. 26. "Hidden people" means no gospel witness, according to Ralph Winter.

there was a witness in Judea and Galilee, Samaria was geographically removed from both testimonies. There was no reasonable way either would be able to carry out an effective witness in their midst. It would clearly call for a special ministry. Therefore, Jesus ordered it to be done in each of the gospel accounts: Matthew 28:19; Mark 16:15; Luke 24:47-48; John 20:21. Finally, in Acts 1:8 it was spelled out geographically: Jerusalem, Judea, and SAMARIA.

There are numerous "Samaritans" in the United States—those who, for whatever reason in the midst of Christian America, have been virtually unreached by the gospel witness of the churches.[3] It is those "Samaritans" that this study primarily addresses.

3. Ibid. "Unreached" means fewer than 20 percent Christians.

1

America as a Mission Field?

The title of this chapter suggests that America is a mission field. It will be our purpose to marshal evidence to substantiate that thesis. It is feared that for the average Christian the idea will raise questions generating either a mild wonderment about its veracity, or a much more reactionary disbelief. After all, is not this Christian America with churches on every corner and the mass media exposing everyone to the message of salvation? Certainly a country that is providing the lion's share of foreign missionaries and funding the same would not itself be considered a mission field.

Perhaps it will be wise to consider the seeming success story of American Christianity that has in part blinded eyes to areas where evangelistic programs have been less than successful. Another problem is the disturbing misconception, widespread among Christians, that all Americans could hear the gospel if they wanted to do so, or the equally false idea that no one should hear twice before all have heard once. It is a most disquieting fact that many citizens will live and die in Christian America having been insulated from hearing the gospel, sometimes within eyesight of the church or even after having lived next door to a born-again believer.

Who are those who have escaped the orchestrated program of evangelism of the church? How have they been neglected? The larger answer to the first question will be the subject of the ensuing chapters. In pursuance of the latter question it will be necessary to note the programs whereby the church seeks to minister to the spiritual needs of the community. It should become obvious that segments of the community are not being reached.

Part of the answer lies in the definition of missions as perceived by the church. Is not everyone a missionary? Are not all programs that reach out to evangelize the community missions? Is it the church's responsibility to evangelize all segments of the community? Perhaps it will be necessary to help the Christian develop a larger vision of his responsibility to reach all segments of the society. Programs have been designed to meet some needs, but there are untargeted and unchurched in most communities.

America is a mission field for numerous reasons, not the least being that the United States is an integral part of the "world" mentioned in John 3:16. There is little question in anyone's mind that the field is "the world" (Matthew 26:13; Mark 16:15) or that foreign service is in fact missions. But there is confusion, if not outright denial, that any service rendered in America should be known as other than evangelism and certainly not as missions. Finally, we shall seek to establish clearly that home missions and foreign missions are integral parts of a world mission field. We shall view the mission world as God sees it—as saved or lost wherever they are geographically. The United States is a very needy part of the mission world, even if it may seem to be virtually Christianized.

SPREAD OF CHRISTIANITY

The transplanting of Christianity into the New World began with the Pilgrim fathers and continues to the present as a fascinating success story. Some might compare that growth with the triumph of those nameless saints of the second- and third-century Roman world who were accused by Pliny of emptying the pagan temples[1] or with vigorous Korean Christianity, which was introduced by missionaries and carried so successfully by national Christians over the countryside. Here, too, great numbers of Americans who have become Christians have been the direct result of intense lay activity.

From the very beginning churches were established as a desired result of continuing evangelism. In 1609 the Anglican church was established in Virginia (with compulsory church attendance), and was followed by the Baptists, Lutherans, Presbyterians, and finally the

---

1. "Pliny's Letter to Trajan," as cited by Earl E. Cairns, in *Christianity Through the Centuries,* 4th ed. (Grand Rapids: Zondervan, 1961), p. 99.

Methodist church. As the people moved west they built new churches and taught their children to fear God.

Church growth was relatively steady, but at points in history it was exceptional. In the mid-1700s there was a great awakening when the preaching of Jonathan Edwards, Gilbert Tennent, and George Whitefield especially stirred the people. Again, a century later, a great revival began under the influence of such men as Charles Finney. Tens of thousands turned to Christ.[2] Today 343,000 churches minister to a religious community of 130,000,000 or 60 percent of all Americans. It is certainly amazing that one in three citizens insists that he is born again. In the midst of all this is said to be a colossal boom of fundamentalist religion so that the growing evangelical community may be one of the most important forces in American society.[3] In the words of Quebedeaux, "The evangelicals . . . once a despised minority, are rapidly becoming the respectable (or chic) religious majority, the new religious establishment in America."[4] This is happening because of intense evangelistic activity.

EFFECTIVE EVANGELISTIC PROGRAMS

The church is aware that it must go out into the community to compel the lost to listen to the evangel. Evangelistic preaching in the church is of little avail if the lost are not there to hear it. Therefore, the church has its visitation night when all are invited to join in this corporate venture. Furthermore, Sunday school teachers are encouraged to visit their students and make new contacts. Youth leaders urge those who attend to invite their friends. Bus visitation captains are zealous in their campaigning. Annual evangelistic meetings are another opportunity for intense community action. Churches sponsor the pastor on the radio or television as a direct appeal to the public. Other opportunities abound such as radio or television evangelism. Radio Bible teaching is very popular, but the "electronic" church is being viewed with mixed emotions.[5] The city-wide campaign by a renowned evangelist is a popular evangelistic option.

2. William W. Sweet, *The Story of Religion in America* (New York: Harper & Row, 1950), p. 284.
3. Jeremy Rifkin and Ted Howard, *The Emerging Order* (New York: G. P. Putnam, 1979), p. 100.
4. Richard Quebedeaux, *The Worldly Evangelicals* (New York: Harper & Row, 1980), p. 168.
5. George Gallup, Jr., and David Poling, *The Search for America's Faith* (Nashville: Abingdon, 1980), pp. 116-24.

Literature blitzing is another possibility. Concerned churches have used numerous available methods to reach every soul possible. They have blitzed the country so intensely that the Christian community has burgeoned. There has been such success that Jeremy Rifkin and Ted Howard have dubbed this evangelical community a "Second America."[6] Evangelicals own and operate 1,400 radio stations or one in every six in the United States. Six hundred offer only "gospel radio." It is suggested that through this medium alone potentially three-fourths of the population can be included in the listening audience.[7]

It is further suggested that programming of Christian-owned and operated television stations can potentially include 20 percent of the viewing public, and a new station is being added each month. At least two Christian TV networks using earth satellite stations beam live programs twenty-four hours daily. A fourth Christian news network—CBN (Christian Broadcasting Network)—has been established.[8] All in all, Americans are exposed to nearly 2,000,000 religious programs annually, aired over some 7,000 radio and TV stations. In 1983 Arbitron research estimated that Robert Schuller's "Hour of Power" telecast commanded first place with an audience of 2,667,000; Jimmy Swaggert was second with 2,653,000; Oral Roberts was third with 2.4 million; Rex Humbard's program was fourth with 1.8 million, and 1.4 million watched Jerry Falwell. Combined they tallied perhaps 4 percent of the population.

Evangelical Americans, numbering 45,000,000, purchase nearly one-third of the religious books on the market, which runs to 2,000 new titles annually.[9] Evangelicals send 2,000,000 students to 7,000 Christian elementary and high schools and are opening three new schools daily.[10] What a success story! Pollster John Crathers Pollock suggests that three-fourths of Americans are "susceptible to a call of faith."[11] But let us not be deceived into thinking that every American can hear the gospel, even if he wanted to do so. It is a larger task and far more complicated than the preceding glowing report may indicate.

In reality, Americans are in deep trouble emotionally, socially,

6. Rifkin and Howard, p. 101.
7. "Religious Radio Stations Combine to Get More Advertising," *Evangelical Newsletter*, May 1981, p. 1.
8. William Martin, "Video Evangelism," *Washington Post*, June 1978, p. 4.
9. Rifkin and Howard, p. 112.
10. *Evangelical Newsletter*, March 1981, n.p.
11. Ibid., April 1981, n.p.

and religiously. Emotional instability is revealed by alcoholism, which dominates the lives of 13 percent of the populace. Incapacitating phobias afflict another 12 percent and depressions another 6 percent. How do we explain a national suicide rate of 11.4 per 100,000, which disguises the fact that ten states, including Nevada, which is perennially the highest (17.6), have rates far higher. Also, certain groups, such as persons over 65 and the Eskimo have rates that are respectively three and ten times the national average.

Social problems are in epidemic proportions. A 50-percent divorce rate does not spring from a deeply religious society. ABC-TV reported that 1.2 million divorces were granted in 1981. Some two-thirds will remarry into a society that readily accepts serial monogamy as an acceptable way of life. The other third will swell the ranks of the singles industry, many as single parents, now an alternate lifestyle, even though it may well produce overwhelming problems. The instability of the American home often leads to child abuse, and that to runaways. Some one million children run away each year (1984). According to Dotson Rader of *Parade* magazine, the average age of today's runaway is 15 and most turn to prostitution and theft for survival. Then, there are the homosexuals who so frequently contract AIDS (acquired immune deficiency syndrome), an incurable disease. Each of these emotional and social problems tend to produce pockets of Americans who are essentially beyond the sound of the gospel.

A DISTURBING MISCONCEPTION

There is a disturbing misconception within the evangelical community that with all of the evangelistic activity going on 90 million unchurched Americans can be reached by means of the programs already in place. The message is pouring forth; therefore, all that need be done is somehow to inspire the unchurched to listen and act. Missionaries are not needed. Christians can evangelize all Americans.

Even foreign missionaries, zealous for those overseas who have never heard, jealously speak of a "gospel-saturated American society," and solemnly declare that "no one should hear twice before all have been able to hear once." That is a grand, emotionally charged missionary appeal, but it has no biblical basis. In fact, many Christians did not accept Christ on their first hearing of the gospel. There are also those who are concerned about the 264 English translations of the Bible[12] when 70 percent of the world's nearly 6,000 languages do not have one word translated into Scripture.[13] The implication is clear: America is overevangelized. This is an oversimplification and clearly misses the point. Every evangelistic effort should be cause for rejoicing because there are still those who have not heard. However, in calling for more attention to evangelism overseas, that case should stand on its own merits without drawing the misleading comparison that everyone in the States has or could hear the gospel.

The fact is that America is not nearly as evangelized as it may at first appear. Consider for a moment the 130 million citizens attending 343,000 churches.[14]

1. 70 million are Protestant, attending 300,000 churches
2. 49.7 million are Catholic, attending 23,500 churches
3. 6 million are Jews, attending 5,000 synagogues
4. 2.8 million are Mormons, attending 6,900 churches
5. 1 million are Orthodox, attending 1,600 churches
6. 500,000 are Jehovah's Witnesses, attending 6,000 churches

It may be that 60 percent of Americans are religious, but notice that all but the 70 million Protestants (32 percent of the populace) are a mission field of 60 million. If that 28 percent is added to the unchurched 40 percent, then 68 percent of Americans are a mission field.

That is assuming, of course, that all Protestants are saved, which few would accept. Even George Gallup indicates that the evangelical community includes only 45 million, or 20 percent of all Americans. He also notes that only 68 percent attend church regularly; therefore active evangelicals number only 35 million, or 15 percent of the populace. That would seem to indicate the mission field has now mushroomed to 85 percent, or 191,000,000 souls.

Finally, a closer look at the 70,000,000 Protestants reveals that they can be subdivided into the following associations of churches:

1. 42 million; National Council of Churches
2. 13 million; Southern Baptist Convention

12. Pat Aherne, "Priority of Christian Investment," *Brown Gold*, March 1981, p. 3.
13. Portions of the Bible have been translated into 1,739 languages. These represent languages spoken by 97 percent of the world's population. (Figures from the American Bible Society.) Leo Rosten, ed., *Religions of America* (New York: Simon and Schuster, 1975), p. 348.
14. Ibid., pp. 437-44.

3. 3 million; National Association of Evangelicals
4. 2.5 million; American Council of Christian Churches
5. 120,000; Independent Fundamental Churches of America
6. 9.4 million; unaffiliated with an association

By means of the above information and depending on one's theological orientation, the extent of the need for evangelism within the American Protestant community can be determined. Gallup also indicates that over the last several years Protestant church attendance has held steady at 38 percent. This means that church attendance is nearly double the size of the evangelical community but far less than the 60 percent who claim church membership.

According to the *Yearbook of American and Canadian Churches* there are nearly 490,000 clergy in the United States. Of this number 271,000 are pastoring 343,000 churches.[15] Those figures mean that about 62,000 churches have only a part-time pastor, or none at all. Just how many preach the gospel is not indicated, of course, but each pastor of a church would have a parish of 807 persons if all of America's 235,000,000 people were evenly distributed. However, the average Protestant church has less than 150 in membership.

It may seem that the American church is alive and well, but when churchgoers were asked why they attended, nearly half responded that it was because they were brought up in the church. They have a "belief without a strong conviction,"[16] as demonstrated by the polls that indicate that less than 20 percent of churchgoing Americans read their Bible daily or pray more than three minutes a day. The ministers admitted praying but only eight minutes a day. The Southern Baptists report that less than 50 percent of their members give any money to the church.

The church it would seem is really not as prepared to reach the unevangelized as it may have appeared. Edward Dayton reports in *Unreached Peoples 84* that the churches in Europe and North America are losing 2,765,000 members per year to nominalism or unbelief, more than offsetting any evangelical church growth. Leighton Ford further comments that high on the agenda for the future must be the reevangelization of the West.

---

15. Constant H. Jacquet, Jr., ed., *Yearbook of American and Canadian Churches*, 47th issue (Nashville: Abingdon, 1979).
16. "Do Americans Believe in the Church?" *American Shriner* article, *Yearbook of American and Canadian Churches* (Nashville: Abingdon, 1979), p. 258.

A DISQUIETING FACT

The disquieting fact of the matter is that there are vast multitudes of Americans who will live and die in the United States
without ever once hearing the gospel. The task of evangelism may
not be mathematically impossible, for if everyone in the evangelical
community would win just five others (45 million × 5 = 220
million), America could conceivably be won to Christianity. But
unfortunately most Christians, unlike their ancestors, seem to have
delegated their personal responsibility in evangelism to the church
and its organized programs. The average American Christian has
never reproduced himself spiritually.

Beyond the fact of the vast numbers needing to be reached with
the gospel, there seems to be a great ignorance of the fact that
America is a pluralistic society. It never has been a melting pot where
all ethnic differences have been merged into a mythical "American,"
ostensibly reachable with a gospel presented by the dominant
society. American subcultures are nearly as isolated from the gospel
preached in English as they would be in their native countries.
Edward Dayton says that every country, including America, is filled
with people groups who share language and religious ethnicity or
class that causes them to perceive themselves as having an affinity
for one another. He suggests, for example, that Los Angeles is a city
with a vast mosaic of people groups. If this is true, then the church
needs to recognize that the several worlds of the unchurched are not
a homogeneous group.[17]

It is not difficult to find those gospel-neglected segments of
society. They are frequently well defined by language, culture, and
geography. There are the ethnics such as native Americans (Indians),
blacks, Hispanics, and Chinese to name a few. There are those in the
inner city, now called central city, from which the established
churches have fled. Multitudes of Jews, Catholics, Muslims, Buddhists, Hindus, and cults practice their religions here in America.
Millions are forgotten in institutional America, such as those in
prisons, hospitals, asylums, children's homes, rest homes, and the
military. In 1984 one hundred million identified with 200 language/
culture groups other than Anglo-American, such as the French-
speaking Cajuns of Louisiana, the New Englanders who live adjacent
to French Quebec, the Haitian immigrants, the Spanish, the blacks,
and recent emigres. The educational world of the high school,

17. J. Russell Hale, *The Unchurched* (New York: Harper & Row, 1980), pp. 186-87.

college, or graduate school campuses, including the international and exchange students, are other identifiable groups virtually beyond the message as proclaimed or the gospel outreach of the typical American church. Urban migration continues to endanger adequate gospel proclamation in rural and mountain communities. Hawaii may be a tourist paradise, but most of these Americans will never hear the gospel. Alaska is over 70 per cent unchurched.

God has given His church a far-reaching responsibility to preach the gospel to all peoples (Matthew 28:19). The church is seeking to reach the lost it knows about both at home and abroad. Denominationally structured churches have developed departments commissioned with the responsibility of surveying needy areas and developing evangelistic programs to reach them. Commendable efforts have been made, but the responsibility to evangelize America is too massive for anything less than total mobilization of the evangelical community. All churches and Christians must awaken to the cause of discovering the gospel-neglected of North America who are frequently to be found in the shadows of gospel-preaching churches. Programs must be developed to make the evangelical community aware of these needs. The evangelical church, which has been the inspiration of missionary activity overseas, became aware of the needs abroad through the preaching of concerned pastors, information provided by foreign mission boards, itinerating missionaries, and mission conferences.

But how is that same church to learn about needy souls, communities, and peoples here in the U.S.? The pastor does not know about them and is inclined to speak of missions as foreign. Home mission boards have been less active in supplying the information, perhaps because of inadequate funding. Home missionaries may not have been as zealous in declaring the need or they may not have been given as much opportunity to present the needs at home in the local church.

DISCOVERING THE TOTAL COMMUNITY

It is necessary to take note of the various programs whereby the church seeks to reach the community for Christ. It can be shown that the people of any community can be divided into various subdivisions, each with its own particular needs for evangelism. Each community will not have all the subdivisions possible, but most churches discover that there are people groups they had not realized they should be servicing.

It will be noted that some groups either do not or cannot attend. It should be asked if these groups are targeted by the visitation program, radio ministry, special evangelistic meetings, or bus ministry. Having charted each program, note which segments of the community receive minimal or no evangelistic thrust. What about them? How shall they hear? Does any church in the community have a program whereby the spiritual needs of those segments are to be met? If not, what responsibility does the church have with respect to those people? What organizations exist or should be developed to assist the church to reach all of the community?

There are parachurch organizations to assist the church in evangelism. Those organizations can be categorized into two kinds of ministry. One group of organizations sells or provides a service and is, therefore, financially self-sufficient. These parachurch services include publishers, evangelists, and Christian bookstores. Other ministries include radio and television pastors and Bible teachers, Bible conferences, Christian film producers, the Gideons, and Christian Businessmen's Committees.

The second group of parachurch organizations depends on the church for regular support. They are missionaries and mission organizations that oversee the ministry. They exist to assist the church in its total ministry, but especially in those areas where the internal programs of the church, its various outreach programs, and the self-sustaining parachurch organizations serving the church and Christian community have left definable groups of society virtually unserviced. Various mission organizations have emerged to assist the church and serve by-passed groups by means of highly specialized programs.

Some confusion exists concerning the priority to be given to the order of evangelism. Some suggest that evangelism must begin at home, for "if American Christians become so preoccupied with 'the regions beyond' that they continue to neglect the foundation at home, the entire missionary enterprise will collapse."[18] There are also those who feel that first priority must be given to those who have never heard. "People can hear the Gospel in the U.S.A. if they want to. The gospel is available. This is not true in other lands, especially among the tribal people .... There is no way for them to hear other than through cross-cultural means."[19]

18. Kenneth H. Good, "Shall We Destroy Foreign Missions?"(Elyria, Ohio: Fellowship of Baptists for Home Missions, n.d.), p. 18.
19. Letter from Macon G. Hare, Vice-Chairman, New Tribes Mission, 3 April 1981.

Balance must be maintained, however. As David Hesselgrave points out, Acts 1:8 indicates that both must take place simultaneously.[20]

It is to be noted that in recent years many citizens of the "mission" world have come to visit or reside in the United States. The newcomers have become one of the larger gospel-neglected segments of American society. The time has come for the church to realize that her mission includes more than her primary targeted peoples in her near community and her "foreign" interests. Peter Gunther suggests that those people in between are "completely ignored" and then calls them the "important gap, home missions."[21]

The church's responsibility is to provide the gospel for all segments of society. How can this best be done? It will first be necessary to determine what realistically can be accomplished through the people and programs within the church. Parachurch organizations can be engaged to assist her complete the work. Whatever the church can accomplish internally ought to be called evangelism, whereas what she commissions to be accomplished through external organizations should be called missions. Next, it is necessary to explain this rationale by determining who is a missionary among the workers of the church.

DEFINING THE TERM *MISSIONARY*

Although the Scriptures are clear that every believer has been "saved to serve" (1 Thessalonians 1:9) and gifted for that service (1 Corinthians 12), there seems to be considerable confusion about the implementation of that truth. First, the average Christian considers his service basically to involve church attendance, Bible reading, prayer, offerings of time and money, and an occasional kind act or word of testimony. It seldom dawns on him that he is to reproduce himself spiritually in the life of another. Over and over the Scriptures enjoin that a father is to teach his son and his neighbor about God (Deuteronomy 4:9-10; Psalm 145:4; Isaiah 38:19; Jeremiah 31:34). Second, wherein the Christian is involved in living out his Christianity, it is determined that he is involved in "missionary activity." "If we are Christians, we are missionaries."[22] The idea is enshrined in the saying "You are either a missionary or a mission field." Even

20. David J. Hesselgrave, *Planting Churches Cross-Culturally: A Guide for Home and Foreign Missions* (Grand Rapids: Baker, 1980), p. 94.
21. Peter Gunther, *The Fields at Home* (Chicago: Moody, 1963), p. 8.
22. *Northern Lights,* March-April 1981, p. 2.

pastors and missionaries fall into this verbal trap. Consider the following from a missionary who is a church planter in the Philippines:

> The Bible mentions nine churches in Asia. It seems that eight of these were started by persons other than Paul, persons who traveled to Ephesus, were saved and trained and went home with the message . . . EVERY BELIEVER A MISSIONARY. (emphasis added)[23]

If every Christian is a missionary, then what do we call the person gifted by God, commissioned, and sent out by the church as a missionary? We have by this technique effectively emasculated a perfectly good term that should designate a definite sphere of Christian service. It is necessary to distinguish between what is Christian service and normally expected of all believers and the distinctive kind of service we have traditionally labeled "missionary service."

The Scriptures indicate that for the Christian there is a "reasonable service" (Romans 12:1-18, KJV*) involving the use of one's body and mind in service in ways acceptable to God. It will include membership in a church ("one body" verse 4), where he will be exercising spiritual gifts (verse 6) and lovingly serving the Lord (verse 11) in a prayerful manner (verse 12) and peaceably (v. 18). These would seem to be minimal requirements of service for all believers. Every Christian is to be a witness, actively communicating his faith and talents as his reasonable service.

Beyond that, the Bible declares that the church is to be aware of those serving in the church who can be singled out for special service at the Lord's bidding. Note that some were set aside in the early church to serve tables (Acts 6:3) so that others could give themselves to the ministry of the Word and prayer (Acts 6:4). Then there were those who were "sent away" to other places (Acts 13:3), out of the midst of those serving in the church at Antioch (Acts 13:1). Those "sent away" ones are those defined in our day as missionaries.

A study of Acts 13—15 reveals certain characteristics about missionary service:

1. They were tested servants of the church whose spiritual gifts were obvious to the Christian community (13:1).

---

23. Roger Walwitz, field report entitled "Forward on the Philippine Field," published by Far Eastern Gospel Crusade.
   *King James Version.

2. The church under the influence of the Holy Spirit set them apart for special service, not in the home church (13:2).
3. They were commissioned (laid hands on) by the church (13:3).
4. They were sent out to make disciples (to preach the Word of God, 13:5).
5. They were reportable to the sending church (gathered the church and rehearsed all, 14:27).
6. They spent their furlough at that church (abode a long time with the disciples, 14:28).
7. They again ministered in their home church (teaching and preaching in the church, 15:35).
8. They helped the church see the spiritual needs of others (declared the conversion of the Gentiles, 15:3).
9. They were sent out again (recommended by the brethren, 15:40).

It should be obvious that not all Christians are missionaries. Missionaries are Christians who, because of service within the church, have risen to places of leadership in that body and have been commissioned and sent to areas of service where the church recognizes its responsibility to extend its ministry. The missionary is sent by that church to perform a service the local church could not offer through any of its other channels of ministry. He is usually sent through a parachurch organization called a "mission," which gives oversight to the particular service the organization renders for the church. Because of this relationship the mission is often called the "arm of the church."

It might be well to note that there are certain mission organizations whose sphere of service is primarily devoted to assisting the church minister more effectively by its in-house programs. Examples of such programs are Child Evangelism Fellowship and Awana. They provide expertise, materials, and trained personnel to inspire and train church members to more effectively function within the church.

Notice that the definition of missions says nothing about geographical or cultural difference. Distance is only part of the issue. Isolation from the gospel for whatever reason does not ipso facto determine a mission situation. The crucial factor that determines whether or not a particular group is a mission field signaling the need for parachurch assistance is a decision by the church that she cannot effectively evangelize that group by any other means. The making of that decision will involve the developing of a larger vision of the church's Christian responsibility within the total community.

DEVELOPING A LARGER VISION

Developing a larger vision of Christian responsibility is necessary because success in some areas of evangelism has blinded the church to the spiritual needs of other segments of society. Evangelistic programs do not target all peoples and as a result bypass some.

America is a mission field because the Christian community has not been disquieted by the fact that some within potential hearing will never be able to respond to a gospel that is not intelligible to them. Others will never hear because the church has not realized that her evangelistic outreach is woefully inadequate and is not reaching into areas where many are effectively shielded from the gospel. Finally, we suggest that America is a mission field because the church's definition of missions is inadequate. Because she does not see some of those whom she is not reaching as a mission field, they remain unevangelized while mission boards stand poised, ready to help reach them.

To aid the church in developing a larger vision of her Christian responsibility, the following eight propositions are offered.

1. The church must become aware of the spiritual needs of all segments of society. The immediate community must be surveyed to determine who is not being evangelized. The concerned church will enlarge the project to include information about the unreached in the larger community of the fifty states and possessions. Information from the total mission world will be necessary.

The information-gathering process is being greatly enhanced by the work of the Evangelical Missions Information Service.[24] It is now preparing an American PULSE that will share current information concerning the unreached in the United States. The editors of the *Evangelical Newsletter*[25] and *Fundamental News Service*[26] also include information important for home missions. In the ensuing chapters, many of the unreached segments of American society are singled out for deliberate consideration. These introductions will help the church become more aware of the spiritual needs of the many segments of

24. Evangelical Mission Information Service (EMIS) publishes *Missionary News Service* on the first and fifteenth of the month, *Evangelical Mission Quarterly*, and six area PULSES.

25. *Evangelical Newsletter* is published biweekly by Evangelical Ministries, Inc.

26. B. Robert Briscoe, ed., *Fundamental News Service*, published by the American Council of Christian Churches.

the community and larger society that are beyond the adequate hearing of the gospel.

2. The church must determine what can be realistically accomplished within the framework of the in-house evangelistic programs already in place or those that can realistically be developed to reach the total community. In some instances, with only slight modification of an ongoing program, a neglected segment of the community could be reached. It might be that a new program could be initiated without great difficulty or cost if the need were known.

It should be noted that, generally speaking, evangelization should take place within the aegis of the local church, using in-house programs and local church people. When it is determined that this is not feasible, then the specialists of a parachurch organization should be considered.

3. The church must develop a realistic definition of missions that recognizes that any people she cannot service with the gospel through her in-house programs of evangelism are a bona fide mission field, whether at home or abroad. The church should not only have a philosophy of evangelism but also a philosophy of missions, for where in-house evangelism is not possible, then out-of-house evangelism must begin.

4. The church must alert her people concerning the community needs that are beyond her in-house programs and send those who are gifted and respond to those needs to approved training institutions to prepare for service. If the church does not take this initiative, then those who leave for training without a particular goal in mind will be challenged with other opportunities for service, which may take them away from their home community and its need. This is not to bypass the work of the Holy Spirit but rather to enhance it. How is a person to be burdened for a need he does not know exists? It may be noted that the church at Antioch was used of the Holy Spirit to challenge her members to evangelize peoples beyond the reach of her in-house programs (Acts 13). The evangelical American church must be awakened to the fact that in 1982 only 2 percent of seminary graduates went into world missions.

5. The church must call for her training institutions to initiate programs to alert and prepare her students for missionary service to evangelize at home as well as abroad. It should be a concern

that of all the Bible schools surveyed in the United States, only a few offer a course in home missions. It may also be noted that not one seminary offers a course by that name. A further problem has existed in that no textbook has been available that details home missions.

Most training institutions have missionary guests on campus to present their work and mission to the students. Undoubtedly the overwhelming majority represent foreign missions. This is not to suggest that foreign mission works are overrepresented, but rather that more attention should be given to the spiritually destitute segments of this pluralistic society. Some of these segments will only be reached for Christ by mission organizations using evangelistic experience gained overseas.

6. The church must prepare internship programs for her graduates to mature and display their spiritual gifts after their return from training institutions. While at school the student may or may not have had Christian service opportunities. Even if the student did, he needs further opportunity to grow in grace and learn to serve well in the church family under the direction of the home pastor. Such experience will prepare the candidate for missionary service.

7. The church should encourage foreign missions to develop home departments to assist her to reach foreign citizens resident here. Why should not a foreign mission be best prepared to help the church reach those who have moved here from the country where the mission serves? This may require that the church and mission do a little soul searching, for there may be some feeling that such a policy might deemphasize the foreign missionary cause. Mission leaders have voiced the opinion that pastors are not as interested in supporting home missions; therefore, they are reticent to open home departments.

One missionary executive writes: "Some North American churches would more readily support a missionary going overseas, even though his living conditions there may be better, than if he were to minister in Newark or Detroit."[27]

8. Finally, the church should recognize home missions to be as valid as foreign missions. Virginia Miller of Gospel Recordings pleads for prayer for home missionaries in their *Together in Prayer*

---

27. Charles Koch, Latin America Mission, quoted by Jack Houston in "When Latinos Reach Latinos," *Moody Monthly*, July-August 1975, p. 25.

bulletin. "Some churches do not think that people in Christian work within the United States such as Gospel Recording, where the majority of the staff do not go to a foreign field, are missionaries in the full sense of the word. Therefore, they do not pray for so-called "home" missionaries. So your prayers for us here ... are doubly appreciated."[28] Both are assisting the church to evangelize segments of society that she cannot reach with her in-house program. In his syndicated column, Paul Harvey notes:

American missionaries have preferred preaching and teaching on far-away islands and remote jungles to the neglect of the asphalt jungles in our own cities. Dollars flow readily to such ministries.
It will be less of an ego trip for the home front missionary ... [he] is without status, is more pitied than applauded ... we will have to try to learn to salute and support the home front missionary.[29]

There should be no home-foreign dichotomy. Ralph Winters suggests new designations: "domestic missions" to indicate areas where there is an established church, and "frontier missions" to indicate where there is no established church. Such designations are to apply to both home and abroad. It is necessary for pastors to face the issue squarely and then to lead their people into a realistic understanding of their responsibility in the total community. Such an understanding is not possible without the assistance of home missions and their missionaries. It may come as a surprise to learn that God has quietly raised up nearly 400 home mission agencies to assist the church in areas where she may be unaware that she has a spiritual responsibility.

The tragedy is that these organizations are often understaffed and poorly financed in the midst of the most affluent church in history, which seems to be totally unaware of the need all around her. It may be that home missions and home missionaries today are not as well organized and represented as they were in the past. It may also be true that home missionaries have felt almost apologetic about presenting the needs of their work in the light of the overwhelming conditions overseas. But, alas, has this not been somewhat the attitude of the church toward home missions?[30]

28. Virginia Miller, "Together in Prayer," printed by Gospel Recordings, January 1981, n.p.
29. Los Angeles Times Syndicate, quoted in Grit, 18 December 1980, n.p.
30. Harold Cook, "Basic Principles and Practices for Home Missions," in The Fields at Home, ed. Peter Gunther (Chicago: Moody, 1963), pp. 21-22.

Perhaps part of the reason for this may be that a feeling of guilt comes over the church when she thinks of home missions. If she had done her job properly there would be no need of home missions, would there? The answer is twofold. Wherein the church has been derelict in her evangelism, she should feel guilty. But the truth is she never will be able to reach the total community without specialists trained to do what her laymen cannot do. In this sense she should not feel guilty, but rather praise God for missions available to assist her.

On the other hand, home missions themselves need to develop a more positive self-image. They need not think of themselves as stepping stones toward that ultimate service, which is overseas. Yet, such negative feelings have been so persistent and widespread among churches and missions that even the accrediting association of home missions, known as the National Home Missions Fellowship, felt more comfortable with a new name, the Association of North American Missions. Let it be stated unequivocably that the church is responsible to see to it that the world community is evangelized. The church will be able to accomplish that only through the services of her parachurch agencies we call missions, both home and foreign.

It is the burden of this research project to gather under one cover five sections of information concerning many of the gospel-neglected groups of America. It will be noted where these peoples are likely to be found as well as some indication of their comparative numbers. That the reader may gain some understanding as to why they are unevangelized, a brief historical introduction will be presented.

Many of these groups have had some exposure to the gospel; therefore, the size of the evangelical community in their midst will be noted if available, and the mission organizations that are ministering to their spiritual needs are listed. This list appears as an appendix at the end of each chapter for ready reference. Where appropriate, sources for materials slanted toward the needs of the group, which are available for their evangelization and edification, are noted. At the end of the book will be found an alphabetical listing of mission societies ministering in North America, with an indication of the groups they service and the number of missionaries ministering to them. The list includes foreign missions that have some work in the United States. This is the only extant listing of missions working at home, and it is not exhaustive.

2

A History of Home Missions

The history of missions in the United States began with the founding of the country. In fact, there were those in England who promoted the colonization of the New World as a missionary project. Perhaps for some this was but pious fraud.[1] However, it is clear from the record that the Pilgrims, on arrival, immediately charged one of their number with the responsibility of converting the Indians, and soon it was mandated by law that two would be given that responsibility each year. Thus, "when the Mayflower dropped anchor off Plymouth Rock, there began the most momentous missionary enterprise since the days of the Apostles."[2]

Even the charters of some of the colonies stipulated that one of the primary purposes of the community would be the conversion of the Indians.[3] Who could have predicted that from those meager beginnings home missions were destined to become the harbinger of a larger missionary enterprise to reach around the world?

John Eliot was clearly a home missionary in 1646. He learned the language of the Indians and translated the Scriptures into their

1. Warren W. Sweet, *The Story of Religion in America*, rev. ed. (New York: Harper & Row, 1950), p. 156.
2. P. O. Miller, *The Imperative of Home Missions* (Richmond, Va.: Whittet and Shepperson, 1931), p. 25.
3. Oliver W. Elsbree, *The Rise of the Missionary Spirit in America* (Philadelphia: Porcupine, 1980), p. 25.

language. He should not only be remembered as the apostle to the North American Indians but also as the morning star of the British and American missionary movement. His work and that of his son preceded by half a century the founding of the Society for the Propagation of the Gospel in Foreign Parts in 1701 in England. Herbert Kane suggests this is the "oldest missionary society in the English-speaking world."[4]

It may be further noted that David Brainerd in 1744, a century after Eliot, was also preaching to the Indians as a home missionary. That was fifty years before William Carey, the father of modern missions, and Henry Martyn were sent to India and before the founding of the first American foreign mission board, which sponsored Adoniram Judson as a missionary to Burma.

Between 1607 and 1732 the major Reformation churches were all planted in the United States. However, it was not until the 1800s that those same churches developed home and foreign mission departments. Why it took nearly two centuries for them to develop organized efforts in missionary endeavor is not clear. Without question the missionary spirit of the colonial period was primarily focused on church extension and Indian missions. There appears to have been very little effort expended in evangelizing the blacks or sailors.

The early American church was not unaware of the spiritual needs of others around them, for they sought to evangelize the fishermen of the coastal regions. Then, as the frontiers moved westward, the churches sent their missionaries to plant Sunday schools, sell gospel portions, and plant churches.

COLONIAL CHURCH MISSIONARY ACTIVITY

The colonial church brought over from the Old World was clearly an established or state church in most of the colonies.[5] A long and hard-fought battle took place before the disassociation of church and state. The leaders of the churches in the Old World were in most instances very much in control of the New World churches.[6] That may give some insight into the limited involvement in missions of the Anglican church as originally established in Jamestown, Virginia, and then throughout the South.

4. J. Herbert Kane, *A Global View of Christian Missions* (Grand Rapids: Baker, 1971), p. 91.
5. Sweet, p. 173.
6. Elsbree, p. 47.

Although there is record of some early education of the Indians in Virginia, after the massacre of 1622 the attitude of the colonists completely changed toward the Indians.[7] It was not until a century after the founding of Jamestown that the Church of England formed its foreign mission board, the Society for the Propagation of the Gospel, and proceeded to send 300 missionaries to the colonies. As Kane points out, all but 79 of those missionaries were foreign born.[8] Their concern seemed to be primarily directed toward church planting among the colonists, but some activity was directed to the Indians and still less toward the blacks.[9]

The Congregational church dominated the northern colonies. Although loyal to the Church of England, the colonists' love of liberty was clearly expressed in their church government and in their missionary activity. They were not tolerant of other religious ideas but were concerned about their rights to freely live and express their own convictions. They were aware of the British fishermen who frequented the Massachusetts coast and set about to find ways to care for the moral welfare of these transients.

Although John Eliot was not a typical New Englander of his time, he did emulate the attitude of the Congregational church toward missions. Eliot studied the Indian language by befriending one who had been captured and who had decided to stay with the colony. This Indian accompanied Eliot on numerous preaching tours to the villages. Within six years that team was responsible for 3,600 Indian converts in fourteen villages called "praying towns." Eliot also translated the entire Bible into their language. This Bible became the first to be printed in the United States.

Eliot wished to alert the church at large about the need for evangelizing the Indians. He wrote tracts that found their way to Parliament, which was impressed to form the President and Society for the Propagation of the Gospel in New England. This Society was charged with the responsibility of holding land and raising money to evangelize the Indians. The administrators of this company were the commissioners of several New England colonies.

The islands off the coast of Massachusetts were also a concern of the church. Five generations of Mayhews gave themselves to the evangelization of the Indians on Martha's Vineyard and Nantucket.

7. Sweet, p. 35.
8. Kane, p. 91.
9. Sweet, p. 247.

Whole families came to Christ, and by 1674 there were 1,800 Christian Indians.

Home missions were successful in eastern Massachusetts among the weaker tribes, but over a period of time the Christian Indians intermarried with the blacks and were absorbed into the larger culture of New England. The work dwindled after 1675 as a period of lethargy set in, and the end of an era came with the death of Eliot in 1690. Indian work was not revived until after the Great Awakening.

PRE-CIVIL WAR MISSIONARY ACTIVITY AND THE GREAT AWAKENING

Prior to the Civil War there was a period of increased missionary activity, which had two sources. The Moravians were well known for their intense missionary activity. They came to the United States from Germany when the state Lutheran church began to persecute them for forming their own separate church. Upon arrival they immediately established industries to fund their missionary efforts among the colonists and the Indians. One historian indicates that "the prime reason why they came to America was to evangelize the Indians whose spiritual destitution had given them great concern."[10]

In 1741 Nicholas Zinzendorf arrived in Philadelphia to organize the various German peoples into a united church. After failing at this, he turned his attention to nurturing a most successful missionary effort among the various Indian tribes.

Although the French and Indian War of 1755 disrupted the work, men like David Zeisberger, the best-known Moravian missionary leader,[11] moved a group to eastern Ohio and continued to establish Christian communities. The efforts were so successful that the "churches were unable to accommodate the great numbers of Indian worshippers."[12] Those noble efforts were almost totally destroyed by the opposing forces of the Revolutionary War. This history is preserved in an outdoor drama, "Trumpet in the Land," which plays each summer near Dover, Ohio.

Another source of pre-Civil War missionary activity was the Great Awakening (1734). It stirred the church to again notice the spiritual needs of those who were not included in her ministry. George Whitefield accepted the burden of Charles Wesley to estab-

---

10. Harry Stacker, *A Home Missionary History of the Moravian Church in United States and Canada* (Winston-Salem, N.C.: Moravian Church, 1924), p. 15.
11. Elsbree, p. 23.
12. Sweet, p. 109.

lish an orphanage in Georgia in 1740. The next year Henry Barclay began a work among the Indian tribes of New York. One of his congregations grew to number 500 Indians and included most of that tribe. Barclay was the most successful of sixteen Anglican missionaries working among the Indians.

Perhaps David Brainerd is the best known of the Indian missionaries of this time. Although his ministry was short, his dedication was total. The publication of his diary was used of the Lord to stir many to Christian service. It has been suggested that "Brainerd dead was a more potent influence for Indian missions and the missionary cause in general than was Brainerd alive."[13]

Jonathan Edwards was not only a great intellectual preacher and writer but also a successful missionary to the Indians among whom he worked at the settlement called Stockbridge. It was to his daughter that David Brainerd was engaged when he died, and it was Jonathan who had Brainerd's diary published.

Dartmouth College was another outgrowth of the Great Awakening. Eleazer Wheelock, a revival preacher, established the college as Moor's Indian Charity School in Connecticut to train Indians and colonists for missionary service. As the Charity School developed into a college, its primary purpose was enshrined on its seal in the words "Vox Clamantis in Deserto," the "voice of one crying in the wilderness." It meant that the school was dedicated to train whites for missionary service among the Indians; however, it was not very successful in its avowed purpose.

As the revival fires spread, concern for missions grew. In 1761 the Presbyterians fielded Samuel Kirkland, James Davenport, and Simon Horton among others to work with the Indians and blacks. The Quakers developed an extensive work with the Indians and began to voice opposition to slavery.

But then the Civil War captured everyone's attention, and missions suffered as joining the war effort became equated with Christian activity. A great period of spiritual deadness settled upon the nation.

POST-CIVIL WAR MISSIONARY ACTIVITY AND THE 1800S

It was not until the Second Awakening in 1786 that the nation renewed its interest in missions, and then a "great wave of enthusi-

13. Ibid., p. 162.

asm for missions swept across the American Church."[14] The church began to reorganize its programs. Mid-week prayer meetings were added as a stimulus to prayer, and the Sunday school was instituted for instruction in the Word of God. Numerous colleges and seminaries were established for the instruction of church leaders, and an organized missions program was initiated to reach out into the larger community.

DENOMINATIONAL MISSIONS

The Missionary Society of Connecticut was organized in 1798 by the state church "to Christianize the heathen of North America and to support and promote Christian knowledge in the new settlements."[15] One by one the New England states followed this example and established their own mission organizations. Thus, New England became "the fountainhead of the broad river of national home missions."[16]

These mission societies took great interest in the Indians. They were given financial assistance by the federal government through its Bureau of Indian Affairs.

Throughout the 1800s the churches developed departments of missions. At first they were home missions charged with extending the church's outreach to those who were either near by or on the frontiers. Some mission departments were responsible for both home and foreign efforts. In many churches separate boards for home and foreign activities were established.

The Presbyterians sent Shelby Jackson to the Rocky Mountains under their home mission board to plant churches among the whites and Indians. After a successful ministry there, he was sent to Alaska. While evangelizing the Eskimos he became aware of their dwindling food supply and was instrumental in introducing the reindeer.

INTERDENOMINATIONAL MISSIONS

A new innovation in missions was expanded as the nineteenth century dawned. The churches had been experimenting with interdenominational cooperation in several areas of ministry including missions. As the country grew, the churches expanded their mission

14. J. Gordon Melton, *The Encyclopedia of American Religions*, 2 vols. (Wilmington: McGrath, 1978), 1:384.
15. Elsbree, p. 56.
16. Kane, p. 98.

programs. For instance, various denominations had founded over 100 Bible societies. In 1816 many of those were united into the American Bible Society. A similar plethora of tract societies were amalgamated into the American Tract Society in 1825. Those organizations sought to produce Bibles and literature for the growing population that had almost no Christian literature. Colporteurs traveled the country selling the literature and evangelizing everyone including Roman Catholics and immigrants.

By 1826 the Congregationalists and the Presbyterians determined to form the American Home Mission Society for church planting in New England and on the western frontier. This missionary effort was hailed as the "most important home missionary agency among Protestants in the U.S. before the Civil War in the cooperative conduct of missions."[17]

Another cooperative venture was the American Sunday School Union founded in 1824. Home missionaries for several denominations worked together to fulfill the objectives of establishing Sunday schools in every neighborhood and preparing literature to be used in them. Missionaries were sent to visit the Sunday schools and make the literature available. The mission still functions today under its new name the American Missionary Fellowship. As the oldest home mission society, it is primarily involved in church planting and includes ministries among migrants, blacks, and Hispanics.

FAITH MISSIONS

By the end of the century the missionary enterprise had undergone another change. Interdenominational missions became known as faith missions as opposed to denominational missions. Several factors were influential in causing this change. By 1825 the antimission Baptists were deeply concerned about interdenominational missions and not only boycotted them but spoke adamantly against them and insisted that they were unscriptural. The issue was essentially one of doctrinal interpretation dictated by a strong Calvinism, but the controversy helped to undermine the interdenominational concept of missions. Another force for change was the growing liberalization of theology within the denominations. Third, the slavery issue and the Civil War (1861-65) deeply divided the churches and the country. Thus, the churches were embroiled in

17. Jerald C. Brauer, ed., *Westminster Dictionary of Church History* (Philadelphia: Westminster, 1917), p. 24.

issues that did not encourage a missionary vision that focused on the lost.

Faith missions developed as a reaction to the lack of interest in missions in the various denominations. Individuals within the churches saw the spiritual need of those not being reached and established parachurch missions to assist in reaching them. Where church leaders once directed the evangelistic efforts of the missionary outreach of the church, now mission societies, with their separate leadership, gave oversight to this ministry. By default the church transferred its God-given responsibility to parachurch organizations that did a Herculean job.

The missions that developed, both home and foreign, became the main source of information concerning missionary needs. The obvious needs at home were the expanding frontier, alcoholism, lumber camps, and the growing number of immigrants, including Jews, Catholics, and Hispanics. The American Sunday School Union (1824) worked the frontiers, and the American Rescue Workers Mission (1896) sought to help alcoholics. Lumberjacks were the concern of the Shantyman's Christian Association in Canada (1908), and Christ's Mission, burdened for the Catholics and Spanish, was formed in 1891. About the turn of the century the American Board of Missions to the Jews (1894) and the Cleveland Hebrew Mission (1904) were founded.

Foreign mission boards were also developing. They included the China Inland Mission (American branch, 1888), the Scandanavian Alliance Mission of North America (1890; now TEAM), Sudan Interior Mission (1893), and Africa Inland Mission (1895). Both home and foreign missions were receiving their candidates from Christian colleges and the fledgling Bible college movement, spearheaded by Nyack Missionary College (1882) and Moody Bible Institute (1886).

Missions was a growing concern on the campuses. On Williams College campus Samuel Mills and several friends met frequently for prayer. These friends, the Haystack Group, vowed to become America's first foreign missionaries. In 1810, through their efforts, the Congregational church formed America's first mission board, the American Board of Commissioners for Foreign Missions. The board sent several of these friends to foreign fields, but "From the beginning the board was concerned for home as well as foreign missions. At its second meeting it expressed the hope that 'this board will not lose sight of the heathen tribes on this continent.' "[18] They sent many missionaries to the American Indians.

Samuel Mills traveled widely on the United States frontier between 1812 and 1815 and was "deeply impressed everywhere with the famine of the Word."[19] He helped organize numerous Bible societies, including the American Bible Society mentioned earlier. By 1886 the Student Volunteer Movement was focusing the attention of collegians on the needs of the developing missions overseas. John R. Mott became a prime mover in the organization and wrote *The Evangelization of the World in This Generation*. That concept fired the hearts of "100,000 students to dedicate their lives to Christ's global cause" on 600 campuses.[20] Within fifteen years 5,000 had been sent to foreign fields.

Home missions were thus eclipsed and grew at a much slower rate. There was no campus organization or influential leader who was able to capture the imagination of the students for home missions as there was for foreign missions. Missionary interest on the campuses was encouraged by the Foreign Missions Fellowship (FMF). On some campuses groups seeking to maintain a balanced emphasis in missions called themselves Prayer Bands or Warriors.

The regular emphasis on foreign missions in the colleges and churches helped turn the attention of pastors, churches, and missionary candidates toward the needs abroad and away from those neglected at home. Even so, home mission organizations and staff quietly grew in numbers during the twentieth century.

THE TWENTIETH CENTURY

The twentieth century may well be remembered as the century of missions. American churches alone spawned over 1,000 mission organizations to continue what Kane calls "the Herculean effort" begun the century before to herald the gospel to the ends of the earth.[21] Today 600 missions carry the gospel overseas. Nearly 400

18. J. Herbert Kane, *A Concise History of the Christian World Mission* (Grand Rapids: Baker, 1978), p. 87.
19. Philip Schaff, *The American Church History Series*, 13 vols. (New York: Christian Literature Company, 1897), 13:256.
20. *Perspective*, published by Institute of International Studies, April 1981, p. 1.
21. Kane, *History of the Christian World*, p. 93.

agencies are working the fields at home, thus underscoring Stephen Neill's observation that this is the American century of missions.[22]

LIMITED WRITTEN HISTORY

The history of the development of home missions in the twentieth century is only sparsely recorded. The Bureau of Missions published *The Blue Book of Missions for 1905*. It was intended to include "in outline some of these works, classed in America as Home Missions, because without remembrance of these the term 'missions' is not half defined." (See Appendix 2.) When the book was readied for publication, it was noted that "after collecting a considerable number of records it became evident . . . that the great difference in forms used by these societies . . . made this matter one of peculiar difficulty . . . requiring study and time. . . . The scheme has been regretfully given up for this year."[23]

A few years later the Interchurch World Movement of North America published a two-volume *World Survey of Missions*. One volume gave detailed information about home missionary efforts of thirty denominations. A great amount of time and money was expended surveying cities, town and country, blacks, new Americans, migrants, Indians, Hispanics, Orientals, Alaska, Hawaii, and the West Indies.[24] The encyclopedic knowledge gathered about the great need for more missionaries was carefully preserved in detailed charts produced in color. The studied conclusion of the investigators was:

> If you are sincerely interested in the spiritual condition of America, you cannot fail to be impressed, even if you are not appalled, by these disclosures of the religious condition of your land. There is no phase of American religious life that is functioning as completely or efficiently as it should . . . [remember] as you read: This is my country that I am reading about. This is my church that is failing in its duty. . . . Here is the chance to "lose yourself" in some absolutely compelling task that cannot be denied.[25]

The investigators gathered much information about the many

22. Samuel Wilson, ed., *Mission Handbook: North American Protestant Ministries Overseas*, 12th ed. (Monrovia, California, 1979), p. 19.
23. Henry Otis Dwight, ed., *The Blue Book of Missions for 1905* (New York: Funk and Wagnalls, 1905), p. 6.
24. Ibid., p. 179.
25. Peter Gunther, ed., *The Fields at Home* (Chicago: Moody, 1963).

home mission opportunities, but they gave almost no information about what was being done to meet the need.

In 1963 the first survey of home missionary effort undertaken by the faith missions was published. (See Appendix 1.) Leaders in the various fields compiled valuable information about the needs in their areas, but little information was given about the history of missions and the development of faith missions.

HOME MISSION SURVEY

In an effort to preserve some of the above information, a list of home missions was compiled and an instrument distributed. Fifty-nine percent return yielded the following incomplete but revealing information.

Nearly 400 missions are working in the United States. They are primarily home missions; however, a few also maintain a work overseas. This number includes forty missions that are known as foreign missions but also have some work in America. A few of the foreign missions have a substantial work here, but for the majority it is a small, growing ministry.

Most home missions (62 percent) were founded in the thirty-year period following 1930. During the nineteenth century a few missions (5 percent) began. Two of those were foreign missions that started their home mission work much later. In the first three decades of this century 8 percent of the agencies were born. Most of those were established after World War I (1914-1920).

The growth of home mission societies parallels the growth of the Bible institute or college and the independent church movement. The Scopes trial (1925) galvanized the attention of the fundamentalists on the Word of God. The depression caused people to think about spiritual values. Preaching included a large emphasis on personal evangelism and helped Christians to become aware of the unsaved around them.

NUMBER OF HOME MISSIONARIES

Exactly how many missionaries are involved in home missions in the 1980s is difficult to ascertain. The survey revealed that 12,000 are working under the auspices of the responding societies. It is not clear how many are working under the other 157 missions. Perhaps the above number of missionaries should be doubled.

There are other missions and their respective staffs that are not reflected in these statistics. First, almost every major city has its gospel or rescue mission. The International Union of Gospel Missions (IUGM) directory lists 1,000 members working under 250 missions.[26] Those figures include several other countries, but the larger percentage is from the United States.

Jewish missions present another complex picture. *The Handbook of Jewish Mission Agencies* indicates that 46 agencies listing 470 missionaries work in 118 locations in the larger cities of twenty-eight states.[27] Most of the Jewish missions are included in those figures.

Third, dozens of children's homes are constituted as missions. They do not have a fellowship organization that maintains a listing of the various homes or the number of their workers. Some of the homes are members of either or both the IUGM and the National Association of Homes for Children.

Fourth, the directory of Christian Camping International lists 750 camps and conferences that represent 4,000 workers, many of whom are missionaries.

Finally, denominational home mission figures have not been gathered. Denominational interest in missions varies widely. For example, the home mission board of the Southern Baptist Convention lists 2,800 personnel and the Assemblies of God have 322 missionaries. Both of those denominations have highly developed programs deploying missionaries in the many home mission fields. They also publish excellent home mission magazines.[28]

GROWTH PROBLEMS

Numerical growth of home mission agencies has been slow. The overwhelming majority of agencies are small, for 94 percent have fewer than 100 missionaries. Twenty-six percent of all missions have fewer than 10 workers. Only 6 percent have more than 100 missionaries, but these twenty-two missions represent 87 percent of the missionaries. Two missions with over 1,000 staff members are Campus Crusade with 3,000 and Youth For Christ with 1,000. Child Evangelism Fellowship has 600 members, and three other societies have over 400.

---

26. International Union of Gospel Missions lists rescue missions and children's homes in the 1980-81 directory.
27. *The Handbook of Jewish Mission Agencies,* compiled by Fellowship of Christian Testimonies to the Jews, lists agencies and workers by states for referral purposes. Published by the American Board of Missions to the Jews, 1976.
28. *Missions USA,* Home Missions Board, Southern Baptist Convention, and *Home Missions,* Assemblies of God Home Missions.

A number of factors have contributed to this phenomenon. First, the leaders of the early missions were often strong individualists who established very independent works. Little thought was given to cooperation with other ministries or the sharing of ideas among missions. The ministry consumed all the leader's time so that almost no time was left for administration. One observer reports that leadership was in many instances ineffective.

Second, there was minimal organization. The board of directors often lived some distance from the field and, therefore, found it difficult to be directly involved with the work. Clearcut goals for expansion of the work were generally missing. Little time was available for deputation or recruitment. Literature explaining the work and personnel needs had not developed, nor was a mission organ produced to keep the churches informed. Although missionaries regularly reported to their supporting churches, only a few recruits were inspired to join them in the work. New leadership personnel was not readily available. In short, in the words of an oral historian, "The missions were often unorganized."

Another factor was the continual shortage of funds. Most of the missionaries went to the fields of service undersupported, with only a limited clientele that was aware of and praying for the work. There was, and still is, a much greater inclination on the part of churches to support overseas missionaries. However, only limited effort was expended in informing the larger public about the need for expansion of the work at home. Without proper funds for supplies and equipment, the work suffered.

Fourth, at times the mission work was established in an isolated place apart from population centers. Difficulty in communication and travel further separated the missionary from large groups of people. In rural areas the ministry often took the form of school visitation, daily vacation Bible schools, and summer camps. It was difficult for a self-supporting church to develop under those conditions.

Finally, a sufficient number of men was not available. In some instances missions were established by women and were predominantly staffed by them. They found it difficult to attract men to expand their ministry. Further, it was difficult to find male leadership for founding local churches. This was especially true in the mountain areas.

In more recent years that image has radically changed. Home mission leaders have learned much from the more sophisticated foreign mission organizations. A national organization has developed to encourage organizational growth and the sharing of ideas and expertise.

THE ASSOCIATION OF NORTH AMERICAN MISSIONS

It was Harry Ironside who said in 1941, "Give us a home mission organization that will compare to foreign missions."[29] He was suggesting an organization that would be comparable to the Interdenominational Foreign Mission Association organized in 1917 as an association of missions which had met certain requirements for membership.

At this time there were groups of individuals meeting for fellowship in areas of the country where they were serving. The Mountain Gospel Fellowship (MGF) was such a group meeting in the Kentucky mountains. They met for the first time in 1932 in the home of Elmer Wagler, founder of Southern Highland Evangel Mission. Later, as the group grew to more than 100, they met at Camp Nathanael of the Scripture Memory Mountain Mission (SMMM). Garland Franklin, the founder of the SMMM and president of the MGF, was one of those who heard Ironside's challenge for a home mission organization. Several mission leaders and pastors organized the National Home Missions Fellowship (NHMF) at Moody Memorial Church in 1942. The NHMF continued for more than thirty years to have its annual meetings in conjunction with the home missions conference of Moody Church, where the missionaries met for fellowship.

The name of the fellowship was changed to the Association of North American Missions in 1980, when it was determined that the organization should be more than a fellowship of missionaries and become an association of missions as Ironside had originally suggested.[30]

Richard Matthews was appointed executive director in 1982 to promote the cause of home missions among leaders and missionaries. The Association maintains six regions: Appalachian, Great Lakes, Ozark, Northeast, Southeast, and Southwest, as well as a national conference that meets annually. It publishes the *Roundtable* quarterly and maintains a national headquarters.[31] The list of member missions

29. Letter from Ralph Tulley, *Southern Highland Evangel*, August 1981.
30. Wilson, *Mission Handbook*, p. 125. (The *Mission Handbook* gives a list of these requirements.)
31. *Roundtable*, published by Association of North American Missions.

as published in the *Roundtable* now numbers forty-three, representing 1400 missionaries.[32]

THE THIRD ERA OF MISSIONS

Home missions, like the rest of world missions, has entered into what Ralph Winters calls the "third era" in modern missions.[33] During the first era (1792-1910) missionaries evangelized the coastlands of the countries. Then came a major thrust into the interior areas (1865-1980). That second era overlapped the first with forty-five transitional years. Finally, Winters suggests that in 1980, after a forty-six-year transition, missions began to be concerned about those who had been bypassed, called "hidden people." Although there is an established church in most countries of the world, these hidden peoples cannot be reached by those churches without a cross-cultural ministry. For those churches it will mean a home missionary effort. For the rest of the world, it will call for foreign mission assistance.

Those same stages can be recognized in home missions. Colonial missions could be equated with the first era. During the second era there was the western advance into the interior with the successful planting of thousands of churches. Home missions also stand on the threshold of a new era that began in the 1930s with the founding of scores of missions ready to assist the church in reaching those who have been bypassed in the great thrust to plant new churches at home.

The home mission agencies that stand ready to assist the church are essentially what Kane calls "specialized missions."[34] They minister to people who are isolated from the message because of certain characteristics such as religion, ethnicity, handicap, institutionalization, geographical identity, or a combination of those. Many people are hidden from the gospel by linguistic and cultural barriers. Even in America "we now realize that subtle cultural differences, being invisible, make even city sub-spheres hidden peoples."[35]

Hidden peoples are to be found in every American community. They are those segments of society that are not Christian and not involved in local Bible-believing churches. If the members of the

32. Ibid., March-May 1981.
33. Ralph Winters, "The Concept of a Third Era in Missions," *Evangelical Missions Quarterly*, April 1981, pp. 69-82.
34. Kane, *History of the Christian World*, p. 95.
35. Winters, "Third Era Missions," p. 82.

local churches cannot effectively reach them, then the expertise of a home mission may well be the answer.

The greatest single problem that home missions face in this twentieth century is not the de-Christianization of American society, although Kenneth Latourette the church historian contends that home missions are helping stem that tide,[36] but a sleeping church, unaware of the spiritual needs of those in its community. It can be said that "America is missionary territory . . . and the great majority of church members in this country have not become alive to this fact."[37] Without the church's being aware of the needs, the mission society cannot help the church accomplish its task.

In rural West Virginia, south of Wheeling, a Hare Krishna temple has been built at a cost of half a million dollars. Not ten miles away is a fundamental church. Should this church consider contacting International Missions to help them determine how to reach the practitioners of that Hindu cult? It should be self-evident that the only way those cultists will hear is for those who know the truth to arrange for the gospel be given to them.

The church in America today must regard itself as being in a characteristically missionary situation. What we call "home missions" is not an eccentric or marginal or optional activity. It is the main business of every local church, every church school, every Christian institution and program. It is the business of every Christian. For the church in America, as everywhere else in the world, is called to further the Christian movement in a society whose dominant presuppositions, standards, and goals are frequently in direct and massive opposition to those of Christianity. In a far more radical sense than has been understood, the church in America must be a missionary church or it will die.[38]

36. Kenneth S. Latourette, *The Twentieth Century Outside Europe*, 5 vols. (Grand Rapids: Zondervan, 1969), 5:25.
37. Truman Douglas, *Mission to America* (New York: Friendship, 1951), p. 8.
38. Ibid., p. 14.

Part 2

Ethnic Ministries

Introduction

A study of missionary activity focusing on the peoples of the United States can properly begin with ethnic Americans, because they are the oldest inhabitants of our country. They include the earliest immigrants (the American Indians), the Hispanics (who preceded the Puritans by at least a century), and the blacks, who are the largest ethnic group. Others from the Old World have come by the millions from 134 backgrounds making America truly a nation of immigrants. Today 40,000,000 are either immigrants or the children of immigrants, 25 percent are foreign born, and one-third do not speak English in the home.[1] Ethnics are those who did not want to lose their cultural identity in the "melting pot" of that day, thus creating a pluralistic society.

The ethnics are culturally identifiable people groups "who perceive themselves to have a common affinity for one another."[2] They tend to congregate in homogeneous groups, often in the inner or central cities where they maintain their Old World ways. Most noteworthy is their native language and religion. It should be noted that their cultural distance from the majority was at best not understood and at worst gave rise to prejudice, animosity, and outright discrimination.

1. *Interlit* (Elgin, Ill.: David C. Cook), October 1977, n.p.
2. C. Peter Wagner and Edward R. Dayton, eds., *Unreached Peoples,* 1981 ed. (Elgin, Ill.: David C. Cook, 1981), p.23.

Although federal laws have sought to force their enculturation and coerce the majority society not to discriminate, social integration has been extremely slow. Jobs available to them are insecure and usually for unskilled laborers. Primary and secondary education continues to be of inferior quality and college remains beyond the reach of most. That locks at least one-third of all ethnics into a cycle of poverty, forcing them to live on income below the poverty line.

Some evangelistic concern has been generated by the evangelical church as evidenced by foreign language churches that have existed for years as a functional part of denominational home missions work.[3] But ethnics remain as large segments of American society, usually unevangelized. Efforts put forth have been meager at best and usually poorly funded. Evangelism has frequently involved enculturation, that is, to be saved meant that the ethnic had to dress and act like the majority culture. Even today many of the churches established in the ethnic community are pastored by "outsiders," for only minimal effort has been made to train ethnics to reach their own groups for Christ.

The successful evangelization of the ethnic will usually involve what Ralph Winters calls "E-2" or "E-3" evangelism.[4] This means that because the ethnic speaks another language and/or does not fully understand the American culture, a missionary will need to be prepared for this cross-cultural ministry beyond the normal evangelistic ability of the average Christian. This will require the expertise and oversight of mission societies to assist the local churches in efficiently planting churches in their communities. Some home mission boards are already effectively functioning. Other foreign mission agencies, whose primary ministry is working overseas among similar language and cultural groups, have established ministries here at home. It is to be desired that other missions will also consider establishing North American departments. These agencies are already well established with experienced executive leadership and seasoned missionaries who for various reasons may not be able to return to the foreign field but who could continue an effective and desperately needed ministry here at home.

These missions already have deputation departments and other agencies through which effective communication could be channeled to the church at large, helping her to realize the importance of

3. James H. Davis and Woodie White, *Racial Transition in the Church* (Nashville: Abingdon, 1980), p. 87.
4. Wagner and Dayton, *Unreached Peoples*, p. 20.

eliminating a home and foreign mission dichotomy. The field is the world, and the "regions beyond" start in the region just beyond where "I" am. Why is it that fundamental churches can have a burden for the blacks in Africa but be totally oblivious to the spiritual needs of the blacks of their own city? Or, how can a fundamental church within only a few miles of an Indian reservation not feel some spiritual responsibility? Perhaps the simplest answer is ignorance of the need or outright spiritual indolence.

The ministry to ethnics is complex and urgent. It is complex in that some of the older ethnics are the children of immigrants who have been here for several generations. Others are immigrants themselves. Then there are the recent children of immigrants who as youthful citizens are demanding their rights through militant political power. Finally, there are the refugees who are more recent arrivals. They are not only a problem to the country but also to some of the resident ethnics, who perceive them to be competition in the job market. The earlier immigrants came here looking for jobs—any job was better than starving to death. Our developing country not only welcomed them but also sought these as abundant cheap labor for our farms, railroads, and mines. The more recent arrivals, however, face a markedly different milieu. Thirty thousand in 1983 sought political asylum. Although many have skills, all must compete for scarce jobs in a highly competitive market. Housing is tight, often resulting in overcrowding in ghetto apartments of the central city as immigrants move in with relatives.

It is to be recognized that these new arrivals are of a radically different stripe. As guests in a new country, they are impatient with the system. Those who have no relatives or sponsors are detained for extended periods. Some riot in the processing centers and demand assumed rights. Other thousands of illegal aliens blatantly reside and work here openly violating the law. A few who become disillusioned choose bizarre ways of returning home. Another part of the complex picture is the changing attitude of the government. It has begun to abandon its mandated English for bilingualism in education and government offices. This has added to the serious problem of functional illiteracy, which has mushroomed to 20 percent of all adults.[5] Functional illiteracy is defined as inability to read the Bible or newspaper. The evangelical church will need to recognize that the foreign mission field has come to the United States as evidenced by the fact that 20 percent (32.4 million) of the populace uses a language

5. *Interlit*, August 1981, p. 2.

other than English (1983). The Los Angeles police department uses forty-two languages in its work.

Finally, ethnic community composition is constantly changing. Although a community may be predominantly of one ethnic majority, it is usually also mixed and changing. The church then faces a fluid situation for which it is ill-prepared and obviously incapable of coping with. They just move out. James Davis and Woodie White from their six-year study *Racial Transition in the Church*, have documented this phenomenon copiously.[6]

The ministry is urgent, for the ethnic is tired of waiting to be treated like any other American and is now on the move politically. Second, many ethnics have a Roman Catholic religious veneer but have found that their church is basically unresponsive to their spiritual needs; therefore, they feel neglected and adrift in a humanistic and secular society. Third, especially those coming from the Latin world, come out of an atmosphere where religion is being infused with an incipient Marxism taught under the guise of the theology of liberation. According to that school of thought, the villain, of course, is the American businessman who has ostensibly exploited his country and now offers him no job here. It is urgent that they feel the Christian community does care—enough to tell them the truth about salvation in Christ Jesus before they become settled ethnics and far less receptive to the gospel.

At least one major denomination has fielded a thousand "language missionaries." Their mandated policy is to establish ethnic congregations. They have produced a manual listing several methods of "cross-cultural outreach."[7] It would be well if every evangelical church would be so concerned.

The concerned Christian who wishes to read about reaching ethnics for Christ may wish to consult missiologist Alan Tippett's *Bibliography for Cross-Cultural Workers.*[8]

6. Davis and White, p. 18.
7. Home Mission Board, Southern Baptist Convention.
8. Alan Tippett, *Bibliography for Cross-Cultural Workers* (Pasadena, Calif.: The William Carey Library, 1980).

3

The Native American

The American Indian is a mission field because 92 percent of all Indians do not go to church; most likely fewer than 8 percent would be Christians. Tom Claus of the American Indian Crusade, an Indian himself, estimates that between 3 and 5 percent are Christian.[1] Most Indians are involved in native religious ceremonies including the fast-growing Peyote cult, incorporated as the Native American church.

The Indian is a mission field because he is effectively isolated from the normal evangelistic programs of both the evangelical Anglo and Indian churches. The Indian is isolated from the gospel in many ways. First he is isolated by *location*. Indians live either on or around a reservation or in a major city. If he lives on the reservation, he may live miles from the nearest neighbor or church. This is common on the Navajo reservation. When he lives in the city he does not live in groups as do other ethnics, but is scattered within the inner city. Many cities have no Indian church. Furthermore, the Indian does not feel comfortable in other inner city churches, including the black and Hispanic.

The Indian is isolated *linguistically*. The older Indian speaks only the native language. Few others can speak his language, which narrows the possibility of there being any Christians in the group

---

1. David Kuchersky, "Toward a Red Theology," *Christianity Today,* May 1975, p. 46.

and increases the probability that a missionary has not learned the tongue. The younger Indian may be bilingual, but his ability to communicate with missionaries in English is limited.

The problem of his limited ability to communicate is further complicated by widespread illiteracy. The older Indian can neither read nor write. The native language probably has no body of literature, including Scripture portions. Many of the younger Indians are functionally illiterate in English because of a high dropout rate from school. The issue is further aggravated by a lack of English literature written on a level he can understand.

Culture also isolates the Indian from the gospel. The biblical message as proclaimed by the Anglo is culturally distant from the Indian philosophy of life, which may be summarized in the words of a song:

> I stand in good relation to the earth;
> I stand in good relation to the gods;
> I stand in good relation to all that is beautiful;
> I stand in good relation to you;
> I am alive.[2]

He is very much attached to the tribal culture which, in most aspects, is diametrically different from that of the Anglo Christian.

The Indian is isolated by his *religious orientation*. Most Indians are deeply religious, but their religion does not include the Christian concept of a personal God. That is evidenced by the fact that many Indian languages have no word for deity. The Dakotas refer to deity as the Great Mystery.[3] Indian religiosity is expressed in seeking to live a life that is in harmony with nature, not by worshipping a divine being.

Tribal diversity is another factor isolating the Indian from the gospel. Anglos tend to think of all Indians as culturally close when in reality there are great differences among the more than 100 tribes. One urban Indian family frequently lives isolated from another because it is from a different tribe with which it has little in common. The urban Christian, either Anglo or Indian, who desires to be a witness must first determine the tribal allegiance to contextualize a meaningful testimony.

2. *The World of the American Indian* (Washington, D.C.: National Geographic Society, 1980), p. 14.
3. Janice Fleming, ed., *The People of the Seven Council Fires* (Pierre, S. D.: South Dakota Historical Resource Center, 1975), p. 51.

The Indian is also isolated from the gospel because there are so *few native churches*. The native Christian population is small and tends to be concentrated in certain tribes. Most Indian churches are too small to adequately support a national pastor or send forth its own people as missionaries. Too few Indians have given themselves for full-time Christian service as pastors and fewer still to become missionaries to other tribes.

Finally, the Indian is isolated from the gospel because of the *dearth of Christian literature available* to evangelize him in his native language or in English. Without Bibles, tracts, or Sunday school literature to supplement or sustain a witness to the Indian, there is little likelihood of his being converted. For those reasons the Indian is a mission field.

EXPOSURE TO THE GOSPEL

From the time white men came to America a witness has been maintained with the original inhabitants. The Spanish (1500s) entering from the south and west brought with them their padres, who immediately included Indians in the parish responsibility and eagerly plied them with the gospel. When the English colonized Virginia and Massachusetts, some effort was made to Christianize the pagans who occupied those lands. The larger effort was made in the New England colonies by such stalwarts as Roger Williams (1636), John Eliot (1646) and his son, and the Mayhew family, who gave five generations to Indian missions. The labors of those along with others were rewarded with thousands of Indian converts extracted from paganism and established in the Christian way. John Eliot's enduring achievement was the translation and publication of the Bible (1661) into Mohican (language no longer used), one of hundreds of Indian languages.

By the dawn of the eighteenth century England began to send missionaries to the New World under the Society for the Propagation of the Gospel in Foreign Parts. Hundreds of workers were dispatched to ply colonists and Indians alike with the Good News.

Frontier life was a grueling and demanding business, and Indian missions were not the most rewarding enterprise. Interest in evangelism soon waned and was not revived until the Great Awakening (1734) again stirred concern for Indian Christianization.

By mid-century (1741) the Moravians had established enterprising communities whose sole purpose was to support missionaries. Many communities worked among various Indian tribes and established Christian towns. The weakness of their effective labors was the penchant for not establishing converts in local churches.

David Brainerd's love for and service among the Indians (1743) were greater than his physical strength could endure. The posthumous publication of his diary by his fiancée's father, Jonathan Edwards, was used to inspire many for missionary service. Edwards (1758) himself served as a missionary for a time among the Indians.

Without question the primary purpose of missionary activity among the Indians has always been evangelism. Considerable evidence can be marshaled to substantiate that thesis. However, colonial Indian missions were not very successful. Several mitigating factors can be noted.

First, not all colonists were of the opinion that the Indian should be evangelized. According to some researchers, "The interest of the great majority of the settlers in the Indian was not his salvation, but his elimination."[4]

Second, the clergy were not in accord about Indian missions. Not all ministers believed that the Indian should be evangelized, but those who accepted the idea that he should be Christianized could not agree among themselves who should be responsible to carry it out. It was finally settled by legislation that one or two of their number would be responsible each year for Indian missons while they kept up the performance of regular parish ministries. The record reveals that "most missionaries who served the Indians were ordained over white, English churches and were missionaries to the aborigines on a part-time basis, or they were ordained as ministers of a white church sometime previous to missionary service."[5]

Third, some colonial churches refused to let their pastors do double duty. Those churches willing to share their clergymen insisted that they keep up the parish ministry or give oversight to an assistant. John Eliot was able to labor among the Indians and do translation work because his church hired an understudy to assist with the parish duties. When Eliot's son determined to work among the Indians, he was permitted to do so only every fortnight.

That arrangement was sanctioned by the New England Company, which appointed the clergy and paid their salaries. Therefore, most missionaries, including the Mayhews of Martha's Vineyard, were pastors first and missionaries second as dictated by the powers that be. In fact, it has been observed that "although the evangelical

4. R. Pierce Beaver, *Pioneers in Missions* (Grand Rapids: Eerdmans, 1966), p. 11.
5. Ibid., p. 4.

movement was dedicated from the start to the conversion of lost persons, it also began to serve the political concensus in the young country."[6]

Finally, history records that concomitant conditions were placed upon the Indians as a prerequisite to conversion. In fact, meeting those conditions was tantamount to Christianization. On the other hand, those same prerequisites were a strong deterrent to the Indian desiring to become a Christian.

One such condition widely held was that the Indian could not be evangelized until he had been civilized. That meant he had to leave his culture, clan, and people. He had to dress and act like Euro-Americans. He must speak their language and become a productive citizen.

> In the missionary perspective, Indians could not be Christians until they first abandoned native habits and accepted "civilized" customs. Conversion meant both the invasion of the Indian body and the conquest of the Indian soul. In nearly every mission these two distinct but interrelated goals were operative. Indians were urged to abandon their "wild" ways and become sanitized Euro-Americans.[7]

That philosophy of missions developed very early, for John Eliot wrote in his diary that he was convinced that it was absolutely necessary to civilize as well as evangelize. Evidently, Eliot articulated the majority opinion, because that system was the pattern for Indian missions until recent years.

To implement the civilizing process, missionaries extracted the Indian from his tribal life and established him in mission towns. The Spanish first did this in the South and West. Eliot created "praying towns" in New England, and the Moravians built villages in the region surrounding Ohio.

Contrary to popular opinion not all Indians were nomadic. Many tribes were more or less sedentary and tilled some of the best land. They taught the colonists which crops grew well in the New World. However, the Indians were not adept at domestication of animals; therefore, they hunted over large tracts of land to provide meat and skins. They also moved to new areas periodically.

One of the greatest conflicts between the colonist and the Indian

6. David F. Wells and John D. Woodbridge, eds., *The Evangelicals* (New York: Abingdon, 1975), p. 99.
7. James Ronda and James Axtell, *Indian Missions* (Bloomington: Indiana U. 1978), p. 30.

involved ownership and use of land. The colonist would not accept the idea of Indian usage of large tracts of land that were held in joint ownership by the tribe. Therefore, several problems were solved by establishing Indian towns. By that means, land was freed, and the Indians were being civilized. Other radical ideas suggested that an area west of Missouri be established where Indians could create for themselves a "holy, civilized life on individual farms."[8] Or, some saw the ravaging of the Indian by European diseases as "Divine intervention." John Winthrop, governor of Massachusetts, said, "God hath hereby cleared our title to this place." At times the government encouraged outright murder. Belden Menkus, Fellow of the American Association of Criminology, reports that at least one time the government encouraged wholesale slaughter of Indians and that at times bounties were offered for their killing.

Mission schools were established in the Indian towns or mission centers for the acculturation process. The Indian was taught to read and write English and how to become a participant in the recognized society. It was found that this was best accomplished in boarding schools where he was under twenty-four-hour supervision. Government agents were inclined to approve funds for these schools because they perceived that "Indian education existed wholly to remake Indians in the 'civilized' image."[9]

How effective were the early Indian missionary efforts? There is record of truly amazing Indian conversions. Samson Occum became a renowned Mohegan preacher. An Indian writer, William Apes, was saved out of the Pequot tribe and George Copway, a Chippewa chief, became an Indian missionary. Scores of others could be mentioned, but these are the exceptions, for a majority of the Indians were never converted.

Much has been written about the success of the Indian towns. However, the record indicates that even the much-heralded Stockbridge community, where the renowned missionary Jonathan Edwards labored, became a white town because the Indians felt pressured into leaving. They moved to Pennsylvania and ultimately to Wisconsin.[10] Indian towns were never properly integrated with whites. Indians were never fully accepted or trusted as bona fide citizens. As evidence, note that many towns were systematically destroyed during the periodic wars. "Even Christianized, politically

8. Ibid., p. 12.
9. Ibid., p. 36.
10. Beaver, *Pioneers in Missions*, p. 79.

neutral Indians made convenient scapegoats for white zealots who literally believed that the only good Indian was a dead Indian."[11] Even the missionaries who labored among the Indians were mistrusted as those who worked with the enemy. Even though attempts have been made to evangelize the Indian, it should be no surprise that wherein he had an honest choice, he rejected the white man's religion. In many instances the Indian had no choice.

RESISTANCE TO THE GOSPEL

As previously mentioned, 92 percent of all Indians are not going to church in the 1980s. Resistance to the gospel in the twentieth century is rooted in the past. It should not be thought that Indians are irreligious or atheistic. In fact, "religion permeates all the daily life."[12] Then why have they resisted the gospel? The truth is that they have not resisted the gospel so much as they have rejected the concomitance of the gospel. They reject the package in which the gospel has been presented to them.

Indians have rejected a gospel that requires cultural suicide. Without judging the motives of the early missionaries, it is quite clear that they thought that an Indian could not be a Christian in his native culture. He had to renounce his way of life before he could be saved.

Indians have also found it difficult to accept the gospel message from the lips of the white man whose word was seldom trustworthy in other areas. Indians trusted the early colonists and shared with them their food and land. Some colonists purchased needed land from the tribe, but others took lands by right of eminent domain with or without remuneration. The Indian made treaties with the increasingly land-hungry newcomers only to find again and again that the word of the white man was not firm, because he had an insatiable appetite for Indian lands.

War was inevitable to protect Indian rights. Although the Indians were able to win a few skirmishes, in the long run they lost the battle. Three hundred seventy treaties were signed between 1789 and 1871, but all were violated.[13]

When reservations were created by the U.S. government in 1786, ostensibly it was, among other things, to protect Indian lands.

11. Ronda and Axtell, p. 21.
12. D. Clarence Burd, "The Indian American," in *The Fields at Home*, ed. Peter Gunther (Chicago: Moody, 1963), p. 56.
13. *Encyclopedia International*, 1970 ed., s.v. "Indian Policy of the U.S."

Within those boundaries no one was allowed to encroach under penalty of law. But by 1830 there was no longer room for Indians east of the Mississippi River under any circumstances. The state of Georgia insisted that the government remove the Indians who were farming some of the state's best land that was needed for the rapidly expanding cotton industry and plantations. Impossible as it may be to believe, Congress passed the Indian Removal Act in 1830 and within ten years 100,000 Indians were rounded up from every state east of the Mississippi River and removed to Indian Country,[14] which later became the state of Oklahoma (1907).

In North Carolina the Cherokee nation resisted. They were one of the Five Civilized Tribes, so called because they had basically adopted the white man's ways. Without provocation, 20,000 were put in stockades, where several thousand died. Then, through the dead of winter, 16,000 were herded to Indian Country, over the 1,200-mile Trail of Tears that required nine months of travel. Twenty-five percent of the tribe died on that death march, which was ordered by President Andrew Jackson. Ironically, his life had been saved earlier by the Cherokee chief Junaluska, at the Battle of Horseshoe Bend. Thus, it became obvious that "the destiny of the country did not provide for the survival even of the Indians. This was to be a white man's country."[15]

The Indians west of the Mississippi were also encapsulated over a period of time within the reservation system. Some nations were restricted to areas with which they were familiar, but others were removed to new areas to start life all over again. The Navajo tribe as a nomadic people was a special problem.

The Navajo felt that homesteaders from Mexico were encroaching on their hunting grounds and carried on a running warfare in which both Indians and Mexicans were killed, plundered, and made slaves of the other. After the United States's war with Mexico (1848) and the westward movement of the whites had begun, further conflict was inevitable. Kit Carson and the army was dispatched in 1864 to round up the entire tribe. The seemingly impossible feat was accomplished by destroying the Navajo's crops and flocks and starving them out. Upon surrender, 10,000 Navajos were forced to make the "long walk" 300 miles to Fort Sumner, New Mexico. Four years later (1868) the Navajos were permitted to return to the Arizona reservation.

14. *Encyclopedia Americana*, 1975 ed., s.v. "American Indian."
15. Wells and Woodbridge, p. 99.

A second negative experience with the whites occurred in 1924. The Indians were forced to reduce the size of their stocks of cattle by killing them. They lost their main source of income. Memory of those events is passed on to new generations, thus keeping hatred for the white man perpetual. "These two events, more than anything else, made the Navajo people a non-receptive people to American missionaries during the first fifty years of missionary activity."[16]

The opening up of the West was directly connected with the westward expansion of the railroad. Although reservation land given to Indians was at the time thought to be of no use to whites, some of it was now found to be needed for right of way for the railroad. Ironically, the Choctaw leaders had predicted nearly forty years before, when they were asked to trade their lands in the East for western lands, "The red people are of the opinion that, in a few years the American will also wish to possess the land west of the Mississippi."[17] True to form, Congress passed the Railroad Enabling Act (1866), which condemned Indian lands and made them available for the roadway.

Following the Civil War (1861-65) the flow of whites westward became a mighty flood. As the population increased and new areas were organized into territories, the Indian resisted by going to war. Thousands of troops were stationed along the thoroughfares through the West to control them.

> One of the unfortunate consequences of the pushing of settlers into the trans-Missouri region and the building of the transcontinental railroads was the unrest produced among the western Indians. . . . This general situation was particularly hard on Indian missions, for many missionaries were compelled to flee for their lives, and religious and economic conditions among the Indians were rapidly going from bad to worse.[18]

The Quakers, articulating the feelings of many humanitarians, encouraged President Grant to consider what was happening to the Indians and change federal policy toward them. The government response was to recognize thirteen Protestant denominations working on the reservations and provide them with funds to help make peace

---

16. Thomas Dologhan and David Scates, *The Navajos Are Coming to Jesus* (Pasadena: William Carey Library, 1978). p. 118.
17. D'Arcy McNickle, *The Indian Tribes of the United States* (New York: Oxford U., 1970), p. 39.
18. William Sweet, *The Story of Religion in America* (New York: Harper & Row, 1950), pp. 337-38.

with the Indian. Grant's Peace Policy (1869) in effect appointed missionaries as Indian agents. The experiment failed because the missionaries were poor administrators and they neglected their missionary responsibilities. The Indians were doomed to nothing more than a social gospel.[19] Later (1881), the reservations were opened to all the denominations for ministry, but at best the Indians were receiving a confusing message.

By 1871 the government had determined that the Indian was no longer a separate power with whom it must negotiate, but rather people who were part of the country over whom it had the power to legislate. One of the first pieces of legislation was the General Allotment Act (1887) designed to break up the reservations and parcel the land in small acreages to Indian families. The ultimate purpose was to destroy any Indian homogeneity and absorb them into the dominant society. This was the action of Protestant North America, which was deliberately trying to stamp out the Indian as a people.[20] They were nearly successful, for the Indian population was now at its nadir, or only 25 percent of the 1,000,000 souls when the white man first came to America.

The Indian was not, however, the "vanishing American" so many had hoped. Even the awarding of citizenship (1924) had not provided incentive for him to become one of the many. Then a new administration revolutionized its Indian policy and determined to allow the red man to live under his own tribal government. This was known as Roosevelt's Reorganization Act (1934). The new attitude of the government was to free the Indians from federal supervision and control; however, that has yet to come to pass.

The government found that it was continually embroiled in problems involving the Indian tribes. Many of the government's concerns with the Indian involved armed conflicts. It therefore established the Bureau of Indian Affairs (BIA) and placed it under the jurisdiction of the War Department. In 1848 the BIA was placed under the Department of the Interior, where it still remains.

The BIA has far-reaching powers that touch every aspect of Indian life. Through its thirteen area offices it administers eighty-two agencies in twenty-seven states. It has been called "an extra state scattered piecemeal over the face of the country. In this shadow-state

19. Gordon Frazier, *The Native American Christian* (Flagstaff, Arizona: Southwestern School of Missions, The Indiana Bible Institute, 1977), p. 13.
20. William Brandon, *The American Heritage Book of Indians* (New York: Dell, 1961), p. 245.

all services, roads, schools, and courts are furnished."[21] This bureau-cratic octopus has always been rife with corruption and unresponsive to the needs of those for whom it was created. It has always been unresponsive because it has never understood the Indians, and has seldom employed them in high positions. This lack of understanding has created an "unbridgeable gulf separating whites and Indians from direct communication and understanding."[22] To what extent is this true of Indian missions?

Indian missions today must recognize that the memory of past injustices dies slowly. Missionary activity has not always taken place with the purest motives. Indian grievances may well be blown out of proportion as evidenced by the 852 claims filed against the federal government in 1946 for land redress. The claims total more than the entire United States acreage! But their feelings are nevertheless real. Sins of the past can be no excuse for spiritually neglecting the Indian, who, in his hurt and anger, still sits in ignorance of biblical truth. That message must be carried across the country to the Indians who are to be found in every state, most counties, and almost every city.

INDIAN PRESENCE

Where are the Indians in the United States? About half the Indian population lives on or around nearly 100 reservations under the jurisdiction of the Bureau of Indian Affairs (see Figure 3.1). The other half is scattered among major cities. Eighty percent of all Indians live west of the Mississippi River, yet two-thirds of the twenty-four states in the East have more than 5,000 Indian residents. The largest populations in the East are in North Carolina (65,000), Michigan (40,000), and New York (39,000), with 10,000 living in New York City.

The largest concentration in the United States is in California (201,300), with one-fourth living in Los Angeles. The next largest concentration is in Oklahoma where 170,000 are divided among sixty-seven tribes. The city of Anadarko is said to be the Indian capital of the country. Arizona (153,000) is third in size and hosts the major part of the Navajo reservation. Fort Defiance is the capital of the Navajo nation (200,000), which is the largest tribe. The reserva-tion straddles four states and includes 30,000 square miles. To the

21. Ibid., p. 371.
22. Ibid., p. 243.

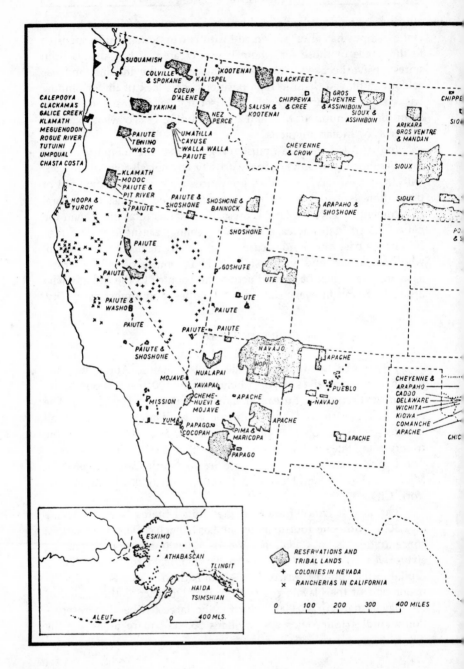

Figure 3.1

PRESENT DAY LOCATION OF INDIAN TRIBES

east the reservation spills into New Mexico (105,000), which has the fourth largest population.

Indians today are to be found in all fifty states (see Figure 3.2) and in more than half of all counties.[23] In recent years the Indian has been moving to the cities to find jobs. Indians living in the East are 84 percent urbanized, whereas of those living in the West, only 40 percent live in the city. Nationwide, 45 percent are urban. Pierce Beaver gives a list of cities with populations over 30,000 and notes the Indian population and churches in each when available.[24]

Indian reservations are to be found in the West. A majority of the reservations have less than 6,000 residents. More than half of all reservation Indians reside on one of twenty reservations. The Navajo reservation is the largest, and three others have between 20,000 and 27,000 residents.[25]

The concentration of Indians in the West may be traced to two contributing factors. Because of the Indian Removal Act, most of the Red Men were forcibly removed from all of the eastern states and relocated in Oklahoma (1830-1840). Some were able to escape the roundup, such as those who hid in the Florida Everglades and in the mountains of North Carolina and New York. Others made their way back to the eastern cities so that today the Indians once again live in every state.

Perhaps a more important reason for explaining the western concentration may be found in discovering the origin of the Indian presence in the western hemisphere. The Americas were peopled very early by a branch of the Mongoloid race, which probably came from the Far East across the Bering Strait. There seems to be evidence that "the fathers of the first-known tribes were Chinese" and that on early maps America was "properly known as Fu Sang."[26] Most Asiatic distinctives are now missing, except for the straight black hair, high cheek bones, and little body hair; therefore, they are called American Mongoloids.

They came from the northwest through Alaska and Canada into the western United States. The larger portion of the 20,000,000 travelers settled in Latin America, more specifically the Andean

23. *Number of American Indians by Counties of the United States: 1970* (Washington, D.C.: U.S. Government Printing Office, Superintendent of Documents.

24. R. Pierce Beaver, *The Native American Christian Community: A Directory of Indian, Aluet and Eskimos* (Monrovia: MARC, 1979), p. 301-6.

25. *Information Please Almanac* (New York: Simon and Schuster, 1980), p. 798.

26. Hendon M. Harris, *The Asiatic Fathers of America* (Taipei, Taiwan: Wen Ho Printing, n.d.), p. 31.

Mountains. When Columbus discovered what he thought was the Indies, there were already two advanced civilizations at their height— the Aztec and the Inca. The former was an empire of 5,000,000 in Mexico and the other 7,000,000 in Peru.

In the United States 1,000,000 Indians moved along the western coast, to the south, into the eastern forests, and up the eastern seaboard. Finally, the plains were peopled in the 1600s, when the horse was introduced. Ironically, the horses the American Indian used to conquer the plains had been brought by the Spanish to destroy the southern empires a century before. We conclude that probably the larger number of Indians has always lived in the West.

The Indian must be recognized as a highly diverse people that are not one homogenous unit. The original hoard of Mongoloids may have spoken 5,000 languages or dialects. They became isolated in Alaska (64,000), Canada (300,000 living on 2,200 reservations), the United States (1,400,000), Mexico (13,000,000), and Central America (3,000,000). The diversification continued in the United States.

Some 460 tribes and 300 languages have been identified. Today there are fragments of 280 tribes left using up to 170 languages. Parts of the Bible have been published in 35 languages spoken by Indians in the United States. The American Bible Society publishes New Testaments in six Indian languages. The Old Testament is being prepared in Navajo. Wycliffe Bible Translators (WBT) has determined that of the many Indian languages, 55 are extremely bilingual, 49 are nearly extinct, and translation work is in progress in 26. There is need for work to begin in 5 others.[27] In 1984 the North American branch of the WBT determined that the need for God's Word in the Indian language has never been greater.

The Indians are to be found almost everywhere again across the United States. The concerned Christian will find them hidden away in his state or city somewhere and should encourage his church to include the evangelization of Indians in the missionary budget.

MISSIONARY ACTIVITY AMONG INDIANS

Missionary interest in the Indian has had a roller coaster history. In 1810 the American Board of Commissioners for Foreign Missions was created and "Indian mission history entered a vital new phase. . . . This interdenominational Protestant society . . . between 1812 and 1865 supported more Indian missionaries . . . than any

---

27. *Ethnologue*, published by Wycliffe Bible Translators Academic Publications, p. 33.

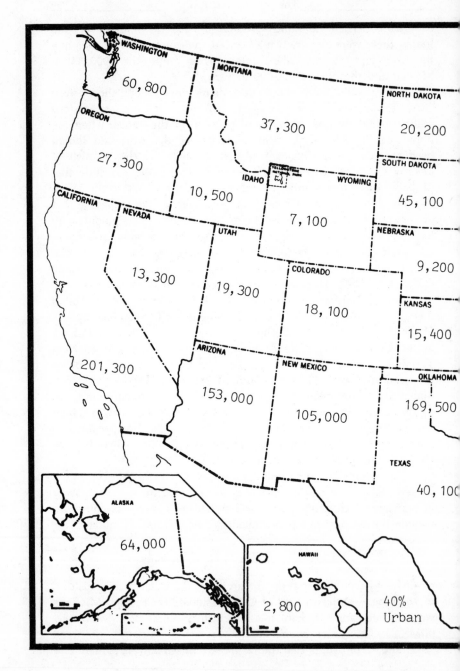

Figure 3.2

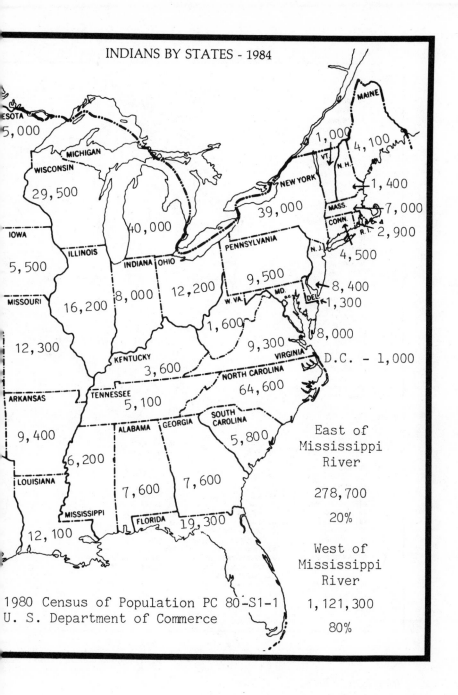

INDIANS BY STATES - 1984

ESOTA
5,000

MICHIGAN

WISCONSIN
29,500

40,000

MAINE

1,000

VT.

N.H.

4,100

NEW YORK
39,000

MASS.
1,400

CONN.
7,000

R.I.
2,900

IOWA
5,500

ILLINOIS

INDIANA
8,000

OHIO
12,200

PENNSYLVANIA
9,500

N.J.
4,500

MISSOURI
16,200

W.VA.
1,600

MD.

DEL.
8,400

1,300

12,300

KENTUCKY
3,600

VIRGINIA
9,300

8,000

D.C. - 1,000

ARKANSAS
9,400

TENNESSEE
5,100

NORTH CAROLINA
64,600

ALABAMA
6,200

GEORGIA

SOUTH
CAROLINA
5,800

LOUISIANA

7,600

7,600

East of
Mississippi
River

278,700

20%

MISSISSIPPI
12,100

FLORIDA
19,300

West of
Mississippi
River

1,121,300

80%

1980 Census of Population PC 80-S1-1
U. S. Department of Commerce

APPROXIMATE LOCATION OF NATIVE TRIBES

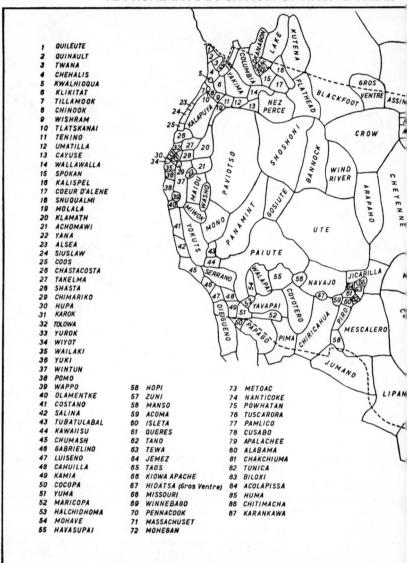

Figure 3.3

Source: D'Arcy McNickle, *The Indian Tribes of the United States* (New York: Oxford Press, 1970), p. 8 (inset).

other mission organization."[28] However, board minutes reveal that they felt the ministry was mostly disappointing.

After 1814 most denominations created their own boards, both home and foreign. Their activity, at home especially, was deeply curtailed by the Civil War. After the war, denominations allowed their missionaries to become Indian agents. However, that move did not enhance church planting among the tribes.

Most denominations sought to plant stations on the Navajo reservation, which contained the largest concentration of Indians. Several found the work too difficult and withdrew. One of the deficiencies of Indian missionaries was the inability to use the native language. It was not until 1914 that a missionary became fluent in Navajo.[29]

Early twentieth-century missionaries were still learning the lesson that civilizing is not the same as evangelizing. It was relatively easy to establish hospitals and schools, but "subsequent years have shown them to be ineffective as a means of evangelism. Where establishing churches and preaching the gospel has been the sole goal, evangelism of the Navajo has been more effective."[30]

Another lesson to be learned from this period of Indian missions is that there were too few nationals trained as pastors. Mission schools had trained leaders for the schools and tribe but not enough became church leaders. After a century of Indian missions (1910), twenty-six American societies had fielded 163 missionaries. They had trained 155 native pastors to minister to a Christian community of 28,000 gathering in 534 churches.[31]

In the 1980s the Southern Baptist Convention is the most active denominational agency with 381 churches ministering to 36,000 communicants. Only the Catholics claim more churches (454) and a larger communicant community (178,000). Among the groups associated with the National Association of Evangelicals, the Assemblies of God represent 80 percent of the work on reservations. They report 204 missionaries working among 161 tribes on 98 reservations in 129 churches.[32] The largest Indian Episcopal church has 800 members, and the second largest (Methodist) claims 670 members. The average

28. Ronda and Axtell, p. 25.
29. Dologhan and Scates, p. 33.
30. Ibid., p. 88.
31. Beaver, *Native American Christian Community*, p. 23.
32. *1980 Survey of Indian Ministry of Assembly of God* (Springfield, Mo.: Division of Home Missions, 1980).

membership of 1,500 denominational churches is 72. These churches are affiliated with forty-two denominational groups.[33]

Pierce Beaver concludes from his survey that 43 percent of the Indian community consider themselves to be Christianized. The 320,000 communicants are divided among Catholic (178,000), Protestant (122,000), and Orthodox (22,000) communicants. Protestant communicants equal 15 percent of the Indian Christian community. Church attendance on a given Sunday among the Navajos averages 12,400, or 8 percent of the populace.[34] A list of Indian churches with their addresses is given in Beaver's survey. They are catalogued according to affiliation: denominational, non-denominational societies, or independent churches.

Faith missions began work among the Indians in 1930 and have grown to twenty-two societies during the decade of the eighties. Three hundred twenty-six missionaries serve twenty-seven churches in a Christian community of 2,800. Half of those churches have national pastors. The average church has thirty members. United Indian Missions, Incorporated, has the largest number of missionaries (80) and Navajo Gospel Mission, Incorporated, has the greatest number of churches (11) (see Figure 3.4).

Since 1960 Navajos have become more receptive to the gospel.[35] There are still 143,000 Navajos who need to be saved, which is 89 percent of the nation. According to one study conducted in 1978, 10 percent of Navajos are nationalistic, militant, and anti-Christian.[36] Another 20 percent are being acculturated but still feel at home in the Navajo culture. They want to learn English. The remainder, or 70 percent, are seeking religious fulfillment. They are only mildly anti-Anglo; therefore, if they are not evangelized, they will probably turn to one of the indigenous cults.

Other tribes may also be receptive to the gospel. Beaver's study indicates that the Lumbees (30,000) of North Carolina, which make up one-half of the state's Indian population, are mainly Christianized. The Five Civilized Tribes of Oklahoma are said to be in a post-Christian era, for they were Christianized before they walked the Trail of Tears. Seventy-five thousand call themselves Christians. These tribes should also be included in a gospel offensive in the eighties.

33. Beaver, Native American Christian Community, p. 18.
34. Dologhan and Scates, p. 95.
35. Ibid., p. 88.
36. Ibid., p. 55.

NATIVE AMERICANS

1. American Indian Bible Missions, Inc.
2. American Indian Crusade
3. Baptist International Missions, Inc.
4. Baptist Mid-Missions - 1950
5. Berean Mission, Inc.
6. Bible Mission to the American
   Indians, Inc.
7. Chief: Christian Hope Indian
   Eskimo Fellowship, Inc.
8. Christian Indian Ministries, Inc.
9. Fellowship of Baptists for Home
   Missions - 1950
10. Flagstaff Mission to the Navajos
11. Good News Mission to the Navajo
    Indians, Inc.
12. Navajo Gospel Crusade - 1951
13. Navajo Gospel Mission, Inc. - 1932
14. Navajo Missions, Inc.
15. Oak Hills Bible Fellowship - 1926
16. Sanders Bible Mission
17. Southwest Indian Missionary Assoc. - 1957
18. United Indian Missions, Inc.
19. Western Indian Ministries - 1937
20. World Gospel Missions
21. World-Wide Missions - 1962
22. Wycliffe Bible Translators

Addresses given in Appendix 1

Figure 3.4

Missionaries	Churches	Christians	Ordained Indians
	4	105	7
19			
24	5	100	
6			
	1		1
8	2		
29	6	450	5
4	3	75	
10	3	90	
39	11	500	
30			
13			
5	1	25	
10			
80	4	225	1
43	9	500	
17			
13			
60			
410[1]	49	2,070	14
	67	2,800[2]	

1. Number of missionaries from Survey 1981.
2. Statistics from Pierce Beaver, *The Native American Christian Community*, 1979, p. 40.

How effective the Anglo missionary can be now is open to question. Gordon Frazier, editor of the *Native American Christian*,[37] says that the white missionary is no longer able to preach in Indian country; therefore, he should spend his time training native evangelists. Without question Indian Bible schools should be given top priority so that Indians can be prepared to evangelize and pastor Indian churches. Beaver lists nine Bible schools presently training Indians for ministry.

One of the greatest problems facing Indian missions is the evangelization of urban Indians. Half of all Indians are hidden away in the central cities. One-fourth of urban Indians are to be found in cities over 30,000. Beaver lists sixty-six urban Indian churches and nineteen others where Indians attend but are not a majority. Those churches each have a mission field of 1,700 Indians. He mentions another ten cities with a combined Indian population of 52,000 and no churches.

The urban Indian presents a unique problem for evangelizing and church planting. There are no native American neighborhoods in the city, for "Native Americans do not seem to cluster together in the same blocks to form tight Indian communities with recognizable boundaries."[38] Jack Waddell and Michael Watson made a detailed study of urban Indians and also corroborate this phenomenon.[39]

Urban Indian church planting is needed because ". . . many Indians do not feel welcome in most urban churches . . . and that they are made to feel uncomfortable, conspicuous, and unwanted when they have attended European-American churches."[40] Neither black nor Hispanic churches fulfill their spiritual needs.

ISSUES THE MISSIONARY MUST FACE

The missionary who desires to reach the American Indian for Christ must face several serious issues.

The Indian capital of the country is Anadarko, Oklahoma. Located there is the Indian Hall of Fame and Indian City, but, more

---

37. Frazier, p. 13.
38. James H. Davis and Woodie W. White, *Racial Transition in the Church* (Nashville: Abingdon, 1980), p. 85.
39. Jack Waddell and Michael Watson, *The American Indian in Urban Society* (Boston: Little, Brown, 1971), pp. 55-56.
40. David Franchak and Sharrel Keyes, eds., Metro-Ministry "Ways and Means for the Urban Church" (Elgin, Ill.: David C. Cook, 1970-9), p. 185.

important for missions, in this center are created trends and movements that affect all Indian tribes.

In Oklahoma sixty-seven tribes, which have been transplanted from other places, now live in proximity to each other. This has made possible periodic intertribal gatherings to dance and sing. Whereas tribal distinctives have been jealously guarded, certain similarities have surfaced giving rise to the concept of a mythical Oklahoma Indian. The commonalities are race, a strange land into which they were forcibly placed, hatred of the whites, and widespread fear that they seek to appease by animistic ceremonies interpreted by a shaman, or witch doctor. The greatest coalescing factor is the desire for a unified voice to speak out for all the tribes.

It was logical that Oklahoma would be the cradle of Pan-Indianism. At the gatherings the dances and songs rehearse the glory of the past, present grievances, and hope for the future. The future is envisioned in terms of a super Indian race that would give rise to a "New Great Indian America."[41] Various national organizations have emerged from the Pan-Indian spirit. In the area of religion, Peyotism developed. The National Congress of American Indians is likened to the United Nations of Indian tribes for political clout in civil rights. By late 1960 Pan-Indianism evolved into Red Power complete with hostility toward Christianity.

Nothing happens on the reservations without some reference to the Bureau of Indian Affairs. Education is controlled by the BIA. Free hospitalization is provided also. All legal matters are handled through its offices. The government assumed those responsibilities "under a treaty-based trust relationship it assumed largely in exchange for Indian lands."[42] In due season the Indian will lose his "special status" with the federal government, for President Reagan is turning federal programs over to the states. This was manifest in the 1982 budget cutbacks. Housing programs were cut 96 percent even though 10 percent of Indian homes are still substandard. Development programs have been cut 82 per cent. Job training programs were cut 45 percent. Indian legal aid programs have been abolished. Those developments will affect the attitude of the Indian toward missions.

Under this rubric are included several problems, some of which have received far too much attention by missions in the past. Church planting must be the primary concern of missions, but social

41. William Powers, *Indians of the Southern Plains* (New York: Capricorn Books, 1972), p. 205.
42. *Sojourners*, June 1981, p. 6.

concerns will affect the ministry as the Indian wrestles with these problems.

Unemployment is a perennial problem that may run as high as 80 percent in some areas. The cause of unemployment is often lack of job skills, but discrimination is still a factor. Indian income in 1980 averaged $1,500 annually. A spinoff of joblessness is the American propensity to solve all problems with a handout. Urban Indians are especially vulnerable.

Indian education is a complicated problem. On many reservations the Indians live great distances from each other. This sometimes requires that the children live in boarding schools away from their parents. In BIA schools the staff is often non-Indian oriented and the instruction in English without Indian language transitional classes. At times the children are taught to demean their heritage and are punished for using the native tongue. This gives rise to "the total dehumanization of the Indian from the time he enters school until the time he drops out of society—and can do nothing but leave an indelible imprint of hate on the American Indian."[43]

Dropout rates are double the national average. Leonard Rascher of the Moody Bible Institute researched the attitude of Indians toward education and found that the "most serious and perplexing problem in American Indian education, for both urban and reservation Indians, is the excessively high rate of Indians that are dropping out of school."[44]

Adults have an average a fifth-grade education. Many are not able to read or write their native language. In Navajoland "the majority of adults cannot read or write in any language."[45] Literacy programs have been established by some Indian missions.

The relatively poor attitude toward life can only contribute to emotional and physical problems. The average life-span is forty-five years. Suicide rates are three times the national average, and on some reservations ten times higher.

Alcoholism is a larger problem among Indians than among any other group of people, for one out of three adults drinks to excess.[46] Much speculation still has not revealed a cogent explanation for the

43. Powers, p. 216.
44. Leonard Rascher, "Urban Attitudes Toward Indian Education" (Ph.D. dissertation, Northwestern U. 1977), p. 11.
45. Missiongrams, April-June 1981, published by Berean Mission, p. 5.
46. James Whittaker, "Alcohol and the Standing Rock Sioux Tribe: A Twenty Year Follow-Up Study," study conducted by Pennsylvania State U., 1980.

phenomenon. Regardless, the Indian cannot handle the white man's fire water. It is the number one problem and is nearly universal. Most reservations have alcohol rehabilitation centers, but little has been done to help the urban Indian who has just as great a problem.

Indians have the highest birthrate in the nation. Since 1900 they have quadrupled in number, and in the decade of the seventies they increased 75 percent. The shorter life-span and high fecundity give rise to a nation of young people. Fifty-five percent of the Navajo tribe is under 18 years of age and 80 percent are under 35. Median age for the nation is 30; however, for Indians it is 23.[47] The Indian youth are in serious trouble. It was reported in Senate hearings in 1968 that the Indian youth is alienated from himself and others; therefore, he is not identifying effectively with either the Indian or the white culture.

Most of the tribes are rapidly becoming infected with the American mania for things. The television and pick-up truck are status symbols. At the same time tribal value systems have been greatly weakened; therefore the youth, attracted by both elements of both cultures, stand between two worlds.

Thousands of Indian men who fought valiantly in the armed services were exposed to the larger world beyond the reservation. They returned with new ideas and desires. Multitudes oscillate between city jobs and the more peaceful reservation life and privileges.

All Indians are deeply religious people. Religion is considered to be the responsibility of the individual.[48] They may well participate in corporate ceremonies, but the experience is deeply personal. At puberty some Indians begin the personal search for harmony with nature by making the "vision quest" for a guardian spirit. In fasting and praying alone a youth seeks a vision that is later interpreted by the *shaman*, the spiritual leader. The shaman will also indicate some item that is believed to be representative of the guardian spirit. It may be worn as a charm or placed in the personal medicine bundle that is sacred to him alone. Some animal or plant may also be designated as a totem object that is powerful in the Indian's behalf.

The medicine man is still very much a part of life for healing or determining the affairs of life in the twentieth century. A widespread revival of old religious rites is taking place.

47. U.S. Department of Commerce, Bureau of the Census, *1980 Census of Population*, p. 3.
48. Powers, p. 124.

The ultimate desire for an Indian is to be in harmony with nature. Any problem is interpreted as springing from some disharmony between himself and his world. Therefore, religion is essentially the system whereby that harmony is restored. The procedure for restoration usually involves intricate ceremony. By means of the ceremony a vision, to be interpreted by the shaman, will reveal what must be done by the individual to restore order.

NATIVE RELIGIONS

The Sun Dance, outlawed in 1890, was revived in the 1930s. This ceremony involves marathon dancing for several days, fasting, and staring at the sun. The dance may include self-torture, which involves tearing out of the flesh a wooden skewer imbedded in the chest and attached to a pole by a leather thong. The purpose of the dance is to induce a vision.

The Sacred Arrow ceremony was created by the Cheyenne Indians who believed that a supreme being gave four arrows to one of their heroes. By means of a special ceremony those arrows were imbued with power and, when pointed at man or buffalo, caused the subjects to be helpless. Today, vows are made during sickness, war, or dying. During the ceremony the sacred arrow keeper reveals the arrows that are said to give off a special blinding light.

The Ghost Dance began in the late nineteenth century when Wovoka, a Paiute became the Indian messiah by proclaiming a new doctrine. He taught that through the Ghost Dance ceremony occult power would cause white men to disappear and dead Indians to return. It is hoped that it will yet one day work. Among the Indians there is a great fear of ghosts, which are believed to be spirits of the departed. Indians may still paint themselves with stripes of red paint that cross over the eyes as a witch repellent, or carry two flicker feathers in the pocket as a goodluck charm.

MODERN DEVELOPMENTS

PEYOTISM

Not only is there a revival of old native religions but a new syncretistic religion has developed called *Peyotism*. Through Peyotism, many Indians (40 percent in some tribes) have turned to a religion that draws from two worlds—that of the Aztec and the Christian. The basic structure of the religion is taken from an ancient Aztec ritual with the same name. In the ceremony a hallucinagenic drug, peyote, derived from a sacred cactus named peyot, is used. In the new religion Christian meanings are given to the blend of ancient and modern ritual. Two basic versions of Peyotism have developed.

The more popular sect is called Half Moon, and the other is named Cross Fire. In the latter the Bible is used in the ceremony, although both use Christian ritual.

The ceremony lasts all night. It begins at sundown Saturday night by circumambulating the special tepee and concludes Sunday morning with a traditional breakfast.

In the center of the tepee is a fire. Behind that is a crescent-shaped altar graced by a large peyote button. Each participant carries a personally-decorated paraphernalia box and wears a red and blue blanket.

The service may be likened to a Wednesday night prayer meeting; or it may be called for the purpose of healing, or for celebrating a birthday, funeral, or memorial, or before traveling. The ritual includes smoking hand-rolled corn husk and tobacco cigarettes and sprinkling the ashes on the altar. It also includes chewing sage or rubbing it on the body and burning incense.

During the service peyote buttons, likened to the Eucharist, are eaten as if at a Communion service, and prayer is made to Jesus Christ. Repetitious singing accompanied by drumming is an integral part of the ceremony. Ritualistic staring at the fire also helps to induce visions, which is the desired objective.

Peyotism is without question widespread in the Indian world. The missionary will need to be conversant with its teaching and practice. In William Powers's informative introduction he summarizes:

> Concurrent with the visionary experience is the feeling of a closeness with God. Because Peyotism is now greatly influenced by Christianity, the members pray to Jesus Christ and refer to the peyote as the Eucharist. They equate the consumption of the peyote button with Holy Communion and espouse the basic tenets of the Christian churches in their prayers and songs. The great difference between members of the Native American Church and those who would take peyote for kicks is that the avid Peyotists cannot understand how the sacred plant can be used for anything but prayer.[49]

49. Ibid., p. 146.

THE INDIGENOUS CAMP CHURCH

In Navajoland a new phenomenon called the independent church has developed. In the past the independent churches developed around an Anglo minister, but more recently a class church has emerged with a charismatic leader who is a kinsman of the group. The leader normally has no formal training. Great danger of doctrinal error is inherent within this movement, but it also has great potential.

Navajo Gospel Mission is experimenting with the concept of indigenous camp churches. Great care is taken to operate within the traditional Navajo social structure, including informal services, native instruments, and concluding with a traditional Navajo ceremonial meal. The objective is to develop strong Navajo leadership and identity.

The camp church begins in a hogan; therefore, it is easy to multiply churches, which Thomas Dolaghan and David Scates conclude is the best way of evangelizing the Navajo people.[50] This same principle of multiplying churches is being used by The Evangelical Alliance Mission in Japan.

The indigenous camp church seemingly has great potential, but it will need a well-designed, systematic, continuing Bible training program for its leadership and laity.

The Indian is a mission field. One mission plaintively asks, "Should the 'first ones here' be the 'last ones to hear?' " Our prayer is that the Lord would raise up twentieth-century David Brainerds to reach these precious souls—whether in the cities or on the reservations.[51]

---

50. Dologhan and Scates, p. 63.
51. *Candidate Seminar Manual* (Cleveland, Ohio: Baptist Mid-Missions), p. 154.

4

Black Americans

Black Americans in 1984 numbered 28 million. At least 40 percent of all blacks are not members of any church. Probably not more than one-half of the 15,000,000 who are church members are included in the evangelical community. Adding the 30 percent whose spiritual needs are not being met in their churches to the unchurched, the total is 70 percent. This definable ethnic group, which is virtually beyond the normal evangelistic outreach of the established evangelical churches, either black or white, numbers 18,000,000. That is approximately the population of Kenya, the Sudan, or Tanzania! Thirty-seven nations have a population of less than 10,000,000 each. Only four countries of black Africa have a greater population than black America: Nigeria, 82,000,000; Ethiopia, 31,000,000; and South Africa and Zaire, each with 30,000,000.

The spiritual plight of black Americans is partly because there are few evangelical black leaders. Most Bible colleges and seminaries for many years would not accept black students, and even now most of those have no active recruiting program for blacks or adequate scholarship programs. Perhaps 500 out of a total of 2,000 black seminarians are studying for the evangelical ministry. Blacks in seminaries equaled 4 percent of the seminary enrollment in 1978, which is up from 2.6 percent in 1970. Keep in mind that blacks are 12 percent of the populace.

Most blacks are not reading Christian material because there is a dearth of literature for the Sunday school and adult reading material that has been written either by or for blacks. (See Figure 4.1.)

Their youth are not joining black churches, and others are leaving them because there are few programs designed specifically for them. In short, the spiritual needs of blacks are not being met.

The failure of black churches to meet the spiritual needs of their people is manifest in several ways. First, only a few blacks are giving themselves to full-time Christian service either at home or abroad. A survey of the three largest black denominations, representing one-third of U.S. blacks, reveals that they have fielded only about one dozen missionaries.

Second, without adequate leadership or role models, many blacks are turning to cults and the Roman Catholic church. Consider also the 200,000 who have turned to the Black Muslim movement and the 800,000 who have become Catholic.

A NEGLECTED MISSION FIELD

Not only has the black church failed, but, perhaps more critically, the white church has also failed. How can that happen in evangelical America? Perhaps part of the answer lies in the response to the following searching question, Are blacks welcome in the white churches? Or, put another way, are they made to feel as comfortable as anyone else?

If the answer is yes, then could they become members with all privileges and without causing a stir among the saints? Does the church visitation program overtly include black homes in the community where calling is taking place or in a totally black neighborhood? Now for the most challenging question of all. Would black teenagers be welcome in the youth group? If the answer is even a question mark, then perhaps racial bias is a part of the reason for the neglect. Certainly there is no biblical basis for discrimination. It can only be a decision of convenience based purely on sociological grounds, which is not Christian.

SPIRITUAL BLIND SPOT

Blacks are a mission field because most evangelical Americans have not seen their spiritual plight, even as they have had no vision of the spiritual depravation of the native Americans, Hispanics, and other equally neglected home mission opportunities. Christians for too long have been myopic in their spiritual vision. They have not seen beyond their own kind and class to those in the community or country for whom they should feel spiritual responsibility. In the words of William Banks, "There is an appalling ignorance on the part of both the blacks and whites concerning the religion of the American Negro."[1]

Yet, another strange feature about the spiritual vision of the evangelicals is that at the same time it is hyperopic. They can see at a distance the needs of the 320,000,000 black Africans and send nearly 8,000 missionaries, investing $255,000,000.[2] This is not to suggest that such outreach is wrong, but rather to point out its success, for today black Africa is nearly 50 percent Christianized,[3] whereas black America may be only 30 percent.[4] This hiatus is explainable when an examination of the typical church mission budget reveals that nothing is designated for black evangelism or church planting stateside. Donald Canty, missionary to Liberia, contends that there is something insincere about the white church's concern for reaching blacks in Africa and neglecting blacks in our own American cities.

AN EMOTIONAL ISSUE

Whenever Negroes, Afro-Americans, or blacks are mentioned, it usually evokes an emotional response. The child may remember the first time he saw a black person and his wide-eyed amazement at the difference in color. The teenager may think about the style of clothes or hair that may differ from his in-group. The adult might think of a favorite black athlete. The urbanite may visualize an inner-city slum resident, whereas the suburbanite remembers the anticipated devaluation of property when a black family moved into his area. The employer thinks of cheap labor. The Southerner remembers the plantation or the struggle to maintain what he considered to be his status. Assuming he has even faced the issue, the Christian is embarrassed with ambivalent feelings concerning an issue about which he has found no comfortable answers. The evangelical church leader fears the day he might be confronted with policy-making decisions involving the blacks. Even blacks themselves respond from their own milieu with rapport for those of similar circumstances or distrust for those who have become more successful. Few subjects

1. William Banks, *The Black Church in the U.S.* (Chicago: Moody, 1972), p. 6.
2. Samuel Wilson, ed., *Mission Handbook: North American Protestant Ministries Overseas*, 12th ed. (Monrovia: MARC), pp. 22,35.
3. Herbert Kane, *Understanding Christian Missions* (Grand Rapids: Baker, 1974), p. 216.
4. George Gallup, estimate reported on television, October 1980.

are more emotionally charged. It is extremely difficult to be neutral. Blacks are a mission field because the emotional issue has not been squarely faced and put to rest with biblical answers.

A MIRACLE OF SURVIVAL

Black Americans stand in our midst as one of the most resilient and remarkable peoples in history. In a word, they have survived! They survived the rejection of their own West African people who captured them, forced them to march in coffles, and sold them into bondage at home and abroad. They survived the cattlelike haulage on slave ships and the dehumanizing experience of being sold as property. They survived the destruction of their African culture, especially their language and religion, as well as the withholding of the privilege of becoming an equal part of the new society. They survived the refusal of all "inalienable rights," such as justice, education, and even the hearing of the gospel.

They have also miraculously survived emancipation, reconstruction, segregation, mandated desegregation, and welfarism. They survived denominationalism, cultism, and extremism. They have survived as a highly churched ethnic group (60 percent are church members) while at the same time one of the most spiritually destitute groups. They survive even now with only minimal interest and concern for the evangelical church, for "from the beginning of slavery, there has never been a consistent attempt by whites with the gospel to evangelize the black community."[5] Evangelicals must at long last take a sustained look at the 12 percent of Americans who are black, composing, in the words of Howard Jones, "one of the largest and most neglected mission fields in today's world."[6]

A study of the blacks as a mission field will include a consideration of (1) their roots, (2) their spiritual condition, and (3) their evangelism.

THEIR ROOTS

THE DILEMMA

Eighty-one percent of black Americans today live in an urban, central city setting, whether in the North, where nearly half of all

5. John Perkins, *A Quiet Revolution* (Waco: Word, 1976), p. 89.
6. Howard Jones, "The Black Church in America," *Good News Broadcaster*, March 1973, p. 9.

blacks now live, in the South, or the Far West. They live on about 59 percent of what whites make and are laid off from their employment two to one over the whites. That may well be partly because a disproportionate number of blacks (40 percent) drop out of school and only one in six goes to college. Yet, they have survived.

In their survival has been a lot of hurt. They cannot understand why, as Americans, they were at first refused any education and then offered an inferior education, for separate was not equal. They do not comprehend why there are no jobs available, or why the jobs they are offered are usually for the unskilled, unsecured, and especially for the unequal pay of 59 cents on the dollar. They subsist in substandard housing and collect a welfare check with which they seek to keep their bodies and souls together, but discover that the dole further demoralizes.

Their families deteriorate with 55 percent of the homes having no father, with 86 percent illegitimacy for teens, and with venereal disease soaring 10 to 12 times above the national average. Alcoholism exists in almost every apartment with "nothing less than the survival of the black family at stake" according to Dr. Jay Chunn, president of the National Association of Black Social Workers. Black youth join gangs for survival on the streets and spend millions of dollars on drugs to escape the dead-ended existence. Then to support the habit they turn to crime, which is mostly perpetuated against their own people.[7] The survival rate for gang life is found to be only three out of ten in five years; for four die and three go to jail.

If and when the police arrive to investigate a crime and ultimately arrest, it is frequently accompanied with brutality. Treatment in the jails is often cruel, and the sentencing of the courts quick and merciless.[8] Those who obtain parole often become repeaters.

Drug abuse climbs. At least 300,000 blacks have become addicts and also seem to be oblivious to the dangers of alcohol and alcoholism, which have been accepted without much question. Jesse Jackson observes, "Alcohol abuse and alcoholism represent a far more severe crisis than is generally recognized by the black community. In fact the misuse of alcohol is not always seen as a crisis at all."[9]

7. Three-fourths of major crimes in the cities are blacks against blacks.
8. Seventy-five percent of men in prison and 65 percent of women in prison are black. Charles King, "White People Must Change," Sojourners, May 1981, p. 20.
9. U.S. Department of Health, Education and Welfare publication No. (ADM) 78-478, 1978 reprint, p. xx.

If they turn to the black church, as 60 percent do, they find an unresponsive organization that, according to Martin Luther King, either burns with emotionalism, reducing worship to entertainment or spiritual gymnastics, or freezes with classism that thrives on exclusivism. The black church is not offering the answers blacks need to face the realities of life. As a result, epidemic numbers are committing suicide.

What hope is there without education, job skills, good government, or a spiritual church? They cast about searching for answers. Many black voices clamor for the attention of demoralized blacks, suggesting causes, both sacred and secular, rooted in the past and present, either non-violent or violent, to which they should give their allegiance and through which they are promised answers. The Black Muslim movement is an example. In Los Angeles that religio-political system has built up a community of 5,000 and is growing. Estimates are that nearly fifty black Americans turn to Islam weekly, partially as a result of Muslim missionaries from Africa working in the black community.[10]

It is with nostalgia that they turn their attention to their roots in Africa. By so doing they hope to find answers they desperately want, but an honest perusal of the historic situation only adds to their consternation.

THE SEARCH

It has become popular for blacks to go looking for their roots. Having been transplanted in one generation from a rural South to a universally urbanized setting, the uprooted search for answers to their dilemma is summarized in the question "Who am I?" Having exhausted their obvious sources for answers and having rejected the conflicting solutions as unacceptable, they then ironically look back longingly to the land where, more than 300 years before, their forebears were first enslaved, thus establishing the pattern of denied rights that have haunted them ever since.

In the fifteenth century, Africa was only sparsely populated by a few major tribes in the central and western regions. The western tribes, at least, made a practice of capturing and enslaving other tribesmen. It was no moral issue for them to sell their slaves to the ship captains who put into port with items for sale. William Banks reports concerning this practice using the words of one Dahomian

10. *Zwemer Institute Prayer Bulletin*, October 1980.

king: "It is the custom of my ancestors; and if the white men come to buy, why would I not sell?"[11]

African slavery began in Europe in 1442 when the Portuguese, having obtained a papal grant, began to import blacks into the Iberian Peninsula. The Spanish introduced the industry to the New World, an industry that would ultimately drain Africa of up to 60,000,000 souls. Probably not more than 15,000,000 landed alive. Most were shipped to Latin America with only 2,000,000 coming to the United States.[12]

It was in 1619 that the first blacks were brought to the United States as indentured servants who could earn their freedom working in Jamestown, Virginia.[13] Others were brought as slaves from the West Indies, where by this time 900,000 slaves had already been brought to Latin America from several West African countries. Later they were brought directly to the United States from Africa.

Finally, by 1807 the cruel traffic of human flesh was made illegal in Europe and in the United States. It was England that had started this nefarious business in the same year the Protestant Reformation began. However, slave selling was not over in Africa, for between 1780 and 1880 the "Arabs and Africans began a slave trade on Africa's east coast even worse than the west African slave trade."[14] They were sold to Red Sea and Persian Gulf countries. In 1880 slavery was over, thus ending the biggest enforced migration in world history.

What can black Americans learn from a look at their roots? Precious little beyond the fact that their roots are not unique, nor are their problems. One black leader suggests that it is time to sever the "umbilical cord which sends (us) to foreign shores to attain a validity which in the final essence (we) do not need."[15] Perhaps a panorama of their history in the United States can offer some answers.

THE UNITED STATES EXPERIENCE

The early colonists were of a hardy stock who left kith and kin to come to the New World to escape the tyranny of the Old. They

---

11. William Banks, p. 10.
12. Ibid., p. 12.
13. Peter M. Bergman and Mort N. Bergman, compilers, *A Chronological History of the Negro in America* (New York: New American Library, 1969), p. 10.
14. *World Book Encyclopedia*, 1970 ed., s.v. "Africa."
15. William H. Bentley, *National Black Evangelical Association: Reflections on the Evolution of a Concept of Ministry* (Chicago: William H. Bentley, 1979), p. 108.

threw themselves with vigor into the awesome task of carving out a new existence. They welcomed any and all who came to help, including the twenty indentured blacks who arrived in Jamestown, Virginia, in 1619. Indenturing was common for whites and blacks; therefore, it was determined early that indenture would last from four to seven years at which time the indentured would be free to purchase his own lands.

Those colonial adventurers were also God-fearers who baptized the infants, including blacks. Baptism also had a particular significance later in life, for adult blacks who had been baptized before coming to the United States were given the right to testify in court in those early years, even against whites. Blacks soon began to own property in significant amounts and also owned slaves.[16] In some states land was offered to the settler on the basis of twenty acres for each male slave and ten acres for each female slave brought to the colony the first year.

It was only a matter of time until slavery was introduced into each of the colonies. In the South slaves were needed for the production of tobacco and cotton. In the North it was for manufacturing, such as rum for export. By 1638 Boston became the main port of entry for slaves even though the bulk of the slaves worked in the South.

As the number of blacks increased, inordinate fear concerning them developed. There was concern about intermarriage and the status of the offspring. There was a question about the morality of holding a Christian in slavery after baptism. One by one laws were enacted settling those issues, which slowly stripped the blacks of their rights. The courts determined that baptism had nothing to do with a person's legal status, insuring continuous slavery; intermarriage became illegal; and a black person was not permitted to testify in court.

Those ideas were fostered by colony leaders, who were directly responsible to the king of England. Parliament passed laws to regulate the blacks on the plantations in the Americas. Their attitude concerning blacks was that they were "of a wild, barbarous and savage nature, to be controlled only with strict severity."[17] The Virginia colony held the greatest numbers of slaves; thus it was there that the British directorates were first put into force.

By 1668 the number of free blacks was increasing. There was

16. Bergman and Bergman, p. 14.
17. Ibid., p. 17.

great concern about their privileges; therefore, it was determined that "Negro women set free, although permitted to enjoy their freedom, yet ought not in all respects to be admitted to the full fruition of the exemptions and impunities of the English."[18] The colonies determined that suffrage was only for freeholders. That effectively removed universal suffrage, especially for recent freedmen. Then laws were passed to stop manumission, or the freeing of slaves, unless the slave was given passage out of the colony.

Indenture was very short-lived. The masses of slaves soon discovered that they would never be able to change their status, thus their work suffered and they looked for opportunities to be troublesome or to run away. Where could they go? Some joined "maroon" communities in the mountains or swamps of the slave states. There is evidence that there may have been at least fifty communes.

The designation "maroon" came from the Spanish *cimarron*, which meant a runaway slave. The camps were to be found in abundance in the Caribbean Islands and South America, where slaves often outnumbered the whites. In all slave states the runaways gathered in camps and lived a nomadic life, often depending on banditry for subsistence. Plantation owners tried to discover and raid those camps to recapture the slaves.

Others sought refuge with Indian tribes, where they often intermarried. The larger number, however, sought to escape to the northern states. So many were running away that fugitive laws were established that enabled an owner to reclaim his property. If a particular slave ran away more than once, he was branded with the letter *R.*

By the end of the century 28,000 blacks had made the "middle passage." That meant that they had crossed the ocean cramped, supine, in 3.25 feet of space like cord wood between the decks. If the weather was clement, they were taken out "from the middle" for air and exercise. Those who lived often landed in the West Indies. The triangular trade, as it was called, consisted of carrying food stuffs from Boston to the West Indies, where it was traded for rum. The rum was taken to Africa and bartered for slaves who were returned to the West Indies. Then a cargo of molasses was taken on for Boston, whose major industry was the making of rum.

Only a few voices were raised against this nefarious trade. The first recorded protest was made in 1688 by Mennonite Quakers in Pennsylvania. Their leader denounced those within their circles who

18. Ibid.

owned slaves, saying that their number in Europe heard "that ye Quackers doe here handel men like they handel there ye cattel ... Pray! What thing in the world can be done worse ... than if men should robb or steal us away and sell us for slaves to strange countries, separating housbands from their wives and children.... We are against this traffick of menbody."[19]

Evangelization of the blacks was minimal. One man gave himself as a missionary to serve the blacks during that century. John Eliot in 1674 sought to educate the blacks as he did the Indians. As the eighteenth century dawned Dr. Thomas Bray persuaded the British to establish the Society for the Propagation of the Gospel to send missionaries to the colonies. Later, that organization became known as Dr. Bray's Associates, after Bray, who for many years sought to educate the blacks. Along with those early missionaries Cotton Mather must be recognized for opening an evening school.

With the advent of the newspaper, advertising for slaves became widespread. Although the Quakers prevailed on the Pennsylvania legislature to ban slave trade, the English crown vetoed their action and encouraged the veritable flood of slaves that followed. During the years 1715 to 1750 an average of 2,500 slaves came annually until they constituted 14 percent of the populous. During the next decade 3,500 per year arrived, raising the proportion to 20 percent. The decade ending in 1770 saw an astounding 7,450 enter annually directly from Africa, raising the total to nearly a half million souls among a total population of 2.3 million.

Virginia still had the dubious distinction of maintaining the greatest number of slaves of all the colonies and never lost that position. However, more important to many was the fact that the blacks were now 40 percent of all the citizens of Virginia. Colonel Byrd II remarked, "The saints of New England imported so many Negroes into Virginia, that the colony will sometime or other be confirmed by the name of New Guinea."[20] Steps were taken by the governor to limit the number of slaves entering. Furthermore, the state passed thirty-three acts seeking to stop the importation of slaves, but England rejected them all. Tragically, the governor also renounced their right to vote.

Benjamin Franklin in 1727 began a long battle against slavery. He published articles and books sometimes written by Quakers. He founded an organization called "Junto" to rally those who were

19. Ibid., p. 20.
20. Ibid., p. 33.

against slavery. It was destined to be a long and hard battle, for the pro-slavery forces were deeply entrenched. Feelings ran deep and fears were fed by calamities that were all too frequently blamed on the blacks. A series of fires in New York City in 1741 is an example. Although there was no evidence against them, eleven blacks were burned at the stake and eighteen were hanged just for being in the area.

THE CONTINENTAL CONGRESS

By 1774 a series of grievances over foreign involvement in local affairs gave impetus for a number of colonial leaders to emerge and form themselves into a federal government. Among their many proclamations "Jefferson declared that the abolition of slavery is the great object of desire in the colonies."[21] Two years later, when he drafted the Declaration of Independence, it originally included the following harsh words about King George III:

> He has waged cruel war against human nature itself, violating its most sacred rights of life and liberty in the persons of a distant people who never offended him, captivating them and carrying them into slavery in another hemisphere, or to incur miserable death in their transportation thither. This piratical warfare, the opprobrium of infidel powers, is the warfare of the Christian King of Great Britain. Determined to keep open a market where MEN should be bought and sold, he has prostituted his negative for supressing every legislative attempt to prohibit or to restrain this execrable commerce.[22]

Although Jefferson recognized the wrongness of slavery, it did not mean that he felt that blacks were equal to the whites. He unabashedly projected his bias by suggesting that black were "monotonous," that they "perspired more," required less sleep, were more adventuresome perhaps because of less forethought, were more ardent after the female, only transient in their griefs, inferior in reason, as well as dull, tasteless, and anomolous in imagination. He quipped that in his experience they were wanting in the arts. In only a couple of instances were they equal to the whites—in bravery and memory. He concluded, "I suspicion only, that the blacks ... are inferior to the whites in the endowment both of body and mind."[23]

As president of the American Philosophical Society, he was but

21. Ibid., p. 48.
22. Ibid., p. 52.
23. Ibid., p. 60.

mouthing the opinion of the scientific and philosophical communities that were heavily biased against blacks. Linne, Voltaire, and Hume for instance "considered the Negro as half animal approximating the orangutang."[24] The first to dispute the "race theories" was Johann Blumenbach who garnered scientific evidence to discredit the belief that there were differences in skull sizes.

It is clear that Jefferson articulated the feelings of most of the fifty-five delegates to the Congress. They were concerned that the colonies not be overwhelmed with blacks like Cuba, which was 79 percent black, or Jamaica, which was 95 percent black. In fact, the whole of the West Indies was 86 percent black and had nearly as many blacks as lived in the colonies. About half of the delegates to Congress owned slaves and were not ready for emancipation.

George Washington, who owned 200 slaves, proffered the idea of gradual emancipation. He wrote: "I never mean—unless some particular circumstances should compel me to it—to possess another slave by purchase; it being among my first wishes to see some plan adopted, by which slavery in this country may be abolished by slow, sure, and imperceptible degrees."[25]

But the time had not yet come for gradual emancipation. The best they could do was to legalize slavery for the present, put a $10 per head import tax on slaves, and recommend that slavery be discontinued in 1808. Congress determined that slaves were taxable property and that they would be counted on the ratio of five blacks equaling three whites for purposes of representation.

Abolitionist ideas continued to grow, and by the end of the century twelve abolitionist societies were operating. Vermont abolished slavery in 1777 and Massachusetts in 1783, whereas Rhode Island, Pennsylvania, New York, and Connecticut adopted gradual emancipation a few years later. However, Eli Whitney's invention of the cotton gin in 1793 made the implementation of the idea more remote. Fear of revolt caused slaveholders to severely restrict slave rights.

In 1808 the government officially ended the importing of slaves, but the official attitude changed little. It is estimated that in the following fifty years another quarter of a million slaves were brought in illegally. Several slave states were admitted to the Union after that, although not without controversy, as the Missouri Compromise made clear.

24. Ibid., p. 52.
25. Ibid., p. 63.

Even the blacks themselves were not universally desirous of being manumitted. There is record of blacks betraying the plans of slaveholders who were about to free them. What would they do with their so-called freedom? They had no skills, education, or finances! Most of all they had no land. Freedom would not give them the right to vote, for 93 percent of the freedmen were disenfranchised. The states even determined what work blacks could do. The Federal government would not hire blacks as mailmen.

Not only were the slaves a problem, but so were the 488,000 freedmen. One solution was the formation of the American Colonization Society, which in 1822 founded Liberia, West Africa, as a homeland for freed American slaves. Many whites heralded the idea as brilliant, for it would, in the words of Henry Clay, "rid our country of useless and pernicious, if not dangerous, portion of its population."[26] Only about 12,000 blacks thought it a good idea and migrated. Others saw it as a way to get rid of them.

The abolitionary movement finally became a crusade. Harriet Beecher Stowe's novel *Uncle Tom's Cabin,* focusing the attention of the masses on slavery, sold over 300,000 copies. Many were willing to cooperate with the Underground Railroad established by the Quakers in the 1830s to help blacks escape to the North. It is estimated that 50,000 escaped until Congress passed a strict fugitive slave law. Then many were forced to flee to Canada. Some northern states countered the law by passing personal safety laws that encouraged the protection of runaways.

THE CIVIL WAR AND CIVIL RIGHTS

When war broke out in 1861, abolitionists in the North urged President Lincoln to free the slaves. Jefferson Davis, the President of the eleven Confederate States of America in the South, declared slavery "as necessary to self preservation." President Lincoln's Emancipation Proclamation was essentially a maneuver to save the Union; therefore he freed only the slaves of the seceded states to urge their return. Those in the four slave states in the Union were not affected. It was the Thirteenth Amendment in 1865 that freed the slaves.

Following the war was a time of severe readjustment for the 4,000,000 slaves who were ill prepared for freedom. Most of them had never had to care for themselves and owned nothing. The government made only a token effort to help them resettle and find

26. Ibid., p. 103.

jobs by means of the Freedman's Bureau, which was notoriously fraudulent.

This period was called Reconstruction. Blacks were caught up as pawns in a great power struggle between the hawks and doves of Congress. The hawks (radical Republicans) wanted the leaders of the South to be severely disciplined. They saw blacks as a power base for a strong Republican party in the South; therefore, they propagandized the "black codes" that Southerners had enacted to regulate blacks after the war and pushed the Civil Rights bill through Congress to counteract the codes. That was followed with the Fourteenth Amendment, which conferred citizenship on the blacks.

Although those gains were moral victories for blacks, they were definitely politically motivated. The black vote was needed to keep the new state governments in power as backed by the army. The black vote was sought by the Northern "carpetbaggers" and the Southern "scalawags." In the end, the blacks really lost, for the Southerners could not be forced against their will to treat blacks with respect.

Not many months passed until the Southerners regained control of state government. Even with the Fifteenth Amendment there was no way of ensuring black suffrage. Whites controlled the land and the jobs. Radical groups such as the Ku Klux Klan and the Knights of the White Camelias very effectively controlled the vote by intimidation and violence. States imposed literacy tests and poll taxes to ensure that blacks could not get control of state governments. Reconstruction had reunited the Union but failed in its effort to force the South to accept blacks as bona fide citizens. In fact, "after reconstruction, practically all political rights given the American Negro . . . were retracted."[27]

Following reconstruction the South continued on its pattern of discrimination. Everything in the South became segregated, including housing, schools, all public services, and buildings, including churches. The Supreme Court, with poor bureaucratic insight, gave sanction to segregation by its 1896 decision of "separate but equal" facilities. This became one of the darkest periods of black history, for there was no way that the court could ensure the "equal" part as history would clearly show. For instance, the South continued to spend two to one for white education over black.

27. Ibid., p. 282.

CONCENTRATION IN THE CENTRAL CITIES

The twentieth century brought radical changes into the lives of blacks. First, they migrated to the cities. For instance, by 1982 blacks were 70 percent of the population of Washington, D.C., 66.6 percent in Atlanta, and 63 percent in Detroit. Second, they united for civil action to gain their constitutional rights. Where once the enemy was the white Southerner, now it was whites everywhere!

Two paths were open for them to follow. One was that of nonviolence. Booker T. Washington as leader and educator encouraged blacks to become vocationally trained and educated. He taught them to respect the law and make friends.

The other path as advocated by Harvard graduate Dr. W. E. B. DuBois involved fighting for equal status. When the National Association for the Advancement of Colored People was formed in 1909, DuBois became a chief spokesman. The NAACP's platform included the following: (1) enforcement of equal rights—civil, political, and educational; (2) outlawing racial discrimination; and (3) direct action in various ways.

One of its first campaigns was to alert the public about the violence perpetuated against blacks, especially lynchings. Bergman reports that lynchings were occurring at the rate of one every six days in 1911 for a total of 1,100 in the first fifteen years of the twentieth century. Following this until 1934 there was still an average of thirty-two per year. At least 3,400 occurred in the sixty-five years before 1947.

Second, he founded the National Urban League to assist the increasing numbers of blacks who were migrating in great numbers to the cities of both the South and the North. They needed help in adjusting to urban life and in finding jobs. Blacks were being pulled to the Northern cities by news of jobs created by the advent of World War II. Furthermore, they were pushed northward by the dual natural disasters of major flooding and the destruction of the cotton crop by the boll weevil plus general disatisfaction with life forced on them by Southern attitudes. Perhaps 350,000 moved at this time to be followed by 1.3 million in the 1920s, 1.5 million in the 1930s, and 2.5 million in the 1940s.

Third, the Civil Rights Movement focused the attention of the entire country on the problems facing blacks. Black leaders began to emerge through increased opportunities for jobs, education, the military, and the growing black middle class. The public became accustomed to seeing blacks as equals and in some instances as superior as they gained national exposure on television, in the performing arts, in sports, and in Pulitzer and Nobel Prize winning. A liberal-minded Supreme Court began to strike down restrictive, unconstitutional laws including its own "separate but equal" fiasco. The time had come for Americans generally to become concerned over racial discrimination. That concern would only begrudgingly turn into action.

During the 1950s and early 1960s Martin Luther King, Jr., of the Southern Christian Leadership Conference and James Farmer of the Student National Coordinating Committee began to lead their people in nonviolent, direct action against segregation or de facto segregation by "freedom rides," "sit-ins," "pray-ins," "wade-ins," and "freedom marches." As those marches spread across the country, they grew in size and received massive television coverage. In Washington, D.C., millions heard King speak of his dream that soon a person would be judged by the content of his character rather than by the color of his skin.

Not all blacks were in favor of integration. Elijah Muhammad and Malcolm X of the Black Muslims (now called The World Community of Islam in the West) wanted separation of the races. The Black Panther Party, an extremist group, including Huey Newton, Bobby Seale, and Eldridge Cleaver, was constantly in conflict with the police. But most blacks just wanted to be law-abiding citizens who could attain the American dream.

The decade of the 1970s witnessed great strides in black advancement. There were more opportunities open to blacks in most areas including housing, education, and jobs. More and more blacks were attaining acceptance and affluence in the Great Society, but still the masses languished in the central city with little hope for the future.

How does this lengthy rehearsal of the black experience in the United States fit into a study of blacks as a mission field? First, the average white evangelical has probably never acquainted himself with these historical facts that so vitally affect the thinking and feeling of blacks.

Second, if whites are to understand blacks to better help them spiritually, they must come to grips with black history and black emotional interpretation of it. Although neither living blacks nor whites have been personally involved in the slavery issue, blacks perceive it as a part of the present dilemma, and whites feel guilty by association.

Third, it must be understood that to the extent there still exists the mind-set that allowed slavery to develop and be defended, the present condition of blacks is related to the past.

Finally, blacks believe that the virtual silence of the church in speaking out against the evils of slavery was tantamount to approval. Furthermore, the involvement of Christians in the slavery movement leading them to use the Scriptures and Christianity as tools for keeping blacks obedient has biased many against Christianity. Some blacks believe that "Christianity came to be a prime agency of control in an interlocking system of physical intimidation, legal manipulation, and religious divarication."[28]

This history has very much influenced the black man's religion.

THE SPIRITUAL CONDITION OF THE BLACK

THE SPIRITUAL CONDITION OF THE BLACK CHURCH HISTORICALLY

Only slowly and begrudgingly did established churches begin to recognize the spiritual needs of the slaves. George Washington wrote in his diary about concern for the physical health of his slaves; "there is little evidence, however, of similar concern for their mental and moral well-being."[29] The Anglican church did baptize and take into membership those who were able to pass the catechism classes. It was not until the eighteenth century that it made a systematic effort to evangelize blacks. Even then it was but a small and select group of the more sophisticated and educated who were accepted.

In 1725 the first church of colored Baptists was established in Williamsburg, Virginia. After two religious awakenings much more effort was made to evangelize blacks during the last quarter of the century and the first quarter of the next. Methodists and Baptists did the most to evangelize blacks, who were attracted to their more personal church services and the less formal church polity. Even so, white church services did not really satisfy the spiritual needs of blacks. They sensed that they were only tolerated in the church, for they were usually confined to designated areas and evicted if there was not room for whites.

Blacks were not permitted to have their own separate churches at first because whites feared that they would become places of dissent and foment trouble. When black churches were permitted,

28. C. Eric Lincoln, "Black Consciousness and the Black Church in America," the 1973 Fondren Lecture at Scarritt College for Christian Workers, Nashville, Tennessee.
29. Bergman and Bergman, p. 40.

they were regulated by law and mandated that a white had to be present in the services. That practice continued until the Civil War.

Under such restrictions only a few joined the organized churches. At the dawn of the nineteenth century merely 4 or 5 percent of blacks were church members. That was approximately 50,000 out of 1,000,000 people. By 1860 the number was nearly 14 percent. Eric Lincoln suggests that this failure was because of the "inability of blacks to reconcile the faith of the evangelizer to their conduct."[30]

Other blacks attended an "invisible church" where brave souls met secretly such as on the maroons in the swamps and bayous. There they were able to worship in unrestricted ways without what Lincoln likes to call the "religious narcotic" administered in the white church.

In the North the thousands of freedmen formed "quasi-churches," which were more often than not mutual aid societies caring for widows, orphans, and the sick. They did not form regular churches because of their experience with organized Christianity in the South.

THE SPIRITUAL CONDITION OF THE BLACK CHURCH IN THE PRESENT

When blacks were permitted to establish their own churches during the period of the Reconstruction, they began to leave the denominations and form their own branches. This action was in part a reaction to whites not allowing blacks to worship in ways that were meaningful. However, Lincoln suggests that:

> The religious reasons for the founding of separate black institutions was the failure of all but a remnant of the white Christian establishment aggressively to pursue its mission on behalf of Christ among blacks. Separate institutions were in part a response to the failure of white churchmen to treat their brothers with equity, respect, care, concern, and love.[31]

Now about 60 percent of all blacks belong to churches that are primarily black. There are three National Baptist Conventions with a combined membership of 8.6 million. The three Methodist Episcopal churches claim membership of 2.4 million. There are perhaps 1.6

---

30. C. Eric Lincoln, *The Black Experience in Religion* (New York: Doubleday, 1974), p. 9.
31. Ibid., pp. 12-13.

million integrated into white churches.[32] Another group is the 3,000,000 who have joined the Pentecostal movement. The 16.3 million black Christians belong to about 57,000 black churches.[33] This would mean that the average church should have 286 members. Because no reliable statistics are available, that figure is probably inaccurate. If all blacks were to attend the black churches, then each would have a membership of 456. It would seem that there are enough church buildings to accommodate all blacks, but most of the buildings would not be large enough to accommodate those numbers.

As the black church evolved, it was at first allowed to be only a carbon copy of the white church. Its theology and polity were prescribed. That was both good and bad. It was good because the church's theological position was evangelical. Herbert Hinkle, a black pastor from Michigan, observes, "The preacher of yesterday was a fundamental, hell-fire and brimstone preacher."[34] Lawrence Jones declares, "Blacks were clearly at one with the dominant religious community in affirming the divine inspiration of the Bible."[35]

It was bad because as the white denominational schools (the only schools that admitted blacks) became more liberal in their teaching, the black graduates became more involved with social issues and less concerned with evangelism. Hinkle observes that "in most of the big-time sophisticated black churches, neither the preacher nor the people ever think about soul-winning."[36] He further charges that many black preachers are more concerned with how they sound than how many are saved. Howard Jones agrees that the ministry of evangelism is not given high priority in the majority of black churches. Ronald Behm, pastor of South Side Bible Church of Chicago, concludes that most personal evangelism is to be found among the Pentecostal blacks.

The black church, therefore, has become highly institutionalized. It has so many auxiliary programs that the people become too busy

---

32. Leo Rosten, ed., *Religions of America* (New York: Simon and Schuster, 1975), pp. 375-76. (400,000 are Catholic; 300,000 are Methodist; 200,000 are Northern Baptist. The Southern Baptist churches are nearly entirely white.)

33. Ronald Behm, "What Are the Black Denominations?" *Eternity*, February 1977, pp. 14-15.

34. J. Herbert Hinkle, *Soul Winning in Black Churches* (Grand Rapids: Baker, 1978), p. 94.

35. Lawrence A. Jones, "They Sought a City: The Black Church and Churchmen in the Nineteenth Century," cited by Lincoln, p. 17.

36. Hinkle, pp. 24, 46.

to have time for evangelism. In fact, as Hinkle declares, there is no atmosphere for evangelism. There is a lot of emotion and religion, but spirit-filled Christianity is missing in many churches. The problems of institutionalization, lack of evangelism, and the emotionalism of black churches have caused some to adjudge that the black church is as liberal as its white counterpart. Others suggest that "it has been erroneously assumed that there is very little true evangelical Christianity within the black church as a whole."[37] Richard Mattox, president of the Fundamental Baptist Fellowship Association, suggests that these churches are basically untaught and, as a result, they do not know the Truth or that they should be evangelizing their neighbors.

Perhaps the most revealing characteristic about the spiritual condition of the black church is its attitude toward missions. Joseph Washington states that blacks are difficult to recruit for anything that requires sustained sacrifice for others. Many black leaders agree that there is largely an absence of missionary vision and programs in black churches.

Another problem within the black church is the limited emphasis placed on the Sunday school. Perhaps part of the reason may be found in the lack of interest of blacks in preparing to teach in the church school. Melvin Banks reports from a survey taken that "very few seminarians consider Christian education a vital part of preparation for the minister."[38] Banks further indicates concern that white publishers of Sunday school materials have shown little interest in preparing materials for blacks; therefore, Urban Ministries, Inc., was established in 1970 as the first black-owned independent publisher of Sunday school materials.

The need for black-oriented Sunday school literature is critical, because what is available, according to Starlon Washington, is geared too high for adequate understanding and is rarely related to black culture. Martin Luther King once quipped, "If you want to hide something from the black man, put it in a book."

THE SPIRITUAL CONDITION OF THE BLACK PASTOR

Pastoral education continues to be a problem for blacks. In the past they were only able to attend certain schools that were more

37. Richard Quebedeaux, *The Worldly Evangelical* (New York: Harper & Row, 1980), p. 156.
38. Melvin C. Banks, "The Black Sunday School: Its Strength, Its Needs," *Christianity Today*, July 1974, p. 10.

broadminded. Reluctantly, the conservative schools began to open their doors. As the cost of education escalates, blacks are finding it more difficult to attend. Few schools have enlistment programs for blacks. This is probably less a problem of racial discrimination than the fact that most of the schools' contacts are in the white community. However, it is also necessary for black pastors to encourage their college-aged youth to prepare for Christian ministries.

In some situations the black pastor may not have any formal education, general or biblical education specifically. This is often true in the "store front churches" in the inner city. At times the pastor is old and retired from secular employment. He may have put his entire savings into the church building he personally owns. It is often attended by relatives or a close-knit group of personal friends.

In many circumstances the small church is not able to support the pastor; therefore he must gain secular employment to subsidize his salary. Obviously, he is not able to give the church adequate attention.

All too frequently the pastor and his church are completely out of contact with the spiritual problems of the congregation. One black put it this way, "Since I had never heard the central message of the gospel, I did not see the black church as relevant to my needs."[39] The church had become the center of community activity, but the people came "to eat, court, drink, and gamble," while the associational meetings were "Disneyland, vacation, the state fair, and the Friday night date all rolled into one."[40]

Black pastors who graduated from white schools were often taught to be ashamed of their religious heritage. They were taught to make the black service conform to white, middle class norms and see the black community as colored white people. According to Quebedeaux, most black evangelicalism, having more in common with the white than the black community, is distinctively middle class. However, he continues, the new black evangelical pastor is not berating his tradition and is focusing his attention on the struggle against racism and building up the larger black community.[41] Many black authors conclude that the black pastor is losing the respect he once held.

39. Perkins, p. 17.
40. Ibid., p. 17.
41. Quebedeaux, p. 157.

THE CHURCH IN POLITICS

The black church and its leaders often become involved in the political arena. The Civil Rights movement was born in the black church, received its impetus, leadership, and funding from black churchmen. The black church is the largest and most powerful organization in the black community; therefore, it is the main vehicle for expression of their felt needs. Sometimes it is their only avenue.

Although there are several black denominational groups, C. Eric Lincoln believes that

> the black church evolved, not as the formal, black "denomination," with a structured doctrine, but as an attitude, a movement. It represents the desire of Blacks to be self-conscious about the meaning of their blackness and to search for spiritual fulfillment in terms of their understanding of themselves and their experience of history. There is no single doctrine, no official dogma except the presupposition that a relevant religion begins with the people who espouse it. Black religion, then, cuts across denominational, cult, and sect lines to do for black people what other religions have not done: to assume the black man's humanity, his relevance, his responsibility, his participation, and his right to see himself in the image of God.[42]

Lawrence Jones in his paper "They Sought a City" suggests that blacks who joined the churches in the 1800s were looking for two things: a religious experience and a vehicle to create a new community. The latter often took precedence over the first. In so doing the black church lost contact with the majority of blacks who did not join.

Is there a relationship between the black church today and that of the earlier days? Leon Watts says that there definitely is. He suggests that the black church from its very inception broke with American white Christianity. He questions whether blacks consider themselves a part of traditional white Christianity, concluding that the main thrust of the black church is black liberation, built on the thesis that there are no assumptions that are not built on experience.[43]

Joseph Washington, Jr., has written the book *Black Sects and Cults*. In it he seeks to discover a common denominator in all black religious experience. He suggests that the groups are all "cults of

42. Lincoln, p. 3.
43. Leon Watts, "Caucuses and Caucasians," *Renewal*, October-December 1970, pp. 4-6.

power for black realization in the here and now."[44] He also suggests that they are too numerous to count, for they come and go as the need arises. "Indeed," he says, "the sole criterion for religion among the black masses was its effectiveness in solving their dilemmas. It did not matter in the least what a religion taught or what the leader believed, as long as he or she demonstrated practical ability."[45] His studied conclusion is that "it is not too much to say that in the mainstream of black sectarianism the social, economic, and political concerns take precedence over spiritual concerns and become real religious concerns."[46]

An honest appraisal of the spiritual condition of blacks and their churches must take into account that black society has its various divisions. E. Franklin Frazier in his book *Black Bourgeoisie* speaks of a new middle class that has left its youthful religious moorings and become spiritually bankrupt so that their lives are emptied of both content and significance. They are leaving the church, abandoning the faith of their fathers, and becoming religious illiterates.

The most obvious religio-political involvement of blacks is in the Black Muslim movement. Figures vary from 7,000 to 200,000 as to the number who are involved. The objective in joining is clearly enunciated as the rejection of America. That rejection included Christianity, English, and the American flag. According to Dr. Muhammad Abjul Rauf, the Egyptian director of Washington's Islamic Center, blacks feel that they are returning to their roots by becoming Black Muslims.

AN EVANGELICAL BLACK CHURCH

It is difficult to define an evangelical black church since the term *evangelical* has not been widely used in the black church. Most blacks would consider themselves to be Bible believers without understanding the distinctives raised by terminology. Out of this milieu emerged in 1963 an organization called the National Black Evangelical Association. William Bentley has written a history of the movement. In it he traces black evangelicalism back to the 1930s and the rise of the Bible church and Bible institute/college movement. The leaders of the NBEA are a product of that era.

The organization has oscillated between a conservative leader-

44. Joseph Washington, Jr., *Black Sects and Cults* (New York: Doubleday, 1973), p. 8.
45. Ibid., p. 118.
46. Ibid., p. 147.

ship and a much more inclusivistic orientation. The earlier leaders were theologically fundamental, but Bentley charges that they were not sufficiently aware of black needs and concerns in the community.

In the 1970s the trend reversed and social activists were voted into office. Lines were drawn between "blacks who were identified with a more socially conservative bent, and who, on that account, some felt enjoyed close relationship with the white evangelical establishment, and those blacks who felt that more conscious efforts ought to be made to actively accept their own culture and carefully relate the Gospel claims within that context."[47] Many conservative blacks and whites left the NBEA at that time.

Bentley believes that the majority of blacks want an organization that manifests "unity in diversity without enforced conformity—a cultural pluralism."[48] This idea he calls "the umbrella concept." He insists that the theology must remain evangelical. A move toward a more conservative leadership was evident with Ruben Conner's election, for the radical black liberation movement was not able to capture the imagination of the blacks nor rally them about a cause they could not define. Conservatives believe they can do this, for they have proffered a Black Agenda that includes the following. We are black. We are Christians. We are members of a community of faith with an ethnic identity. We must develop a program of missions, both home and foreign. We must evangelize our own black people, which we can do best. We must produce black-oriented literature for the "bulk of black studies material is contemporarily produced by liberal white scholarship."[49] We must have a program of social action. We will develop a black evangelical theology that is not societally blind nor identified with black culture, but anchored to the rock even while geared to the times! We must develop our own black leadership, using whites only in indirect or complementary ways, for "it stands to reason that those who are struggling with their own identity are in no position to assist others in attaining theirs."[50] We must establish evangelical black churches which can speak out when necessary, for,

we are heading back to a past from which many of us thought we had

47. William H. Bentley, *National Black Evangelical Association,* rev. ed. (Chicago: William Bentley, 1978), p. 20.
48. Ibid., p. 27.
49. Ibid., p. 141.
50. Ibid., p. 109.

clean escaped, and in all this, the church stands for the most part silent and seemingly blind—mute and immobile against primordial wrongs in which she stands implicated by this silence that gives consent. Bad men triumph because good men choose not to speak![51]

Other associations of fundamental black churches have also come into being. One group is headed by Warren Lawrence and is called the Mission Association of Negro Evangelicals. Another is the Fundamental Baptist Fellowship Association including nearly 100 churches with a membership of between 8,000 and 10,000. Richard Mattox of Community Baptist Church in East Cleveland, Ohio, is the president.

What is the spiritual condition of the black church? William L. Banks summarizes it in this way:

A black person even now has to prayerfully seek a local assembly which is without gospel jazz, fashion shows, money-raising gimmicks, and condones immorality, and positively speaking, a church which stresses clean living, preaching of the Word, and the saving blood of Jesus Christ! To find such an assembly is no easy task.[52]

White evangelicals with concern for black America must become aware of the black evangelical and assist him in reaching our mission field of unsaved blacks. Without a doubt, if the job is to be done, blacks will have to do it. But does that exonerate white evangelicals? Obviously not, yet only a few white leaders and churches have been willing to admit that fact and do something about it.

Let us proceed with a survey of missionary activity aimed at reaching the black Americans for Christ, discipling them and establishing them in evangelical churches.

Missionary Activity Among Black Americans

A DISAPPOINTING HISTORY OF MISSIONARY ACTIVITY

Although there were some like John Eliot and Jonathan Edwards, who were early missionaries to the blacks, it does not take long to summarize what missionary activity was being conducted among the slaves during the Colonial period. Gerald de Jong, professor of European history at the University of South Dakota, says that there

51. Ibid., p. 123.
52. Melvin C. Banks, p. 128.

was probably a failure among all denominations, for at the end of that period the majority of slaves were still heathen. They died strangers to Christianity.

Later, as the interdenominational ministries began, a new impetus for missions to blacks should have begun, but it did not happen. Samuel Ward suggests that those ministries also had to bow to the interests of those from whom they received their support.[53]

Nineteenth-century missionary activity showed little improvement according to one black. He suggests that it failed to reach into the black community.[54]

A GROWING MISSIONARY CONCERN

It would appear that missionary activity among blacks has never had a high priority in most white churches or even among blacks. But there is a growing recognition that blacks are indeed a mission field. The American Missionary Fellowship reports that several million blacks in the deep South offer one of the most fertile fields for evangelism, Bible teaching, and church planting in America today. Howard Tannahill, camp director for Cedine Bible Camp, notes that many blacks in America are religious but do not know Jesus Christ personally. Gordon Mumford, president of Southern Bible Institute, suggests that their purpose is to prepare blacks to carry the gospel into the black community, which is virtually without the Good News.

When Baptist Mid-Missions missionaries, Mr. and Mrs. Richard M. McMullen, could not return to the Central African Republic for health reasons, they looked at the American blacks and exclaimed, "Oh, what a need there is for fundamental Bible-teaching Baptist churches in the black community." They settled in the southeast corner of the District of Columbia and are planting the Beracha Baptist Church of Washington, D.C.

InterVarsity Christian Fellowship reports there are thousands of campuses across the United States, and the growing metropolitan campuses with their concentration of blacks have caused them to double their black staff. They also report that 30 percent of those who attended their Washington '80 gathering of evangelical college students were black.

53. Samuel Ward, *Autobiography of a Fugitive Negro—Samuel Ward* (New York: Arno, 1969), p. 64.
54. Lawrence A. Jones, "They Sought a City," p. 23.

Black evangelicals are also concerned that their people are a mission field. William Bentley decries the "traditional practice of exporting abroad what was not practiced at home" and notes the growing concern over "making the forces of missions to consist entirely of foreign ministry."[55]

Howard Jones agrees:

> If white fundamentalist and evangelical churches would have been just as dedicated in evangelizing black America and other non-Caucasians as they have been in evangelizing the great masses of people on the mission fields abroad, America would probably be a different nation today.[56]

He is also concerned that "black evangelicals have not evangelized the unsaved and unchurched masses of fellow American negroes—one of the largest and most neglected mission fields in today's world."[57]

A COMPLEX PROBLEM FOR MISSIONS

There are a number of complexities to be considered in a survey of missionary activity today among blacks. Thomas Sowell points out in his book *American Ethnic Groups* that there are really three black groups in America: the descendants of the "free persons of color" of antebellum America; the descendants of the emancipated slaves who are the largest group; and the West Indian immigrants. Each has his own ethnic identity to be considered for evangelism.[58]

A second complexity to take into account is the great variety of conditions under which blacks live. Most blacks live in the cities; that is, the inner city, or what was once called the ghetto. However, the central city is no longer growing because blacks are moving to the suburbs almost as fast as whites. Nearly one in four metropolitan blacks lives in suburbia, while some whites are moving to exurbia.[59] It is also to be noted that since 1970 many blacks are moving back to the South; others are living in the rural South under circumstances

---

55. Bentley, *National Black Evangelical Association*, p. 54.
56. Howard Jones, "The Black Church in America," *The Good News Broadcaster*, March 1973, p. 9.
57. Ibid.
58. Thomas Sowell, "Three Black Histories," in *American Ethnic Groups*, ed. Thomas Sowell (Chicago: The Urban Institute, 1978), p. 7.
59. George Sternlieb and Robert Lake, "Aging Suburbs and Black Home Ownership," *Annals of American Academy of Political and Social Science*, November 1975, p. 90.

not much different from African apartheid. These complex conditions demand a variety of missionary programs.

Third, there are at least three sources of missionaries. There are the American white missionaries, black missionaries, and foreign black missionaries who are seeking to evangelize the American blacks.

The black denominations have only a minimal missionary activity, but faith missions sustain a variety of programs including Bible schools and camps, literature production, evangelism, inner city work, and church planting to name a few.

Another problem to consider is that there is no centralized coordination of all of those efforts. A variety of white home mission organizations are doing what they think is necessary. American-based foreign mission organizations are experimenting with bringing blacks from overseas to work in the American black community as well as carefully and quietly fielding some of their missionaries here at home. Black evangelicals are beginning to do something through their associations like the National Black Evangelical Association and black mission societies such as the Black Evangelical Enterprises. They are also sending black missionaries through white mission societies. For example, the Fellowship of Baptists for Home Missions now has at least thirty-two serving in church planting in the black community. It might be helpful to have some coordination, but that does not appear to be very likely, considering evangelical history.

MISSIONARY OPPORTUNITIES FOR THE LOCAL CHURCH

Perhaps the place to begin to assess the need for missionary activity among blacks would be to look at one's own turf. Is there a black community within the determined target area of the church? Is it serviced by a fundamental black church? If there is not a witness, then does that church have a program to reach blacks for Christ? Is there a long-range plan to establish a fundamental black church? Is there a fundamental black church servicing the black community of the nearest major city?

As the church becomes aware of the needs of the larger black community, what can the local church do to become involved in a missionary program to reach blacks? First, it can encourage its own young people to see the need and dedicate themselves to serve as missionaries in the black community. It can further prepare to support them financially in that ministry and determine what mission agencies have a black ministry in this country to which they could direct them for missionary service.[60]

Second, it can become aware of schools where special ethnic studies programs have been developed that include blacks in the teaching. On the Bible institute level, Moody Bible Institute is an example. On the seminary level, Dallas Theological Seminary could be mentioned.

Another avenue of involvement is to become aware of Bible schools that are primarily concerned with training blacks for Christian service.[61] Although blacks are generally gaining admittance to white Bible schools, the black Bible school still has a vital ministry. There is the economic factor. Those schools operate as a mission; therefore, they can offer the training at a subsidized price. The staff, either white or black, are dedicated to knowing and understanding blacks and offering courses that are designed to meet the needs of blacks. The educational level and ability of blacks is a vital factor. Every effort is made to help blacks apply the education to their unique circumstances.

Although the teaching medium is English, Bible schools can take into account black English, which is now seriously being studied as a distinct dialect. J. L. Dillard, a linguist, holds that this dialect is rooted in various Creole and West African languages. The purpose of recognizing black English as a dialect is not to begin to teach in it, but rather to better understand blacks and help them communicate in the larger society the glorious truth of the Word of God. In Detroit, the teachers have been told to learn this dialect that they might better teach standard English. Jeffrey Hirshberg, associate editor of the Dictionary of American Regional English (DARE), indicates that they have discovered fifty words or phrases that qualify as long-lived black vocabulary.

Fourth, the church should alert itself to the need for literature that is written by qualified blacks for blacks, using illustrations meaningful to them. Although white publishing houses such as David C. Cook, Scripture Press, and Union Gospel Press have made efforts to include blacks on staff, their materials are primarily targeted for white audiences. It is necessary then to fund publishing houses that are dedicated to producing black literature.[62] Finally, the

60. See Figure 6.
61. See Figure 7.
62. See Figure 8.

church can acquaint itself with the growing number of evangelical black organizations and leaders that need prayer and support.

DIFFICULT ISSUES

It should be noted that the evangelical church will need to consider some seemingly difficult issues as it seeks to assist the black church win black America for Christ. As an ethnic group, many blacks will feel more comfortable in their own churches where they can worship the Lord in ways that are meaningful to them. Willie B. Jemison, a black pastor, says, "People have to be able to identify with our message and our concern. That is part of ethnicity of worship— we are different, and not just in color. Some folks don't want to accept that, but in a worship service, we just don't act the same."[63]

Must blacks act the same as whites in their worship services? Can they have their own music, emotionality, active involvement, and length of service?[64] If it can be different, how different can it be and still be considered evangelical or fundamentally acceptable? Remember, America is not a melting pot. It is more realistically a stew! We have accepted differences in worship services in black Africa. Can we do the same in black America? Other blacks may enjoy participating in a white church. They should be acceptable within the fellowship family. But how should the service be conducted? In ways acceptable to the majority, or in ways all can participate?

Finally, how involved should the church be in social issues? Traditionally, the evangelical white church was only obliquely active, but in more recent times even fundamental churches have become overtly vocal and militant in establishing political organizations such as the Moral Majority. The black church in the past has been condemned for its political activities. Is a new precedent being set? A case in point follows.

John Perkins, a black fundamentalist preacher, in 1961 established the Voice of Calvary Ministries in Jackson, Mississippi. Born in a sharecropper's shack in southern Mississippi, he was trapped, like all other poor blacks, in the "cycle of poverty," including unemployment, lack of education, and poor health. Somehow he

63. David Frenchak and Sharrel Keyes, eds., *Metro Ministry* (Elgin, Ill.: David C. Cook, 1979), p. 61.
64. James S. Tenney, "Singing from the Soul: Our Afro-American Heritage," *Christianity Today*, May 1979, pp. 15-19. This article suggests the whole worship ritual is musical in essence.

escaped to California and there found Christ as Savior. Although he
had vowed never to return to Mississippi, Christ prevailed, and he
went back to Mississippi to preach the gospel. As blacks were saved
and a church was planted, he saw nothing being done to break the
cycle of poverty. The Voice of Calvary Ministries operating in
Jackson, Mendenhall, and New Hebron include educational programs, a chain of thrift stores, a bank, health centers, a farm, and a
Bible institute, all designed to help his Christian blacks improve their
lot spiritually, physically, socially, and mentally. Is this to be
considered home missions in rural Mississippi? It is amazing how
much of this kind of ministry is carried on in foreign missions in
primitive areas. These are far-reaching questions that will not be
easily answered, but they will require an answer.

In conclusion, it should be obvious that blacks are a mission
field as attested by both black and white leaders. There are many
organizations that stand ready to assist the church in accomplishing
the job. The church must face the issues and answer the questions so
that blacks for whom Christ died may hear, for as evangelist Tom
Skinner has observed, "The black man in America is more open to
the Gospel now than ever in history."

Mission Boards Serving Blacks

1. Africa Inland Mission
2. American Missionary Fellowship
3. Baptist International Missions, Incorporated
4. Baptist Mid-Missions
5. Bethel Bible Camp (and Conference)
6. Black Evangelical Enterprises
7. Children's Bible Fellowship
8. Christian United Reaching Everyone
9. Conservative Baptist Home Missions
10. Fellowship of Baptists for Home Missions (serving Fundamental
    Baptist Fellowship Association of Black Churches)
11. Inner City Impact
12. Inter-Varsity Christian Fellowship
13. Open Door Ministries, Inc.
14. Teen Challenge, Incorporated
15. Tom Skinner Association
16. Voice of Calvary Ministries

Black Bible Schools

1. Bay Ridge Christian College, P.O. Box 726, Kendleton, TX 97451 (Church of God)
2. Carver Bible Institute and College, P.O. Box 4334, Atlanta, GA 30302
3. Cedine Bible Institute, Route 1, P.O. Box 239, Spring City, TN 37381
4. Emmaus Bible College, 2570 Asbury Road, Dubuque, IA 52001
5. Manna Bible Institute, 700 Church Lane, Philadelphia, PA 19100
6. Southern Bible Institute, 830 Buckner Blvd., P.O. Box 17734, Dallas, TX 75217
7. Voice of Calvary Ministries, 1665 St. Charles Street, P.O. Box 10562, Jackson, MS 39209

Materials Prepared for Blacks

1. American Tract Society, Negro Division, E. B. Lane, Director, P.O. Box 402008, Garland, TX 75040. Producer and publisher of black evangelical literature written by blacks. A resource catalog is available.
2. Open Door Ministries, Inc., 1044 Pershall Road, P.O. Box 13619, St. Louis, Mo. 63137.
3. Urban Ministries, Inc., 1970 (assisted by Scripture Press and Zondervan Publishers). First predominately black-owned independent publisher of Sunday school literature, developing and distributing literature relevant to urban youth and black youth in particular. Sunday school lessons based on International Lessons in the idiom of black experience and life-style.

5

Hispanics in the United States

The United States is home for the fifth largest of twenty concentrations of Hispanics in the world.[1] There are more Spanish living here than in all Central America or most South American countries. In fact, up to 10 percent of the world's 266,000,000 Spanish-speakers reside here. Reliable figures are tenuous at best, but the U. S. Census Bureau, by means of a list of 8,000 Spanish surnames compiled by the Immigration and Naturalization Service for the 1980 census, has established that this "invisible minority" is 6.4 percent of our population, or 16,000,000. However, mission organizations project that there are 25,000,000, whereas newspaper reporters estimate 40,000,000. It appears that Hispanics are now the second largest ethnic minority after the blacks, but because of a higher birth rate they will soon become the first.[2]

Their presence has already been recognized by the television industry. The twenty-three-year-old National Spanish Television Network (SIN) by 1984 had 199 affiliates interconnected by satellite to reach the 3.1 million Spanish-speaking households across the United States, all in Spanish. Would this not be an excellent method of getting the gospel into these homes?

Hispanics are rapidly becoming a "visible minority" as they agitate for civil rights like those recently gained by blacks, and for

---

1. Antonio Arroyo, *Prophets Denied Honor* (New York: Orbis, 1980), p. 240.
2. Carey McWilliams, *North from Mexico* (New York: Greenwood, 1968), p. 290.

nationwide exposure through "freedom flotillas" and "air lifts" of new arrivals. Most Americans, especially evangelical Americans, seem to be only vaguely aware of the large and widespread Hispanic presence. They are clearly a definable minority who have refused to be absorbed into the greater society, most of whom continue to subsist in the inner sanctums of most large cities. By and large they have been neglected by their own espoused Roman Catholic church and more particularly by the evangelical church. In the opinion of Luis Palau, a well-known Latin American evangelist, they are largely unevangelized. That is attested by the fact that only 15 percent are members of Protestant churches,[3] which is a smaller percentage than any country in Latin America. David Keeler of CAM International observes that only 3 to 5 percent are evangelical.

Hispanics are a heterogeneous people comprised of two dozen ethnic groups having come over a long period of time. That we might better understand their spiritual plight, let us examine (1) their history, (2) their location, (3) the migrant, (4) the social situation, (5) their spiritual condition, and (6) missionary activity among them.

HISTORICAL OVERVIEW

Spanish Americans have had a long and colorful history in this hemisphere. The Spanish conquistadores destroyed the illustrious Indian empires of the Incas of Peru and the Aztecs of Mexico. Spain's explorers based in the West Indies, the nursery of Spanish culture in the western hemisphere, laid claim to most of the lands north of Portugal's Brazilian heartland. In the early 1500s Ponce de Leon discovered and named La Florida. Only a few years later California was discovered, named, and populated by the Spanish from Cortes's capital in Mexico. By 1610 they had also founded Sante Fe, New Mexico. In the late sixteenth century Spanish land-owners cleared the land in the South from the East to the West Coasts. They planted seed grains, fruit trees, cotton, and introduced livestock that transformed the land and the life-style of the inhabitants. Much of that was accomplished by slave labor.

> The laborers they pressed into service were the Native Americans readily available. From the first the key to Spanish productivity was the use of native labor. The horse, gun, and the wheeled vehicle provided physical power to dominate, and there was absolute authority in the

---

3. Estimate by Ricardo Ramierz, executive vice president of the Mexican Cultural Center of San Antonio, Texas.

faith that Christianity was the one true religion, which it was the Europeans' duty and destiny to bring all mankind.[4]

They not only taught the Indians manual skills, that is, silver, gold, and iron work, carding and weaving wool, but also sought to enculturate them with European language, customs, and Roman Catholicism. All of the Indians did not take kindly to the "forced labor, destruction of traditional customs and religion and the extortion of direct tribute."[5] In the Santa Fe territory they revolted and drove out the Spanish. However, permanent settlements were established from coast to coast by 1776 in Florida, the Carolinas, Louisiana, the four southwestern states, and California.

Intermarriage with the mesa-dwelling Indians, the Pueblos, Zunis, Hopis, and Pimas created a new cultural-racial group of mestizos that established a pattern followed throughout the centuries to the present. The mestizo was resentful of both parent cultures and was misunderstood by them. Living in constant fear of the attacks of the nomadic tribes of Indians such as the Apaches, Navajo, and the Comanches, the mestizo nevertheless became the landowner of the Southwest. Through the Spanish missions the sedentary Indians were Romanized, but the nomadic Indians continued in their old religious ways. Thus, the history of the American Indian is intricately connected with that of the Spanish. McWilliams suggests, "Both in New Mexico and in Arizona the Indian population should be regarded, in some respects, as part of the Hispanic element; for they are similar in racial background, language, and religion."[6] It is interesting to note that 40 percent of the Indian population still lives in the southwestern states. So far-reaching was the Latin influence, it led Alford to conclude that the eighteenth century was the Hispanic century in the territory that was to become the United States.[7]

The following century brought the Anglo-Americans to develop the lands that Spain had dominated but never peopled. It was the Mexicans who flowed into the land of the cactus of our Southwest, which was contiguous and similar in terrain and climate. They were familiar with the climate and brought with them time-honored solutions to the many problems of the land. Without them the Anglos would never have been able to develop the land or the

4. Harold Alford, *The Proud Peoples* (New York: New American Library), p. 51.
5. Ibid., p. 53.
6. McWilliams, p. 80.
7. Alford, p. 61.

industries, for the Mexicans brought the original expertise to develop irrigation and mining. The Anglos then developed the massive industries using the Mexicans as cheap labor.

War was inevitable in settling the problem of land ownership. Mexico, which included the lands from Texas to California, had won its freedom from Spain. Then Texas, in the famous battle of the Alamo of 1836, revolted against Mexico. The Treaty of Quadalupe Hidalgo in 1848 established the border; however, those 2,000 miles of border have been nebulous ever since. Because of that treaty the residents of 300 years became strangers and encroachers on their own lands; much as had been done to the Indians before them. Now three cultures vied for supremacy: Indian, Hispanic, and Anglo.

The land east of Texas to the Mississippi and north to Canada also belonged to Spain. In 1800 she gave it to France, from whom we bought the Louisiana Purchase in 1803. Finally, the Gulf states and Florida were purchased from Spain in 1819. Thus was transferred the legal ownership of those southern lands, but this history is still very much part of the "La Raza," the thinking pattern of the modern Hispanic.[8]

The nineteenth century provided opportunity for new waves of Hispanic migration. Gold was discovered in California by a Mexican. Other Mexicans introduced the expertise of quartz mining for gold as well as the skills for silver and copper mining. Cheap labor from Mexico was again abundantly available. Southern Florida received thousands of Cubans who established themselves in the tobacco industry.

It was the twentieth century, however, that provided the great job opportunities that tempted so many Hispanics to migrate. Mexicans were recruited to provide cheap and abundant labor for railroad construction and maintenance. Also, they were recruited for the Texan cotton fields and California sugar beet industry, as well as the Nevada mines. Then World War I spurred industries across the country to expand their output. Thus, it became an established practice to look to Mexico for abundant unskilled labor to fill jobs no one else wanted.

The clearing of the lands of the West created more jobs that were then translated into the digging of irrigation canals and the planting of great orchards and crops that would need harvesting. As laborers followed the ripening crops northward, great streams of

8. Arroyo, p. 12. (La Raza means "the Race" and indicates in the Spanish mind the common Hispanic heritage.)

migrant labor developed, thus creating a need for more seasonal unskilled labor.

Although legal channels had been developed to allow Mexicans to enter, it was easier to bypass the ambiguities of the immigration laws. While officials "looked the other way," thousands of Mexicans were brought in illegally as undocumented workers. Thus a pattern was established that allowed "wetbacks" to clandestinely enter the United States—a pattern that has continued to the present. It is variously estimated that there are up to 12,000,000 illegals residing here, more than the 9.3 million legally residing![9] Only a million a year are caught and deported, but many are back on the job a few days later. The 2000-mile Mexican border is said to be the most crossed international boundary on earth as nearly one-tenth of Mexico's population oscillates across it. Mexicans constitute 60 percent of the Hispanics in the United States. Cubans began coming to the United States in large numbers to escape Castro's Communist paradise in 1959. Alford observes that they came with different needs and aspirations:

> The Cuban immigrants were very different from any Spanish-speaking group that had preceded them. English was already a fluent second language for most of them. Among the refugees were doctors, lawyers, engineers, teachers and successful businessmen, most of whom were . . . more affluent . . . or independent professionals.[10]

Although professionals had to validate their credentials, eventually they were absorbed into the greater society. Businessmen reestablished themselves in small businesses with some difficulty, for they were destitute after leaving their home island. Even so, "in 1970 over 6,000 Cuban businesses and more than half a million Cuban people were contributing more than $450 million a year to Miami stores. In New York more than 10,000 businesses—from grocery stores to banks—were owned by Spanish Americans."[11]

Not all Cubans came with the idea of staying. Many dreamed of the day when their country would again be free. Some joined revolutionary movements that spontaneously smoldered in the Floridian cradle of Cuban independence. Abortive attempts have dissipated much of that dream. Many were encouraged to relocate in

9. Griffin Smith, Jr. "The Mexican People on the Move," *National Geographic*, June 1980, p. 786.
10. Alford, p. 167.
11. Ibid., p. 189.

Spanish Harlem of New York City, Philadelphia, New Orleans, and Atlanta. Few have any interest in Christianity. Six percent of the Hispanics in the United States are Cuban, and half of all Cubans stateside live in Florida.

In 1980 the "Freedom Flotilla" brought more than 125,000 refugees, raising the total number of Cubans in the United States to 665,000. All were looking for a new start in life, but for most it has been be a long, hard struggle. They soon discover that unskilled jobs are becoming less available and that their lot is the ghettoes of the major cities.

Puerto Ricans have found it easy to cross the 1,000 miles of water separating their island from Florida. More than 2,000,000 have entered and have stayed on in Spanish Harlem of New York City.[12] As citizens they are free to come and go at will, and many take advantage of cheap flights. They are the second largest (14 percent) Spanish-speaking group.

It is estimated that 2,000,000 Central and South Americans have come to the United States. In 1982, 100,000 El Salvadorians fled to Los Angeles. In New York City alone 25,000 Uruguayans have overstayed their visitor's visas. Fifty thousand Colombians live in New York City and 100,000 live in Miami. The Central and South Americans total 8 percent of Hispanics. There are also nearly 50,000 Filipinos in the United States, many of whom speak Spanish.

HISPANIC CONCENTRATION

Hispanics have tended to concentrate in the areas surrounding the natural points of entry—New York City, Florida, and the border from Texas to California. (See Figure 5.1.) The Mexicans have fanned out in what McWilliams calls the "borderlands," where from 60 to 80 percent of all Hispanics live in a band 150 miles deep, running parallel to the border, from Los Angeles to the Gulf of Mexico. There they are transforming the Southwest into "Mexico USA," which Griffin Smith, Jr., calls a "Nation within a Nation."[13] California, Arizona, New Mexico, and Texas are home for more than 7,000,000 Hispanics. The state of California is 25 percent Hispanic, whereas Texas is 20 percent. Those two states host one-half of America's Hispanics.

12. John Maust, "The Exploding Hispanic Minority: A Field in Our Back Yard," *Christianity Today*, August 1980, p. 14.
13. Smith, p. 786.

The second largest Hispanic concentration is in the Northeast, where Puerto Ricans entering at New York City move northward to Boston and southward to New Jersey.

South Florida is visited by 13,000,000 foreigners each year, most of whom are Hispanic. One hundred multinational companies maintain Latin American headquarters there. The president of Ecuador has referred to Miami as the "capital of Latin America." By 1981 the Miami area was 40 percent Hispanic. It has been projected that Latins eventually will outnumber the non-Latins.

It is significant to note that in the years 1970 to 1978, 40 percent of the population growth of the United States occurred in California, Texas, and Florida, where there are heavy concentrations of Hispanics.[14]

Hispanics are essentially an urban people, because 90 percent (1983) of them live primarily in the central city of every major metropolitan area of the country. The largest concentration live in Los Angeles, where 2,000,000 Hispanics have created the second largest Mexican city in the world. New York City has the second largest concentration with 1,500,000, predominantly Puerto Ricans. Miami has 700,000 Cubans.[15] But Chicago has a unique situation with 580,000 (unofficially 1,000,000)[16] Hispanics who are dominated by the above groups in addition to Guatemalans and Colombians. San Antonio's population is 54 percent Hispanic.

Most states have at least one county with several thousand Hispanic residents. Several states have counties with growing Hispanic concentrations such as Los Angeles County, California. It is already 25 percent Hispanic and predicted to be 50 percent by the year 2000. Other counties in the southwestern states are now 80 percent or more Hispanic. Dade County, Florida, is predicted to be 80 percent Hispanic by the year 2000.

THE MIGRANT

Migrant workers, two to four million disenfranchised Americans, are basically a little known, though necessary segment of agricultural America. Like slaves through the ages, they are a source

---

14. William S. Ellis, "Los Angeles: City in Search of Itself," *National Geographic*, January 1980, p. 34.

15. *Worldbook Yearbook*, 1980, s.v. "Census," p. 240.

16. John Maust, p. 39.

MAJOR SPANISH-AMERICAN POPULATION CENTERS

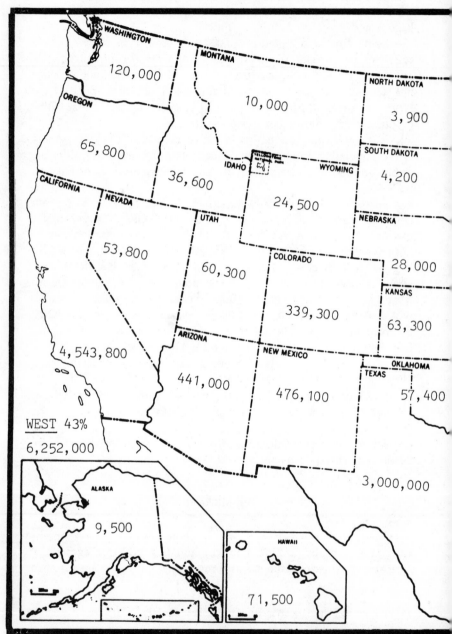

Figure 5.1

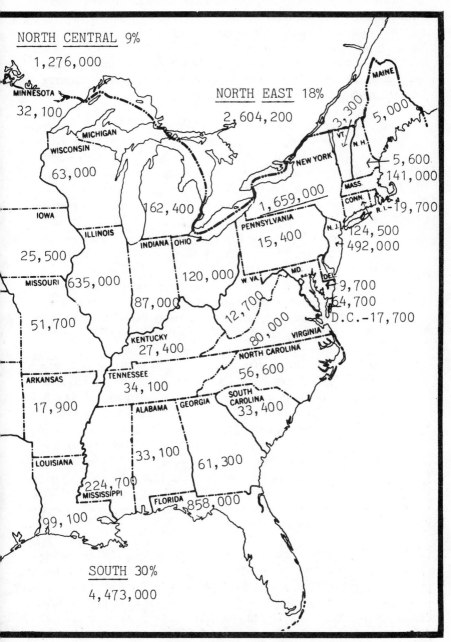

NORTH CENTRAL 9%
1,276,000

MINNESOTA
32,100

NORTH EAST 18%
2,604,200

MAINE
3,300   5,000

VT.   N.H.
MICHIGAN
WISCONSIN
63,000

NEW YORK
5,600
141,000

MASS.
162,400
CONN.
R.I.—19,700

IOWA
ILLINOIS
INDIANA OHIO

PENNSYLVANIA
1,659,000
15,400

N.J.
124,500
492,000

25,500
MISSOURI 635,000
120,000
W VA.
MD.
DEL
9,700
64,700
D.C.—17,700

87,000
12,700
80,000
VIRGINIA

51,700
KENTUCKY
27,400
NORTH CAROLINA

ARKANSAS
TENNESSEE
34,100
56,600

17,900
ALABAMA GEORGIA
SOUTH
CAROLINA
33,400

LOUISIANA
33,100
61,300

224,700
MISSISSIPPI
FLORIDA
858,000

99,100

SOUTH 30%
4,473,000

1980 CENSUS OF POPULATION PC-80-S1-1

of cheap labor. Their jobs are unskilled and seasonal; therefore, they must migrate with the ripening harvests along three major migrant streams. (See Figure 5.2.) Federal government publications delineate these as follows:

Major migrant streams. There are three basic migratory streams with some off-shoots from the main streams. Each stream is different in its demographic and social characteristics.

(a) The major stream is comprised of Texas-Mexican family groups who live mostly in south Texas and start their Northward trek in April or May. In past years the general movement was into the Texas Panhandle, western Oklahoma, and Colorado where the labor stream splits. Some crews go into Wyoming, Utah, Idaho, Oregon, and Washington while the majority swing east to North Dakota, Minnesota, Wisconsin, Michigan, and Ohio. Then they go back south working in Indiana, Illinois, Arkansas, returning to south Texas for winter.

(b) The next largest stream moves along the Atlantic Coast. Most of these migrants winter in Florida working in vegetables and citrus. They are predominately black citizens born and raised in the Southeast. They are not as family oriented as the Texas-Mexican American, speak English, and travel in crews. This stream has perhaps 40,000 workers in recent years. They leave Florida to work in the cultivation and harvest of fruits and vegetables in Georgia and North Carolina, eastern counties of Virginia, Maryland, Delaware, and as far north as upper New York state.

(c) The third movement of migrants occurs mostly within the boundaries of California. Most migrant workers of recent years in California live in the state and follow the crops around the state. Many have almost year-round employment. They are mostly Mexican-American, with some Anglos and Orientals.[17]

Although most states had at least one county with 100 or more migrant workers, ten states use over two-thirds of all migrants; California, Texas, Florida, and Michigan are the top four users.

The state of California has at least 1,000 camps, ranging in size from 100 to 1,000. Frequently the California migrant never leaves the

17. *Manpower Magazine*, U.S. Government Publication, July 1971, p. 29.

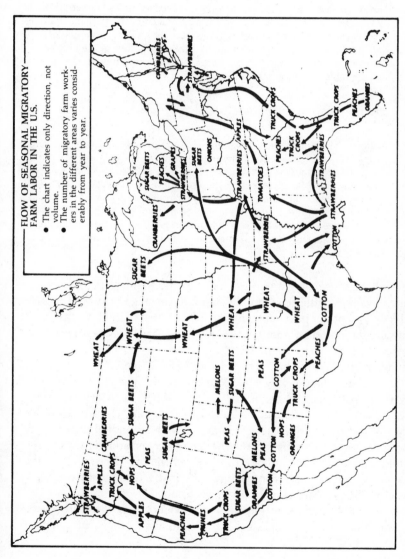

FLOW OF SEASONAL MIGRATORY FARM LABOR IN THE U.S.
- The chart indicates only direction, not volume.
- The number of migratory farm workers in the different areas varies considerably from year to year.

McWilliams, Carey. *Ill Fares the Land: Migrants and Migratory Labor in U.S.* Reprint. New York: Arno, 1976.

Figure 5.2

state. The heaviest suppliers of migrants are Texas and Florida. However,

> a few foreign workers are legally admitted on a temporary basis to do seasonal work. They are from Canada, India, Britain and West India. North Mexicans are allowed since 1968; however in 1973 over 100,000 "wetbacks" were discovered, which is estimated to be perhaps 10% of the total illegally here. Uncle Sam has become greatly concerned about the "national disgrace" of the migrant families who live at the bottom of the socio-economic ladder ... living and working under conditions unacceptable to the other Americans.[18]

He has enacted numerous federal programs such as:

> National Migrant Worker Program. This program assists migrants and their families to settle out of the migrant stream. The migrant worker is given basic education, vocational training, and supportive services (including financial assistance) to help him develop marketable job skills that will enable him to secure stable, year-round employment, either in his home-base area or in states along the migrant stream. The program also includes staff training, research, and experimentation with bilingual skill training and basic education to find the best ways to help migrants.[19]

But all of those programs have only scratched the surface socially and have done little economically about the average income of $2,400 (1984) except to price the migrant out of the market in favor of mechanization. The number of migrants has dropped from 12 percent of the hired farm labor to 7 percent. In other words, the number of migrants has dropped by nearly 50 percent.

Who are these nearly 4,000,000 Americans? The migrant may be white Appalachian, Black, Indian, Oriental, Mexican, Mexican American, Puerto Rican, Canadian, Cuban, or Jamaican. He may work as part of a crew or "freewheel." He may have a second job that is also seasonal. Because of his mobility he seldom votes, and his 1.3 million children usually have little or "broken" education. These urchins are called America's "most forgotten disinherited, educationally deprived youth."[20] Eighty percent drop out of school.

About 40 percent of migrants are Mexican, and therefore speak Spanish and broken English. They are Roman Catholic in name.

18. Ibid., p. 29.
19. Ibid., p. 29.
20. Ibid., p. 29.

Because of the seasonal employment they work only about one-third of the year and have a life expectancy of forty-nine years. The infant mortality rate is 125 percent higher than the national average. They are notoriously poor managers of money and given to alcohol. Many are now receiving relief money.

Migrants form a distinct subculture and tend to be family clannish. All members of the family work together in the fields. They also tend to be authoritative and have a limited view of the world. They see things only with relation to themselves; right and wrong depends on their own experiences. They find it difficult to accept responsibility for their position in life.

Whereas the man may be nominally the head of the household, the woman often makes the decisions. Among blacks, the grandmother still plays the dominant role. Divorce, separation, common-law marriages, and unwed parenthood are still common.

Mexicans live in the extended family structure in colonies. Work crews may be one "family." The woman is usually the center of the home and works in the field with the clan. Babies are always welcomed and wanted, and "toted" to the fields.

This life-style gives rise to a persistent feeling of inadequacy. There is a lack of planning for the future. The migrant's work rarely contributes to a feeling of self-fulfillment or human worth. Money is seen as the sole reward of work.

Some are now using federal programs to break out of the migrant life for a sedentary life. They need to be reached with the gospel, but their mobility makes it all the more difficult to do more than personal work among them.

THE SOCIAL SITUATION OF THE HISPANIC

It is exceedingly difficult to discuss the Hispanic social milieu because of the differences in multinational Hispanic peoples. What is true of the Cuban may not be of the Puerto Rican or Mexican. However, because Mexicans make up at least 60 percent of the legal Hispanic population and most of the illegals, their overwhelming presence tends to speak for all. Also, federal statistics speak of all Hispanics as one unit. It may be generalized that their median age is nine years less than the Anglo. Moreover, most Hispanics work in less skilled trades, but are not at the bottom of the economic ladder. In 1979 when the median family income for whites was $20,000, the

Spanish income was $11,600 and the black income was $11,600.[21] While 60 percent made less than $12,000, 27 percent made less than $7,000 or minimum wage.[22]

The lack of skills coupled with functional illiteracy in English tend to cause the Hispanic to gravitate to unskilled and temporary jobs. The migrant is a prime example. He competes with mechanized equipment in an everdwindling market and moves about following the crops. As better living conditions were forced by the government and better wages were won by unionization, mechanical equipment was developed effectively eliminating thousands of jobs. Central city housing is all that many can afford on the low-paying jobs available. In Miami it is estimated that one-half of all hotel staff and three out of five service station attendants are Cuban. Still, there is open hostility toward Hispanics for taking already scarce jobs. In Los Angeles it is said that if all the illegals were deported, "the area's hotel, restaurant, and garment industries would be paralyzed."[23] In Texas some farm workers "live in abject poverty in jerry-built cubicles of concrete blocks that lack running water."[24] Griffin Smith, Jr., goes on to report that "in Hidalgo County's metropolitan area, the per capita income is only $3,859, one of the lowest in the country. Its unemployment rate is 12 percent. It is the bottom rung of America's economic ladder."[25]

Education is the biggest problem they face. Evangelical Missions Information Service reported that Hispanics are at present the most undereducated Americans. Roger Luna summarizes:

Most Mexicans who came to the United States were from the poorest and most uneducated classes of Mexico. Then, to make matters worse, schools serving the Mexican-American community have traditionally been substandard. The result is that at present of the Mexican-American population twenty-five years or older, only 2% ever started college, and only 1.6% ever graduated. Of this group, only 28% ever graduated from high school. While the situation has improved ... the effects of the depressed educational scene ... are still being felt.[26]

21. U.S. Department of Commerce, Bureau of the Census, Population Characteristics, Series P-20, no. 361, May 1981.
22. Latin American Pulse, October 1980, published by Evangelical Missions Information Service.
23. Maust, p. 41.
24. Smith, p. 796.
25. Ibid., p. 796.
26. Arroyo, p. 163.

The Hispanic, whose median age is 23, is seeking to find himself while lost in an uncaring society. He is asking, "How do I fit into American society?" Griffin Smith, Jr., in trying to define who a Mexican-American is, was told that the Mexican-American is a "citizen of the United States whose family originated in Mexico. Beyond that, it's a state of mind." Another said, "It is a feeling of straddling two different worlds."[27] There seems to be a "brotherhood forged by suffering and a perception of injustice." That camaraderie is expressed in the words La Raza.

There is a growing pride in being a Mestizo, which is defined as being "Indian in blood and soul and Spanish in language and civilization."[28] Thus, there is not only an acceptance of what he is but also the real danger of developing a kind of master race attitude. Jose Vasconcelos verbalized that in his book *The Cosmic Race*. In it he theorizes that the Iberoamerican is superior because he is a mixture of previous world civilizations.[29] In his state of feeling rejected, such a conjecture is very appealing. He is becoming a fifthrace.[30]

On a United States scale, the Hispanic's socio-economic circumstances are inferior, but when compared with the conditions he left behind, he is worlds ahead. He has liberties only dreamed of. He is tasting victories won through organized labor. In short, he is becoming smitten with materialism.

The language question remains unsolved. Some states are instituting bilingual programs in the early grades. That may help in a time of transition, but the Hispanic must be bilingual if he insists on maintaining his Spanish in a predominantly English-speaking society. By the second and third generations English is often the major language. Even so, evangelicals will need to assess the local situation, for as Eli Garza, the dynamic leader of the Baptist work in Detroit has discovered, he must use both English and Spanish in his church to effectively communicate with his congregation.[31]

There is a growing use of Spanish in the mass media. There are hundreds of Spanish radio stations and dozens of television channels and newspapers.

27. Smith, p. 785.
28. Ibid., p. 791.
29. Jose Vasconcelos, "The Cosmic Race," in *Prophets Denied Honor*, ed. Antonio M. Stevens Arroyo (New York: Orbis, 1980), p. 32.
30. Arroyo, p. 34.
31. Latin American Pulse, p. 7.

THE SPIRITUAL NEED OF THE HISPANIC

Most Latins are Roman Catholic in name at least. Statistically they make up 25 percent of the United States Catholic church, but in the Southwest the figure is 65 percent. Yet, most Hispanics do not attend church because they were never made to feel welcome. In some places signs were placed that read, "Mexicans Not Allowed," or, "Mexicans restricted to the Back Four rows."[32] Rather generally they were taken for granted for they were already Catholic. Alert priests are noting that Hispanics have always been second-class citizens in the Catholic church and the "Chicanos remain the most neglected and forgotten people in the church."[33] Not only are 80 percent not attending the Catholic church, they are defecting as one observer reports "to the Protestants, the Evangelicals, and the Jehovah's Witnesses, among others."[34] It is worthy to note that Jehovah's Witnesses claim some 45,000 Hispanics and the Mormons 50,000. The National Council of Churches indicates that 20 percent are members of their denominations.

The Pentecostal and charismatic movements are particularly appealing to the Hispanic, for they appeal to his open, warm feeling and expressive personality. Ramirez articulates this when she says, "Puerto Ricans, especially the lower classes who are a people apt to express openly their feelings and emotions, found in Pentecostalism an adequate vehicle for expressing and communicating their religious feelings and convictions."[35]

Another Hispanic, when asked, What does being a Pentecostal mean to you? replied, "It's what binds much of us poor Puertorriquenos together. It gives us strength to live in these conditions. It's like being part of a familia that is together in Christo and we help each other with the little materials we may possess."[36]

In a similar vein the Charismatic Catholic movement is drawing Hispanics into active participation within that church because it is

---

32. Arroyo, p. 191.
33. David F. Gomez, "Somos Chicanos: Strangers in Our Own Land," in *Prophets Denied Honor*, ed. Antonio M. Stevens Arroyo (New York: Orbis, 1980), p. 132.
34. Arroyo, pp. 41, 308-309.
35. Ana Maria Diaz Ramirez, "Religion in the Melting Pot of the Caribbean—San Juan, Puerto Rico," in *Prophets Denied Honor*, ed. Antonio Arroyo (New York: Orbis, 1980), p. 338.
36. Piri Thomas, "Savior, Savior, Hold My Hand," ed. Arroyo, *Prophets Denied Honor*, p. 152.

responding to their felt needs. Services are in Spanish, with nationals leading.

Would it not be expected that some would bring with them cultic forms of religion? Widespread throughout the Caribbean Islands, wherever the Africans were brought in and a veneer of Roman Catholicism was superimposed, a synthesis evolved. In Haiti this is variously called Vodun or Voodoo; in Trinidad, Shango; and in Cuba, Santerra.[37] Miami residents report that a variety of Voodoo rituals regularly take place primarily in a fifty-square-block area known as "Little Haiti." One Santerian cult "is believed to have 10,000 Cuban-American members, making it stronger in Miami than it ever was in Cuba."[38] The ritual includes offering animal sacrifices whose carcasses are then tossed into a river.

If the evangelical church is to effectively communicate the gospel to Hispanics, it will have to awaken to the fact that these people exist and recognize a God-given responsibility to do something about it. One mission leader charges that "they are found living next to a Bible-preaching church or next door to a born-again Christian family, yet these people live as heathen in a pagan land. Pastors, local churches, and Christian workers do not go after them."[39] One leader estimated that not more than 20,000 of the 6,000,000 in Los Angeles are born again.[40] Another, Al Bergfalk of Chicago, estimates there are not more than 20,000 among the 1,000,000 in his city.

An aroused church will then need to ask itself this question posed by a Puerto Rican: "How can our religious needs be met by a middle class and white church institution?"[41] It is a relevant question, for Piri Thomas goes on to charge, "The trouble with the outside people from nice well-to-do churches who sincerely send people to work among us armed with all the knowledge of the Bible is that he has a complete lack of understanding about what makes us tick."[42]

What does make them tick? All we have reviewed above is part of the question. They must be seen as those drawing from three worlds. As a Mestizos they combine Indian, Spanish, and Anglo

37. Francis O. Michael, "A Shango Religious Group and the Problem of Prestige in Trinidadian Society" (Ph.D. dissertation, Ohio State University, 1958).
38. Worldwide Missionary Crusade, November 1981, p. 10.
39. Florent Toirac, executive director, Spanish World Gospel Mission, Inc.
40. Mike Protasovicki, pastor, as quoted by John Maust in *Christianity Today*, August 1980, p. 12.
41. Arroyo, p. 153.
42. Ibid., p. 158.

heritage and are proud of it. They live in substandard ghettoes, where each community will be either mono-Hispano or multi-Hispano, that is, having several Latin American groups. Each subgroup will have its own special needs. For instance, the Mexicans came here to survive economically; the Puerto Ricans came from an island that has spawned Latin American Pentecostalism, spiritism, and syncretistic cults. They are "not so much a religious people as a people in search of religion."[43] Chicanos, on the other hand, are nonreligious, having little interest in the church.[44]

The multicultural heritage of the Hispanics will of necessity need to be considered in establishing churches that will be meaningful to them. Elizondo suggests that their "Indian and African roots ... give a different rhythm to their religious practices."[45] Caesar Chavez, a Mexican, observes, "Our mentality is quite different from the Anglo-Saxon mentality."[46] That may be seen in the fact that the Mexican is one who often stands aloof, for "between reality and his person stands a wall of impassivity and distance, which although invisible is still impenetrable. The Mexican is always distant, distant from the world and from others. Distant also from himself."[47] He has an identity crisis.

Hispanics have been spiritually abused and neglected. Their former religious leaders have promised and not delivered. They are educationally deprived and economically exploited. They are citizens needed, but only tolerated. They are angry at themselves and the world and now demand their rights and get them through power, as Caesar Chavez has proved. However, the blacks are angry at Hispanics for taking their jobs. Bilingual education and official offices (although promised) are only partially available. Even the Catholic church tried unsuccessfully to "Americanize" them. Thus, they turn to radical forms of politics, cults, or distorted forms of Christianity. It should be obvious then that we must help Hispanics find the truth, to establish a church and Christian community to train their own leaders with whom they will feel comfortable.

MISSIONARY ACTIVITY AMONG HISPANICS

Missionary activity among the Hispanics is pitifully small and

43. Ibid., p. 273.
44. Ibid., p. 350.
45. Ibid., p. 12.
46. Ibid., p. 351.
47. Ibid., p. 44.

scattered. (See Figure 5.4.) Although most denominations have some Hispanic ministry, it has been limited primarily to the Baptists and the Pentecostals. The Southern Baptists have established 1,400 churches, most of which have Hispanic pastors, serving a Christian community of 150,000. The American Baptists report 300 congregations. The Assemblies of God list over 700 groups, while the Church of God (Cleveland, Tennessee) has a membership of 10,000 and the Church of the Nazarene claim eighty-nine churches. The Missouri Synod Lutheran churches have developed thirty-nine congregations with 3,800 members. There are seventy-three congregations affiliated with the Christian and Missionary Alliance.

Few independent evangelical churches are making a major impact, for the evangelical church has no centralized machinery with which to survey the need, to recruit men and money, or to coordinate efforts in church planting. Perhaps it should be noted that the early church did not have either, but evidently there was a widespread conviction that everyone should hear! Thus, responsibility must be assumed by those churches and pastors who are near enough to assess the need and respond to it. Also, mission societies must survey the needs and alert the larger evangelical community about the need through their journals, itinerating missionaries and executives, and the Evangelical Mission Information Service. It is generally conceded that the majority of Hispanics are not being touched by the gospel.

Some pastors have engaged Spanish-speaking men to develop a Hispanic congregation that uses the same facilities as the Anglo church. Others have supported home mission organizations that have a burden to reach the Hispanics of the United States. Some missions give direction to church planting operations in several communities, thus accumulating expertise from their collective activities.

One example is the First Baptist Church of Flushing, New York. This white church of about 300 members has engaged five qualified men equipped to evangelize the Spanish, Portuguese, Chinese, Korean, and Russian communities surrounding the church. They are looking for a Japanese-speaking pastor also. These special language groups each meet throughout the day in their own meetings in the same church facilities and then meet corporately for the evening service.

The Conservative Baptist Association has a number of churches in the five boroughs of New York City seeking to service the Hispanic and Haitian communities.

Inner City Impact, a mission in the Humboldt Park region of Chicago, has found it effective to send workers into the community to work with the youth. They have youth meetings in their own facilities and a summer camping program. Out of their ministry has come a Puerto Rican church, the Good News Bible Church.

A group of Spanish pastors in the Chicago area has formed an association called the Chicago Area Spanish Evangelism (CASE). It is their desire to coordinate the efforts of the 200 Spanish-language churches who are seeking to evangelize Chicago's Hispanics. The efforts include Spanish-language evangelistic crusades.

Spanish-language radio programs, such as those carried over station WMBI in Chicago all day Saturdays; KVMV in McAllen, Texas; KNCB in Houston, Texas; and KMAX in Pasadena, California, are very effective and need to be instituted across the country. Programs are produced by the Spanish World Gospel Mission, the Spanish "Back to the Bible," the "Radio Bible Class," the "Back to God Hour," the "Lutheran Hour," the "Mennonite Hour," the Southern Baptists, the Plymouth Brethren, the Baptist General Conference, and Luis Palau, who tapes his full-length crusade messages. "Back to the Bible" Spanish program, "La Biblia Dice," is aired over twenty stations.

Jaime Shedd, coordinator de programición Hispaña, estimates that 30 percent of Chicago's Hispanics prefer English to Spanish, but he also notes that Spanish is the language of the heart; therefore, the need is great for increasing Spanish broadcasts. As a follow-up program, the telephone is proving to be a more effective spiritual counseling tool than correspondence, for it is quick and personal.

In the Los Angeles area 125 churches joined together and invited Latin American evangelist Luis Palau to hold an evangelistic crusade in June 1980. This first Spanish-language crusade in the area was heralded as very effective and should be repeated in other cities.

Other united efforts include the cooperation of thirty-eight Baptist churches (predominantly Cuban) in Miami to fly in two plane loads of Cuban refugees. As a result, there are at least 100 Cuban churches in the Miami area.

Some mission societies with primary ministries overseas are now working with ethnics here at home. Worldteam, for example, has spearheaded a "partnership plan" in Miami among Haitians. The mission is working together with the Association of Churches in Haiti and a small Haitian congregation in Miami to try to reach the estimated 30,000 Haitians in the Miami area. Perhaps this Worldteam program could be emulated by other missions in their ministry to Hispanic and other ethnic communities. Pocket Testament League is sending its sound trucks and evangelistic literature teams into the inner cities. They say it is one of their most vigorous and vital ministries. Others have found that a Spanish-language bookstore ministry is very effective. Numerous publishers make Spanish-language literature and Bibles available. (See Figure 5.5.)

There is a desperate need to reach the Hispanic community, which some estimate to be less than 1 percent born again. David Keebe estimates that in 1981 from 3 to 5 percent were evangelicals and 5 to 10 percent were members of Protestant churches. Although numerous storefront churches have sprung up, most of them are so small they cannot afford a full-time pastor; therefore, lay preachers holding secular jobs and bi-vocationals are filling a void. There is a desperate need for a trained clergy among Hispanic congregations. Bible college and seminary programs are needed, with funding to make them available. Pastor Alex Montoya of First Fundamental Bible Church of Monterey Park, California, is seeking to develop a graduate program at Talbot Seminary for Hispanic pastors. Moody Bible Institute has an ethnic studies program to prepare missionaries for such service. McCormick Seminary has an urban ministries program as does the Wheaton Graduate School. Fuller Seminary, Northern Baptist Seminary, La Puente Bible Institute, and Rio Grande Bible Institute, among others, also seek to prepare men for Hispanic ministries. The total number of theological students in Hispanic studies in 1978 was 681.

The words of William Conard are a stirring challenge:

> This presents a challenge to returned missionaries, Spanish-speaking Christians, and the whole U.S. evangelical church. Missionary candidates with health problems used to be turned down by candidate boards; now these people could serve the U.S. Hispanic community and still get good medical treatment.
> The need is totally obvious. A positive response must come forth in the U.S. evangelical church. These Hispanics smile, then say, "Hola, amigo. Que tal? Que Dices?—Hi, friend, What do you say?"[48]

The Henry Tobelmann family is an example of a postive response to that question. After thirty-two years of service in Chile with Gospel Mission of South America, health did not permit them to return. Yet, they were challenged to minister to the 2,000,000 Hispanics in metropolitan New York City.

In Newark, New Jersey, they were led to the Evangelistic Committee of Newark, which was willing to form a Spanish depart-

48. Latin American Pulse, p. 8.

ment called HUEP representing Hudson, Union, Essex, and Passaic counties. Some thirty churches backed that ministry, which included open air evangelism using an audio-visually equipped van, sixty to seventy hours of radio programs aired weekly over WXWZ, and Bible correspondence courses from Source of Light Mission, which by 1980 averaged 7,000 lessons a year.

As that ministry grew, a need was felt for an interdenominational mission with the purpose of reaching the Latins of the metropolitan New York area. Henry Tobelmann writes, "We prayed and approached some missions, but they were not ready to assume a 'home missions' program; therefore we felt led to establish the Latin Evangelistic Outreach in 1976, called LEO."

Pastor J. Allen Nicholson of First Baptist Church, Hillside, New Jersey, appreciates this ministry and writes in a church letter:

> What would you do if some morning you woke and found yourself on a mission field? Well, that is just about what is happening in many urban areas of New Jersey. I daily meet folk whose language I don't comprehend, whose culture is far different and who came from some country where we have missionaries. It seems the mission field is coming to us. That is why as a pastor, I'm involved and thankful for the LEO. Henry and Ruth Tobelmann are doing a job I can't do.
>
> This should be the attitude of all concerned Christians—to find some way to reach all the peoples of our communities with the Gospel.[49]

---

49. A letter of pastor J. Allen Nicholson, First Baptist Church, Hillside, New Jersey.

6

Other Ethnics

INTRODUCTION

Whereas American Indians, blacks, and Hispanics, because of size and activist groups, are the more obvious ethnics, other groups also stand in need of specialized evangelism, because "the typical American church does not fit. Its style of operation, government, and communication are unlike what many ethnics need."[1]

Richard Colenso, general director of specialized ministries of the Christian and Missionary Alliance, suggests that there are three kinds of homogeneous groups. They are the *immigrant* or new resident, the *transitional* or people who are passing from the immigrant culture to something else, and the *established* or those who have settled into some part of the American cultural mosaic.

Furthermore, he suggests that the established have adopted one of three possible life-styles. Some have essentially retained the Old World ways and settled in an ethnic ghetto such as Chinatown. In such a setting they may "have no greater opportunity to receive Christ here than they did back home. The popular styles of evangelism pass them by."[2]

Second, a unique cultural life-style may have been created such

1. Richard Colenso, "Evangelism Among Ethnic Peoples in the United States," Reference Library (n.p.: Evangelism and Home Missions Association of the National Association of Evangelicals, November 1976), p. 5.
2. Ibid., p. 5.

as that of the Indian, black, or Hispanic. In chapters 3, 4, and 5 it has already been noted that these people must be encouraged to develop churches that are culturally relevant to them.

Last, there are those who have adopted the majority culture and seem to be basically blended into the "American" society. Even then, according to Colenso, "a homogeneous group will probably form based upon national origin or culture."[3] These people usually become a hidden people group—hidden from the gospel.

According to the 1984 statistics there were 14 million ethnics in addition to the blacks, Indians, and Hispanics within the American context. Others will continue to arrive for some time into the future because the United States government allows 700,000 immigrants to enter legally each year. As the world seethes with political convulsions, millions of people become refugees. Americans open their hearts and pocketbooks, and America opens her doors to relocate thousands of refugees. (See Figure 6.1.) Americans relocated thirty thousand refugees in 1983. In addition, another 100,000 to 1,000,000 enter illegally. Eighty-one percent of the immigrants now come from Latin America (48 percent) and Asia (33 percent) instead of Europe (16 percent), which was the case before 1965.[4] The immigrants scatter across the fifty states, but California (36 percent), Texas (13 percent), and New York (12 percent) receive the lion's share (61 per cent).[5]

Finally, at all times there are 6,000,000 temporary residents living here who are neither immigrants nor tourists.[6] It is clear that the mission field has come to the church in America. Stephen Thernstrom, a social historian and editor of the *Harvard Encyclopedia of American Ethnic Groups,* insists that America's ethnics are being rapidly assimilated; but Don Bjork, formerly World team's North American Ministries director, suggests that the millions of newcomers are changing America and compelling a new thrust for North American missions. That new thrust must include the cooperation of foreign missionaries and their boards because

> the sheer number and kind of newcomers is outpacing timely and effective response from existing churches and agencies. Most of the present waves of newcomers are from cultural groups previously

3. Colenso, p. 5.
4. Thomas Dolmatch, ed., *Information Please Almanac 1980* (New York: Simon and Schuster, 1980), p. 797.
5. U.S. Department of Commerce, Bureau of the Census, 1980 Census of Population "Supplementary Report."
6. EMISary, January 1981. Published by Evangelical Mission Information Service.

unserved by home missions and churches of North America. Foreign missions have the intercultural expertise to reach them.[7]

In this chapter several smaller ethnic groups are examined. They are but suggestive of the plurality of people groups that are hidden away to be evangelized in communities across America. They are sometimes called the great "forgotten foreign fields."

ESTABLISHED ETHNICS

Within America's cultural mosaic are to be found those who continue to use their native language even though they have been living here long enough to learn English. Most of these citizens are more or less bilingual, but they feel more comfortable with the mother tongue. They have come from the Far East or Europe. Their spiritual needs will be fulfilled best by a church that speaks their language.

CHINESE AMERICANS

Americans of Chinese descent numbering 1,000,000 (1984) are a mission field because 94 percent of Chinese Americans are unchurched[8] and could not be reached by the existing churches, either Chinese or English-speaking. The Chinese church is not prepared to adequately minister to the overseas-born Chinese who speak dialects that are not being used in the church. Nor is she prepared to serve the American-born Chinese who speak English and have moved away from Chinatowns to the suburbs.

English-speaking white churches obviously are not able to evangelize the Chinese speaker. But neither are they prepared to either evangelize the English-speaking Chinese or to freely accept him into the fellowship. A majority of Chinese Americans are therefore hidden peoples; that is, they are a mission field.

The Chinese first came in great numbers to the "gold mountain," the Chinese name for America at that time, as prospectors following the discovery of gold in 1848. A great number were brought in as coolies or cheap labor to build the Central Pacific Railroad (1864-1869) and to work the huge farms in the West.

---

7. Don Bjork, "Reaching Newcomers to North America." Paper presented at the joint National Association of Evangelicals and Evangelical Foreign Mission Association Convention at Orlando, Florida, March 1979.

8. *Evangelical Newsletter*, March 1981, published by Evangelical Ministries, Inc.

Widespread persecution of Chinese Americans developed as they became the scapegoat during times of economic depression and unemployment. It culminated in lynchings and the Oriental Exclusion Act (1882). This was the first time the country excluded an entire race by law. The law was repealed in 1943, but even then a strict quota of 100 immigrants per year was enforced. After 1965 the quota was relaxed and 20,000 arrive annually.

Chinese Americans congregated in the cities of the West Coast (53 percent) and then in the Northeast (29 percent). The state of California is home for 40 percent of America's Chinese, and New York State boasts 20 percent. Other groups are to be found in Hawaii (56,000), Illinois (29,000), and Texas (26,000). Typically, the Chinese gathered in ethnic communities called Chinatowns. In this setting the traditional extended family cared for one another and took new arrivals into their flats.[9] Jobs were available from Chinese business men in the community. Although wages were minimal, long hours, frugal living, and pooling the family income afforded younger members opportunities to become educated and move up the social scale. Today the Chinese American has attained a higher educational and economic status than the average white American. For example, one church in Houston, Texas, has 150 Ph.Ds.

The two largest Chinatowns are located in New York City (70,000) and San Francisco (38,000).[10] A recently observed phenomenon (1979) indicates that more Chinese now live outside the Chinatowns than live within. For instance, 100,000 Chinese live outside the Manhattan Chinatown. However, the Chinatown continues to maintain a density that is twelve times that of the rest of the city because of the influx of 7,000 immigrants annually.

In San Francisco the Chinese population is also divided evenly between Chinatown and the suburbs. It is obvious that Chinatowns have become a place of transition for the suburb-bound newcomer. Immigrants are absorbed into the Chinatown economy without going on welfare. From Chinatown educated individuals with marketable skills emerge to take their place in the larger society.

Chinese Americans are therefore polarized into widely differing socio-economic communities. Within Chinatown are the poor, unskilled Chinese-speaking and struggling persons. Some of the so-

9. James H. Davis and Woodie W. White, eds., *Racial in the Church* (Nashville: Abingdon, 1980), p. 86.

10. K. M. Chrysler, "Chinese Americans—Stereotypes Won't Do," *U.S. News and World Report*, July 1980.

called Hong Kong Chinese Americans were ardent propagandists for Maoism.[11] In the suburbs Chinese Americans are English-speaking, affluent, and Americanized. Both communities stand in need of evangelization.

Chinatowns are to be found in the urban portions of all fifty states, but unfortunately eighteen states do not have even one Chinese church and ten do not have a Chinese Christian fellowship.

The first Chinese church was planted in San Francisco in 1853. By the end of the century, eleven denominations had begun Chinese ministries using Anglo missionaries. The ministry was primarily one of providing English classes and other social assistance programs.

The Chinese church grew slowly until Chinese pastors were trained or immigrated and anti-Chinese sentiments diminished. After 1960 Chinese churches multiplied rapidly so that by 1983 there were 600 Chinese churches servicing a community of 2,500 Chinese. The Chinese church is distributed regionally in direct proportion to the Chinese population: 136 in New York City; 126 in San Francisco; and 109 in Los Angeles. There is a serious lack of churches for the rapidly growing, more affluent population of American-born Chinese who do not live in Chinatowns. Joseph Wong, an American-born Chinese pastor from San Francisco, observes that the American-born Chinese are the largest hidden group of American Chinese. Although they constitute more than half of all Chinese Americans, nine out of ten are not Christian because the Chinese church never reached them or they are dropouts claiming neither the gospel nor Christ.[12]

The average Chinese church is less than ten years old, is located in Chinatown, and meets in less than adequate facilities. Location requires that its 135 members commute to hear the older, foreign-born Chinese pastor. The church is growing at the rate of 36 percent every three years with most of that growth attributable to the addition of Christian Chinese immigrants. At the same time the church is losing its young people, for "the Chinese-speaking elders have little success in keeping their own second generation in the church."[13]

Perhaps 25 percent of the 49,000 committed Christian Chinese

11. Thomas Sowell, ed., American Ethnic Groups (n.p.: The Urban Institute, 1978), p. 91.
12. About Face, August 1981, published by Fellowship of American Chinese Evangelicals, p. 3.
13. Christian Witness to the Chinese People: Thailand Report. Published by Lausanne Committee for World Evangelization, 1980, p. 24.

actively witness; therefore, the Chinese church is not able to keep up with the growth of the North American Chinese population, which is doubling each decade because of large numbers of immigrants and a birth rate that is twice the national average.

Chinese evangelical leaders are concerned about evangelizing Chinese Americans; therefore, they formed in 1972 the North American Congress of Chinese Evangelicals (NACOCE), which meets in Chinese fashion on even years. This organization represents all North American Chinese churches (500) including Canadian Chinese churches.

The leaders of the Congress recognize that the American-born Chinese represent one of the greatest challenges before the Chinese church; thus, they founded the Fellowship of American Chinese Evangelicals (FACE). The Fellowship established a quarterly, *About Face* (1979), through which it purposes to alert the Chinese church concerning the spiritual needs of American-born Chinese.

To promote evangelism among all Chinese in North America and to develop a missionary thrust among Chinese churches, the Evangelical China Office (ECO) was opened in 1980.[14] The ECO is sponsored by three groups engaged in Chinese evangelism—the North American Congress of Chinese Evangelicals, the Evangelical Foreign Missions Association, and the Interdenominational Foreign Mission Association. By means of this organization, most North American-based evangelical foreign missions and Chinese congregations are united organizationally in the task of Chinese ministries. The Evangelical China Office disseminates information on Chinese evangelism by editing the *Chinese World Pulse,* which is published by the Evangelical Missions Information Service.

Half of all Chinese churches have been planted by denominational missions. Two missions have planted the majority of the denominational churches—the Southern Baptists (15 percent) and the Christian and Missionary Alliance (12 percent). The Baptists began in the nineteenth century and the Alliance in 1969.

Thirty-nine percent of Chinese American churches are independent. They were planted by independent pastors, retired missionaries, or groups of Christians.[15] In 1982, 400 Chinese students were in Bible college or seminary.

Eleven faith missions maintain work among Chinese Americans.

14. *Chinese World Pulse,* October 1980. Published by Evangelical Missions Information Service, p. 3.
15. "Build Up His Church for My Kinsman's Sake." Paper presented before the North

(See Figure 6.2.) Church planting is the primary ministry of seven organizations. Two have campus ministries, and three provide Scriptures and messages recorded in numerous languages and dialects.

Two schools offer specialized training for Chinese ministries. (See Figure 6.3.) A new Chinese Bible is now available from the American Bible Society. It was translated solely by Chinese linguists and is called *Today's Chinese Version* (TCV).

JAPANESE AMERICANS

Japanese farmers came to the West Coast as early as the 1800s. In 1907 the Gentleman's Agreement slowed their immigration, but as of 1952 all Asiatics who come to the United States within the immigration quota system are able to become citizens.

Seven hundred thousand citizens of Japanese descent live in the United States. The vast majority of Japanese Americans belong to the Buddhist church; therefore, they are discussed in chapter 8.

PORTUGUESE AMERICANS

During the decade ending in 1975, 100,000 Portuguese immigrated to the United States from Portugal, the Azores in the mid-Atlantic, and the Cape Verde Islands off the coast of West Africa. Most Portuguese-speaking Americans settled in New England. Fall River, Massachusetts, which is 50 percent Portuguese, is the heart of New England's Portuguese American community of 150,000.[16] In Massachusetts, the elementary schools of the Portuguese American community are bilingual, such as in New Bedford, where 60,000 Portuguese reside. Baptist Mid-Missions began a church planting ministry in 1983.

Rhode Island also hosts many Portuguese-speaking citizens. Around Narragansett Bay is a large community of Portuguese Americans. Most Portuguese are engaged in farming and fishing. Others have taken jobs in industry, especially in textile manufacturing.

A Roman Catholic veneer hides the true longing of the Portuguese for the truth. Only a token effort has been made to reach these people for Christ. American Mission for Opening Churches has one

American Congress of Chinese Evangelicals, Pasadena, California, June 1980. Available from Chinese World Mission Center.

16. O. Louis Mazzatenta, "New England's Little Portugal,"*National Geographic,* January 1975, p. 90.

couple in church planting in Massachusetts among Portuguese fishermen, as well as the ministry mentioned above.

The Bible is available in Portuguese as are other materials. Gospel Light Publications and Baptist Mid-Missions both maintain publishing houses in Brazil, where all but 26,000,000 of the world's 138,000,000 Portuguese-speakers live. Scripture Gift Mission of Canada, an affiliate of the London parent, provides materials in Portuguese.

FRENCH-SPEAKING AMERICANS

The French world of 200,000,000 reaches into North America where 7.5 million people speak French. French Canadians living primarily in Quebec are 67 percent of the total, but 2.5 million French-speaking Americans live in the United States. Americans who speak French live in two areas: one million live in New England and the rest in Cajun country centered in Louisiana.

The United States has a long history of contact with France. French explorers sailed up the Saint Lawrence and Mississippi Rivers in the 1600s establishing a lucrative fur-trading industry with the Indians. Even though the French built fortresses, the Spanish in the South and the British in the North repulsed them.

The French and Indian wars of the eighteenth century ended with the Treaty of Paris in 1763. By means of that treaty Canada and the lands east of the Mississippi were occupied by England. The lands west of the Mississippi were controlled by Spain. In 1800 these latter lands secretly reverted to France who sold them to the United States as the Louisiana Purchase in 1803. French continues to be spoken in both of those areas.

Three northern New England states (Maine, New Hampshire, and Vermont) border on Canada's French Quebec province. A large percentage of the 2,600,000 residents are bilingual. Many of them speak French in their homes.

Thousands of Canadian men work in the United States several months a year in the paper industry or as woodsmen. They live on both sides of the border and regularly cross the border weekends to be with their families.

Quebecans have migrated to the United States to live and work in industries in Connecticut, Massachusetts, and New York. Other Canadians come down from the St. John River Valley in New Brunswick, the province north of Maine.

Missionaries of the American Missionary Fellowship working in

New England have been surveying the spiritual needs of Francophone, or French-speaking, Americans for several years. They conclude that the

> churches existing in French areas of New England are rarely willing to be involved [in French evangelism]. Most New England cities have one or more evangelical churches. They, for the most part, either do not know how to approach the French problem or else are already over-programmed and will not consider a French work.[17]

The American Missionary Fellowship has determined that they should plant French-speaking churches in towns near the Canadian border in the New England states that are contiguous with Canada. In those towns the French-speaking population may include 80 percent of the residents, as evidenced by the number of bi-lingual road signs. By concentrating the work near the border they are better able to work the French field, which is international. Quebec is said to be "one of the least evangelized areas of North America."[18]

Access to French Quebec is essential not only to follow up those who travel back and forth across the border, but also to ensure a more adequate pool of potential workers. Bethel Bible School in Sherbrooke, which is just north of Vermont, is a French Bible school. Students attend from 100 French evangelical churches in Quebec and three in New Brunswick to train for the ministry. French literature is also available from Canada.

Shantyman's Christian Association of North America is a Canadian based missionary organization which works in the lumber camps among French lumberjacks. In the early days these woodsmen lived in remote places in shanties and were called shantymen; therefore, the missionaries who were burdened to reach them for Christ adopted the above name. The ministry is demanding for the work is in remote places and the men are transient. The mission publishes a monthly newspaper, *The Shantyman*. Christ for the Lumberjack and Lumberjack, Inc., also minister to the woodsmen.

Back to the Bible produces a French-language program in France entitled *La Voix de l'Evangile*, which is also aired in Quebec.

Information about French-language work in New England and

---

17. *Available Ministries*, Fall 1980. A publication of the American Missionary Fellowship.
18. *The French World: A Neglected Field as Seen by Youth with a Vision* (Texas: Youth With a Mission, n.d.), n.p.

other ministries is available from the Evangelistic Association of New England.

Lafayette is the center of French Louisiana, where 1,500,000 Cajuns live virtually beyond the gospel outreach of the state's evangelical churches. The Acadian is the largest minority (36 percent), followed closely by the black (29 percent).

Cajuns came to Louisiana, a former French colony, after they were expelled from Acadia in 1755. Acadia is a region of eastern Canada centered in Nova Scotia, where the French Catholic Cajuns had migrated from France in 1604. The name Acadia was given the region by Henry Wadsworth Longfellow in his poem "Evangeline." When the British banned the Catholic church the Cajuns fled Acadia.

These thrifty, hardworking, fun-loving, and devoutly religious people avoided learning English until the early 1900s. Today they are bilingual but prefer the French language. A French-English patois is used almost exclusively, especially in the bayous.

Although the Cajun is originally from Acadia, because of intermarriage the lineage is difficult to trace. Therefore, anyone who has lived in Cajun country long enough is called and calls himself a Cajun. It is now fashionable to speak French and revive the Cajun culture.

Most Cajuns have a Catholic veneer, but for many it is proper to "spit on the bait," carry a bag of salt on the belt, or wear an amulet under the clothes for good luck. Warren Doud, a former missionary to Cajuns under the Go Ye Mission, notes:

> There is little gospel witness to the Catholic Cajuns. The few evangelical churches in the area from Texas to New Orleans and south of Alexandria, have little to do with the Catholics and mainly minister to the Protestants who have moved in from the outside.
> It is safe to say that the Cajuns are among the least well evangelized in the U.S., having fewer Christians and fewer Christian workers per capita than many places in Africa and India. It is a very needy field and worthy of consideration as a field of service.[19]

Two Bible churches can be mentioned as Cajun churches, those whose members are Cajuns. The Opelousas Bible Church in Opelousas was pastored for twenty-five years by a Cajun, K. J. Fontento. He is now teaching at Southeastern Bible College. The Henderson Bible Church is also Cajun. There is little known mission work among the Cajun people. Bill Hitchfield, of Bible Conference and Mission,

19. Personal letter from Warren Doud.

indicates that their organizational objective is to plant churches in Catholic-populated areas in southeastern Louisiana. A present ministry in Ville Platte by Ken Ardain, a Cajun, is the planting of the Grace Bible Church.

SLAVICS AND CZECHS

European aliens have fled from every Communist-dominated country. Seven hundred ninety thousand Slavics and Czechs live in the United States and Canada. "Radio Bible Class" is now printing in the Slovakian language.

NEW ETHNICS

The new ethnics entering the United States are primarily from the countries of the Pacific basin. Where once the newcomers crossed the Atlantic and entered through Ellis Island, more and more they are now arriving in California, primarily in Los Angeles where 3 million now reside.

Many come for political asylum. In 1980 the United States government eased the grounds on which asylum could be won. In 1978 only 3,700 came, but by 1983, 30,000 were arriving.

In the 1980 census 5.4 million aliens registered from 150 countries. The American Bible Society reports that they provided Scripture in seventy-seven languages for the American public in 1983.

ASIANS

World social and political instability, as evidenced by 10,000,000 refugees (1982), is especially pronounced in Asia. (See Figure 6.4.) These ancient lands where history began bulge with 2.7 billion people or 61 percent of the world's population. Socially, Asians are trying to enter the twentieth century, but 50 percent of Asian adults are illiterate, and 40 percent of the populace is under fifteen years of age. Politically, unseasoned governments struggle with economic development within and communistic expansionism without. No Asian country is immune from either Russian or Chinese Communism; therefore, 7.3 million refugees in 1980 sought refuge elsewhere.

The United Nations has defined a refugee as any person who, because of persecution arising from race, religion, or political opinion, or because of military operations or catastrophe has fled his home and is unable or unwilling to return. Another definition suggests that "a refugee is a soul fleeing from oppression and disaster."[20]

SOUTHEAST ASIAN REFUGEES

Southeast Asia includes those countries east of India and south of China as well as the islands of Malaysia, Indonesia, and the Philippines, down to Australia.

Vietnamese. Since 1975 millions of Indo-Chinese have come to the United States for asylum from intolerable living conditions in their countries.[21] Half of those have settled in California. Seventy percent of the Indo-Chinese refugees are Vietnamese. Congress is now limiting the influx of Indo-Chinese to 100,000 annually. Vietnamese continue to arrive at 4,000 per month, down from 10,000 monthly in 1981.

The Vietnamese tend to congregate where others of their heritage are already living. The greatest number have settled in California, but many others are living in fishing villages scattered along the Gulf Coast from Florida to Texas.

The 2,700,000 Vietnamese are eager, hardworking, and honest folk who desire to quickly become self-supporting. Not all Americans welcome these industrious people, especially the American fishermen, who feel that the outsiders are encroaching upon an already troubled fishing industry.

The newcomers have found America and Americans bewildering. At times they have been received with kindness, but at other times with hostility. The Ku Klux Klan has been guilty of hurling unfounded accusations that the Vietnamese are communist infiltrators.

Vietnamese refugees want to find the peace and acceptance they have never known. Harvey Arden, of the *National Geographic* staff, has written of the troubles of one group of refugees. They fled from Haiphong, North Vietnam, in 1954 to Phan Thiet, South Vietnam. Fourteen years later they fled to Vung Tau. By 1975 it was necessary to move again, this time to Guam. They ultimately arrived in the United States where again and again they have sought to find a place where they could put down roots. One refugee summarized their experience, "All our lives we have been at war, have known nothing

20. Lorna Anderson, *You and Your Refugee Neighbor* (Pasadena, Calif.: William Carey Library, 1980), p. 27.
21. Harvey Arden, "Wanderers from Vung Tau: Troubled Odyssey of Vietnamese Fishermen," *National Geographic*, September 1981, p. 378.

but war. First it was in Vietnam. Now it is here in America—a war for our people to be accepted."[22]

Refugees have a variety of religious backgrounds, including Buddhism, Taoism, and Confucianism, but all are essentially animistic. Some have been exposed to Roman Catholicism.

Southern Baptists have the largest ministry among these refugees. They have founded thirty-five Vietnamese congregations (1981) by deploying some of their foreign staff, who have learned the language, to work with the home staff.

Christian cassette tapes in Vietnamese and other Indo-Chinese languages designed for refugees are available from Project Share or Gospel Recordings. (See Figure 6.1.)

Laotians. In 1975 the Communists took over Laos and thousands of Laotians fled to nearby Thailand to escape the "yellow fire" of the Vietnamese. By 1980, 120,000 had gathered in refugee camps to wait for opportunities to be relocated in the free world. Thirteen thousand located in the ghettoes of the Oakland-San Francisco area. Churches and individuals across the United States responded by sponsoring the resettling of refugees in their communities. The Community Bible Church of Dallas sponsored a Laotian family that is now settled in the Laotian community of Dallas. An evangelical Laotian church has been established in East Dallas to service the Laotian community.

Near Atlanta, Georgia, a large Laotian community has developed. The Forest Hills Baptist Church of Decatur has reached out to the Laotians by adding a Laotian-speaking pastor to their staff. He ministers to a congregation of up to 150 which uses the church's facilities. This church sponsors several ethnic churches on their premises.

Columbia Drive Baptist Church in Decatur, Georgia, also ministers to several ethnic groups. Two hundred Laotians fellowship with them, and 70 have joined the church.

Hmong/Miao from Thailand. Thirty-five thousand Hmong people have migrated to the United States from Thailand and Laos since 1976. The Hmongs originally lived in southwest China. The China Inland Mission had a large work among them before the Revolution. Over a period of a century the Miaos migrated to other southeast Asian countries.

The Christian and Missionary Alliance ministered to the Hmong in Laos beginning in 1951. By 1975 the Communists overran the

22. Ibid., p. 378.

country and the Hmong fled to Thailand. Since 1976 they have come to the United States, where many have settled in southern California.

The Christian and Missionary Alliance Church continues to minister to the Hmong through thirty congregations that include several thousand Hmong Christians.

The Overseas Missionary Fellowship maintains a ministry among the Hmong and Mien refugees.

THAIS

There are 120,000 Thais in America (1984), 60 percent of whom live in Los Angeles. Ninety-six percent are Buddhist, although only about one-fourth practice their religion. A large Thai Buddhist Temple is located in northern Los Angeles, complete with Buddhas. In the Los Angeles area are 50 Thai restaurants, two newspapers, a radio station, and a bookstore.

About 60 percent of Thais are students, many of whom will return to Thailand. The Bible is available in Thai, and three churches have been established to serve the community. Here is a great opportunity to reach Thais who could return to their native land. Other Thai communities are to be found in New York, Chicago, Baltimore, San Francisco, Seattle, Washington, D.C., and in Michigan.

INDONESIANS

A former missionary to Indonesia settled in San Francisco to minister to the Indonesian community. He began by placing an ad in a local newspaper inviting any in the area who would join him to celebrate a holiday having special meaning to the Indonesians. Two hundred responded to the ad and joined in the festivities. Two churches have been planted from the contacts made during that festive occasion.

FILIPINOS

There are 775,000 Filipinos living in the United States. During the decade of the 1970s they became the second-largest Asian group. They are widely scattered, nominally Catholic, and virtually unevangelized. Little is known of their evangelization.

IRANIANS

During the crisis that developed in Iran over the taking of

American hostages in the United States embassy, Americans became aware that 200,000 Iranians are living in the United States. In fact, Iran has the highest number of foreign students studying in the United States. The American government threatened to deport the illegals but later did not follow through.

Iranians have emigrated over the past 50 years. Half of all American Iranians live in the California and Chicago areas. Ebrahim Ghaffari of Iranian Christians International, Inc. (ICI) estimates that there are two to three thousand born-again Christians in a community of perhaps 100,000 nominal Christians from an Arminian or Assyrian background. ICI maintains a bookstore of Persian materials for ministry and various fellowship groups for Persian Christians. A Persian hymnal is available as well as cassette tapes of Persian hymns. ICI's quarterly publication, *Majdeh,* is published in both English and Persian.

PALESTINIANS

By 1981, 110,000 Palestinians had become citizens of the United States. The Palestinians lived in Palestine for hundreds of years before 1948, when their land was divided and renamed Israel, Jordan, West Bank, and Gaza. The majority (67 percent) of the Palestinians continued to live in the area as displaced persons (Jordan, 27 percent; West Bank, 18 percent; Israel, 11 percent; Gaza, 11 percent),[23] but others became refugees in various countries.

Eighty-three percent of the Palestinians who migrated to the United States are now citizens as they have lived here for more than ten years. In fact, 36 percent have lived here more than thirty years.

Many Palestinians are afraid to identify themselves because of the pro-Israel and anti-Palestinian bias that exists in the United States. Even so, they are beginning to join national organizations that exist to promote Palestinian unity. The Palestine Congress of North America, founded in 1979, is the largest, claiming 20,000 members in its many affiliates. Their activities are primarily social in nature.

Twenty years earlier the American Federation of Ramallah Palestine was organized. Its 3,000 associates are more politically active. A third organization, the Association of Arab-American University Graduates (1967) appeals to the 60 percent of Palestinians who belong to the academic or professional communities. Palestinian

23. Elias H. Tuma, "The Palestinians in America," *LINK,* July-August 1981. Published by Americans for Middle East Understanding, Inc., p. 3.

Americans speak Arabic, are fluent in English (85 percent), and some are familiar with Hebrew.

Palestinian American citizens are here to stay. Although active in the American political system (40 percent Independent, 30 percent Republican, and 21 percent Democrat), they have not formed lobbying organizations to influence legislation concerning the Middle East. Only 25 percent of American Palestinians regularly support the Palestine Liberation Organization (PLO), even though all Palestinians believe in creating a home for homeless Palestinians.

The Palestine Liberation Organization (1964) is a political group representing 4.4 million Palestinians with a primary goal to establish a Palestinian state for homeless Arabs. This organization of guerrilla groups and other interested parties was recognized in 1974 by Arab governments and the United Nations as the representative of the Palestinians. The U.S.S.R. established diplomatic relations with the PLO in October 1981.

American Palestinians are nominally Muslim, but "secularism is far stronger than it seems to be among Palestinians in the Middle East and among the PLO leadership." It is questionable that the Palestinians are a homogeneous group. However, John F. Mahoney, executive director of Americans for Middle East Understanding, Inc., declares that Palestinian Americans are declaring themselves as a definable community.[24]

It is essential that evangelical churches become aware of the possible presence of the Palestinians in their community. At present, there is no evidence of any organized effort to present the gospel to the Palestinians.

KOREANS

Koreans coming from the Far East have quadrupled to 355,000 in the United States during the 1970s. As professional people they are to be found in many cities across the country, but especially in Los Angeles, where there are 200 Korean churches; Washington, D.C., and Chicago, where another 100 Korean language churches have been established.

John Song, a Korean working with Galilean Baptist Missions, is planting churches in the Korean community in the Detroit area. Although most emigres speak some English, the church services are conducted in Korean. Word of Life Press, an arm of The Evangelical

24. Ibid., p. 2.

Alliance Mission, has established a Korean bookstore in California,[25] where Korean language literature is available. The most extensive Korean work is under the auspices of the Home Mission Board of the Southern Baptist Convention. They project 1,000 units (church groups) by 1990.

Of all new ethnics, Koreans are the best churched. This may be because they brought with them their pastors from the strong Korean church.

CARIBBEAN ISLANDERS

The Caribbean Sea south of Florida in recent years has come to mean more than a peaceful vacation cruise to the Bahamas or a place where tropical storms are spawned. Fidel Castro has changed all that by using the island of Cuba as a staging point for Marxist revolutionary activity throughout the Caribbean islands and elsewhere. Cubans have fled this communist paradise by the thousands (665,000) for political asylum in the United States. (See chapter 5.) Other Caribbean islanders, looking for jobs, have immigrated.

HAITIANS

Haiti, lying 800 miles southeast of Florida, is the poorest nation in the Western Hemisphere. Six hundred thousand Haitians have migrated to the United States looking for jobs and a better opportunity to live the good life. After 1959, when Dr. Francois Duvalier (known as Papa Doc) began his reform in Haiti, thousands of educated mulattoes fled to the United States. These professionals started in Brooklyn, New York, a Haitian community that has grown to 400,000 and spread into the adjoining states. It is the largest Haitian community in America. Other Haitian communities can be found in southern Florida (60,000), Boston (20,000), and Chicago (20,000).

The United States allows 20,000 Haitians to immigrate annually. Perhaps as many more arrive illegally via the Bahamas each year. The more recent arrivals are seldom bilingual and speak only Creole, which is a patois of French, African, Spanish, and English. They are willing to work hard and are accused by the blacks of taking their jobs. They are 97 percent illiterate.

Within the Haitian communities in Miami, New Orleans, and New York City, Voodoo, a mixture of African religion and Roman

25. Word of Life Press, 1828 W. 9th Street, Los Angeles, CA 90006.

Catholicism, is practiced as it is on the island. It includes the playing of drums, the sacrificing of chickens, and placing hexes on people. It was reported in a New York newspaper that a father killed his son because the spirits told him to do it.

Peter Golinski, a missionary with UFM International for twenty-five years in Haiti, is an evangelist in the American Haitian community. He estimates that there are 130 Haitian churches working in Haitian communities totaling 600,000 people. The largest Haitian church is the First Haitian Baptist Church of Brooklyn, New York. It has a congregation of 2,000 and has planted numerous satellite groups.

The average Haitian church may have fifty members, meets in a storefront building, and is pastored by a Haitian who also maintains a secular job. If the pastor has any Bible training, it was received in Haiti.

There are too few Haitian churches to reach the community. Sixty churches in Brooklyn each are responsible for nearly 7,000 Haitians. In South Florida the ratio is worse with sixty churches trying to minister to 60,000 Haitians. But in Chicago and Boston there are six churches in each area to evangelize a community of 20,000. The American Haitian churches do have a burden to evangelize their own people. Many satellite groups have been started by Haitian Christians.

A greater concern needs to be manifest for the Haitian Americans by our evangelical churches and faith mission boards maintaining work in Haiti. The Southern Baptists have the largest number of Haitian churches but almost no missionary staff assigned to the work. Worldteam maintains a token work in Florida with two Haitian churches working in cooperation with the national church in Haiti.

In conclusion, the 1980 census reveals that there are more than 5,000,000 aliens in the United States from 150 countries. This substantiates the concept that America is an international mission field. In fact, thousands of people from all over the world continue to come to America. What an opportunity and responsibility we have to reach them with the gospel. This is true in many areas of our country and all of us should work to reach them with the gospel of our Lord Jesus Christ.[26]

26. *Worldwide News,* January 1982, p. 4.

MISSION BOARDS SERVING THE CHINESE

1. Ambassadors for Christ (church planting; students)
2. Baptist Mid-missions (Asian Americans)
3. Chinese Christian Mission
4. Chinese for Christ
5. Chinese Gospel Crusade, Inc.
6. Chinese Outreach (tape ministry)
7. Far Eastern Broadcasting Company, Project Share, Box 1, La Mirada, CA 90637
8. Gospel Recordings, 122 Glendale Blvd., Los Angeles, CA 90026
9. International Students
10. Overseas Missionary Fellowship
11. Pocket Testament League
12. Send, International

STUDY CENTERS FOR CHINESE MINISTRIES

1. United States Center for World Missions, 1605 E. Elizabeth Drive, Pasadena, CA 91104.
   A. Institute of Chinese Studies Publication: *Watchman on the Great Wall* (bimonthly) *Extended Family*
   B. Chinese World Missions Center Publication: *Chinese Missions Tomorrow* (monthly)
2. Trinity Evangelical Divinity School, 2065 Half Day Road, Deerfield, IL 60015
   Chinese American Program (CAP) to train leaders for American Chinese churches
   Information about Trinity's summer seminars for Chinese seminarians is available from Hoover Wong, 1054 S. King Street, Honolulu, Hawaii 96814
3. The Billy Graham Center, Wheaton College, Wheaton, IL 60187, is starting a Chinese program for Chinese from overseas.

Part 3

Introduction to Ministries Among Religious Groups

Introduction

The Constitution of the United States guarantees freedom of religion, which means that all citizens have the right to espouse and propagate any religious conviction without fear of governmental interference. Americans have fought long and hard for this freedom that did not exist in the early Thirteen Colonies.

Those who migrated to this country brought with them their religious beliefs and with varying degrees of success evangelized their neighbors. Today Americans espouse every kind of religious expression known to man. Religion is such a popular subject that the *Good Housekeeping* magazine published an article, "The 1200 Religions in America," which merely listed the religions without comment. It included fifty-six Buddhist groups, thirty-one Catholic, forty-six Hindu, twenty Islamic, thirty-four Jewish, eighteen Mormon, nineteen they labeled "pagan," twenty-six witchcraft, and fifty-four that were called "unclassified New-Age groups." The article concludes that there are far more than the 1,200 they listed "in the rich spiritual tradition of our country."[1]

It should be obvious that in most communities there will be groups of individuals who consider themselves to be very religious but who need to know the truth about Jesus Christ. Most of those people will never hear the gospel unless the church recognizes their

---

1. J. Gordon Melton, "The 1200 Religions in America," *Good Housekeeping*, March 1980, pp. 136-78.

existence and devises a plan to present the Good News to them in a manner that takes into account their sensitivities.

A number of mission agencies specialize in ministering to adherents of the major world religions. Perhaps the best known are those concerned with evangelizing the Jews. These missions maintain training programs for their missionaries and provide literature prepared for their ministry. Their house organs provide information helpful in understanding how to witness effectively to those people.

Many of those missions also provide training programs for laymen. By means of this service laymen are exposed to the religious beliefs and practices of a particular group and are then provided with opportunities to observe and take part in personal witnessing to practitioners in the community. Such programs are available for Jewish, Muslim, Hindu, and Mormon witness.

Certain missions target the larger cults such as Mormons and Jehovah's Witnesses. The tragedy is that almost nothing is being done to win the masses who have turned to what William Peterson calls "those curious new cults," which keep springing up without end.[2] The activity that does exist is primarily one of either warnings against the cults or clandestine activities initiated by parents who hire an agent to find, rescue, and deprogram their children who allegedly have been brainwashed by the cult.

A large and growing body of literature is being produced by concerned organizations and missions to alert young people, especially on college campuses, and parents concerning the message and procedures of these groups.

Several missions have targeted the 60 million American Roman Catholics as a mission field. In this study we have not included a history of Catholicism, but the missions concerned are listed.

2. William Peterson, *Those Curious New Cults* (New Canaan: Keats, 1975), p. 265.

7

American Jews

INTRODUCTION

The six million Jews in America are a mission field. Because of their theology, they do not believe that Jesus Christ is the Son of God. Moishe Rosen, a Hebrew Christian and founder of Jews for Jesus Mission, says that most Jews will exit from this life into a Christless eternity. They are also a mission field because they are isolated from the gospel. That isolation is partly because of their own attitude toward Christianity, which they reject, and in part to the attitude of the Gentile church, whose concern for the Jew is too often expressed in the idea that he has already had his chance. Finally, the Jew is a mission field that the church has already recognized as standing in need of evangelization; therefore, it has commissioned 400 missionaries and recognized fifty mission boards to begin to meet that need.

HISTORY OF THE JEWISH PRESENCE

Who is the Jew that the church admits is a mission field? He is variously defined as one who traces his lineage to Abraham, or one who has a Jewish mother. But now a Jew is anyone who claims to be a Jew,[1] for "Jews are no longer certain just what makes them into a people."[2]

American Jews have come from a variety of the countries of the Jewish Diaspora. The earliest Jews arrived with the colonists but not from Europe. They were Spanish and Portuguese Marranos who were fleeing the Inquisitor. The Marranos were Jews who had been forced to convert to Christianity and then encouraged to migrate to Brazil to establish business enterprises. It was feared that the Marranos were really Jews at heart; therefore, the Inquisitor sought to force them to comply with Christianity. The Marranos were fleeing to Holland for asylum when they were blown off course and landed in the colonies, where they were not warmly welcomed.

A second stream of Jews migrated during the later half of the nineteenth century. These Jews were from the European ghettos that had been established four centuries earlier. They were welcomed as entrepeneurs who had entered the world of banking and retailing to help transform America into an industrial nation.

A third group of Jews came from Russia during the years following 1880. Thirty-five thousand per year came from the Pale in Russian-occupied Poland until 3,000,000 poverty-stricken and almost illiterate Jews arrived. They were a complete contrast to the German Jews who had already become Americanized and who now helped the new arrivals to quickly assimilate. The Russian Jews became a real force in helping to organize the American labor movement.

Fourth, between the years 1933 and 1939, 157,000 Jews fled from Germany to escape Hitler's mania to destroy European Jewry. That migration depleted a large section of Germany's intellectual elite, thus transferring "the world's intellectual leadership from Europe to America."[3] In the next decade 200,000 others fled devastated Europe.

Fifth, during the decade of the 1960s, 73,000 Jews fled Fidel Castro's Cuba and the Arab Near East. Since 1970 and the Helsinki Accords, 10,000 Russian Jewish emigres enter annually. This number represents 50 percent of those who flee from the tyranny of Russia, which has 2.7 million Jews, the third largest Jewish population in the world, after America (7 million) and Israel (3 million). Another 4.1 million are scattered in the European Diaspora (1983). There are 16.8 million Jews throughout the world.

1. Max I. Dimont, *The Jews in America* (New York: Simon and Schuster, 1978), p. 165.
2. Jacob Neusner, *American Judaism* (New Jersey: Prentice Hall, 1972), p. 83.
3. Dimont, p. 189.

Why has America become the largest center of the Jewish Diaspora? Here the Jew has found refuge from a worldwide racism that is an outgrowth of neurotic nationalism called anti-Semitism. The Jew was able to flee anti-Jewishness, an effort to convert him to Christianity, by migrating to another country, but anti-Semitism, the mind-set to destroy him, is much more malignant and difficult to escape.[4] In America the Jews have faced and continue to face outbursts of racism that are mostly unorganized except for Ku Klux Klan activity,[5] but according to studies, this racist attitude is merely dormant because fully one-third of the American population is highly prejudicial. Still, anti-Semitism has never been the ideology of the American federal government.

Jews are overwhelmingly an urban people. In fact, more than one-half of all Jews live in seven major cities. Yet, there is scarcely a city in the United States where Jews are not resident. The largest Jewish city in the world is New York, which is home for 1,118,000 Jews. Moishe Rosen says, "New York City is not just another city. It is the city to be reached in Jewish evangelism, the key to evangelism in North America."[6]

Eight states of the industrial north from Illinois to Massachusetts contain 5,000,000 Jews (88 percent). New York State has the largest population of Jews. The second largest population lives in Los Angeles. Five hundred thousand live in Philadelphia and 300,000 in Chicago. Seventy-five percent of Florida's 300,000 live in Miami. Every state has more than 300 Jewish residents and most have several thousand. (See Figure 7.1.) The only way the widely disseminated American Jews will be confronted with the gospel will be through the mobilization of evangelical churches, which are also widely dispersed.

American Jews are not only an ethnic minority; they are also a religious community. That religious community is deeply divided into four unequal sects. The several streams of Jewish emigres through the years brought with them a smorgasbord of religious beliefs. The majority of Jews came from the European ghettos and brought with them a rather strict, legalistic Orthodox Judaism. When they arrived in America, they quickly adopted a life-style that did not include the ghetto or the old religious leaders. Most of the Jews discarded ghetto Judaism and the Yiddish language as they reformed

4. Ibid., p. 158.
5. *Evangelical Newsletter,* February 1981, p. 1.
6. *Jesus NY,* n.d., p. 4.

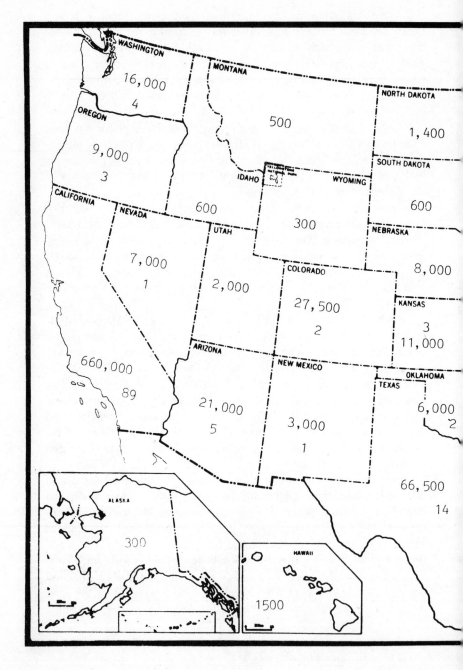

Figure 7.1

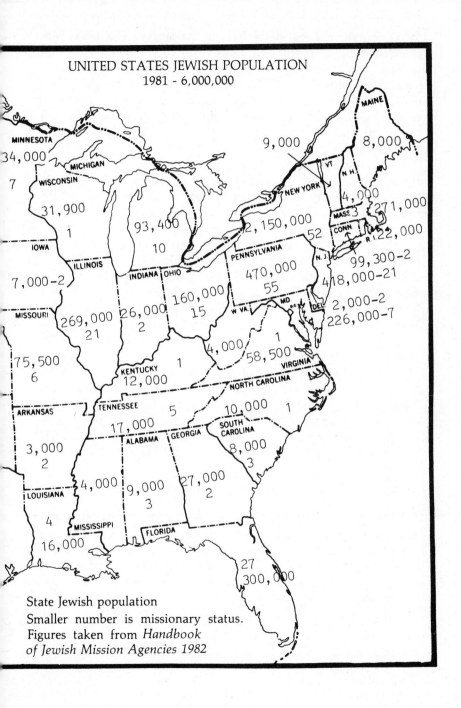

UNITED STATES JEWISH POPULATION
1981 - 6,000,000

MINNESOTA
34,000
7

MICHIGAN

WISCONSIN
31,900
1

93,400
10

MAINE
8,000

9,000

VT.
N.H.

NEW YORK

4,000
MASS. 3
CONN.
R.I. 22,000
271,000

2,150,000

52

IOWA

ILLINOIS

INDIANA OHIO

PENNSYLVANIA
470,000
55

N.J.
99,300-2
418,000-21

7,000-2

269,000
21

26,000
2

160,000
15

MISSOURI

MD.
DEL
2,000-2
226,000-7

75,500
6

KENTUCKY
12,000

W VA
4,000
1

58,500

VIRGINIA

ARKANSAS

TENNESSEE
17,000

NORTH CAROLINA
5

10,000
1

3,000
2

ALABAMA GEORGIA

SOUTH
CAROLINA
8,000
3

LOUISIANA
4

4,000
9,000
3

27,000
2

MISSISSIPPI
16,000

FLORIDA

27
300,000

State Jewish population
Smaller number is missionary status.
Figures taken from *Handbook
of Jewish Mission Agencies 1982*

their life-style and joined the Reform Synagogue. This often hap-
pened in the brief period of a decade. Not all orthodox Jews bolted
the strict practice of Judaism. On the northwest edge of Oak Park, a
suburb of Central Detroit, is an Orthodox Jewish community. In a
two-square-mile area men may be seen wearing black Homburg
hats, long overcoats, and full beards. Nineteen synagogues, ten
Jewish bakeries, as many kosher butcher shops, and two rabbinical
colleges service the community.

A reaction to the radical reforms of the latter movement gave
rise to a middle-of-the-road position called Conservative Judaism. In
Conservativism there was a move to restore Jewishness without the
legalism of the Orthodox. The three sects have about equal numbers
of adherents for each includes 18 percent of the populace.

The fourth and largest group of American Jews is the 2.7 million
unaffiliated Jews. Many of these are business and professional
persons who were earning over $20,000 annually in 1977.[7] They still
affirm that they are Jews and have no inclination to lose their
Jewishness even though a third of their Jewish youth marry Gentiles.
Most Jews affirm an ethical monotheism that may or may not have
any specific boundaries or permanently fixed views. But, they all
declare "faith in Torah."[8]

Finally, the centralization of power in the Jewish community has
gravitated away from the synagogue and the rabbi to the community
federation and its president. Evangelization of the Jew will need to
take into consideration this unique power structure and the concur-
rent loss of power of the rabbi and the synagogue. Surveys indicate
that only 9 percent of Jews attend synagogue regularly each week.

EXPOSURE TO CHRISTIANITY

The concerned Gentile Christian recognizes that Jews are spiritually lost and stand in need of a Savior. He further concedes that one
day the Lord will gather up His Jewish people and return them to the
Holy Land. But for now the Jew is set aside because of unbelief. He
is being punished; therefore, should he be evangelized?

He should be evangelized because that is the revealed plan of
God. Paul wrote to the church at Rome:

---

7. Donald Light, Jr., and Suzanne Keller, *Sociology*, 2d ed. (New York: Alfred Kopf,
   1979), p. 306. (This is double the national average. Twice as many Jews are in the
   professions.).
8. Dimont, *Jews in America*, p. 255.

Dear brothers, the longing of my heart and my prayer is that the Jewish people might be saved. I know what enthusiam they have for the honor of God, but it is misdirected zeal. For they don't understand that Christ has died to make them right with God. Instead they are trying to make themselves good enough to gain God's favor by keeping the Jewish laws and customs, but that is not God's way of salvation.

As you know, God has appointed me as a special messenger to you Gentiles. I lay great stress on this and remind the Jews about it as often as I can, so that if possible I can make them want what you Gentiles have and in that way save some of them. Romans 10:1-4; 11:13, 14 (TLB*).[9]

Jews have been persecuted from the year 70 when Titus destroyed the Temple and the Jews were scattered in the Diaspora until the Holocaust in Germany, when 6,000,000 Jews were slaughtered during the late 1930s and early 1940s. Much of that persecution has been at the hands of so-called Christian nations or their leaders. It is said that John Chrysostom, an early church Father, preached that God hates the Jew and the Christian should also because the Jew was the Christ killer.

The Roman Catholic church banished Jews from the Vatican State in the thirteenth and sixteenth centuries. Spain forced Jews to be baptized in the fifteenth century. The Inquisitors sought to force the Jewish Marranos to live like Christians for 300 years.

Even Martin Luther's brief pro-Jewish attitude soon turned to vehement anti-Jewishness, and he encouraged their expulsion from Christian lands. It is no wonder then that "a latent mistrust of Christians and a deeply rooted prejudice against Christianity possess the soul of the Jewish people because of the long ill-treatment accorded them by instigation of churchmen."[10]

John Calvin was strangely silent about the Jews. In fact, for three centuries Protestant churches did nothing to evangelize them. Although much is being done now to bring the Jews to the knowledge of Christ, the Jewish missionary will most assuredly not want to be unaware of how Christians have treated the Jews in the past. Perhaps this knowledge may also stir a nascent church to greater activity.

---

*The Living Bible.

9. Romans 10:1-4; 11:13-14, The Living Bible (Wheaton: Tyndale, 1971).

10. Albert Huisjen, The Home Front of Jewish Missions (Grand Rapids: Baker, 1962), p. 99.

JEWISH MISSIONS

Organized Jewish evangelism is a relatively recent idea. Jews were not a spiritual concern of the Reformers (c. 1517) or of the denominations that followed. The first mission established to evangelize the Jews was founded in 1809 in England. Originally it was completely independent of the Church of England, but later the London Society for Promoting Christianity Amongst the Jews became an Anglican mission with worldwide ministries.

A similar pattern of Jewish missions in the United States is evident. The colonial churches had little concern for the spiritual welfare of the growing number of Jewish immigrants who were fleeing to America for asylum from various countries of the world. It was not until 1885 that the American Messianic Fellowship was established under the name *Chicago Hebrew Mission*. A decade later in New York City the American Board of Missions to the Jews began work among the largest concentration of Jews in the world. But the greatest concern for Jewish evangelism in the United States is a twentieth-century phenomenon.

By the eighth decade of the century there were fifty mission societies and over 400 missionaries. (See Figure 7.2.) Three-fourths of the missionaries work under the auspices of the ten largest missions, which average thirty members. Fully 80 percent of the missions, however, have fewer than ten missionaries and the average is only three.

The multiplication of societies may be seen as an attempt to establish centers of evangelism in cities across the country where Jews have congregated. However, the task is a mammoth one. One-third of American Jewry live in New York City, but only forty-four missionaries (11 percent) work in this city; therefore, each missionary has a mission field of 45,000 Jews.

The problem is the same in every city. Although seven cities contain 56 percent of all Jews in the United States, only 20 percent of the missionary staff is deployed to reach those cities. Hundreds of cities have no missionary at all. Boston, for example, has 170,000 Jews and no missionary.

It has been established that there are Jews in all fifty states. Missionaries are working in thirty-six states. However, there are no missionaries in fourteen states where thousands of Jews reside. Nine states have more than ten missionaries, including California, which has the largest number (80). Among those with less than ten missionaries is Maryland, which has seven missionaries working among 226,000 Jews. This means that each worker has a mission field of nearly 32,000 souls.

It should be obvious that missionaries to Jewish people are scattered abroad, often working alone among lonely men and women. The Fellowship of Christian Testimonies to the Jews was established with four objectives:

1. To promote fellowship in order to improve, strengthen, harmonize, and expand the ministries of the individual and collective membership in the evangelization of the Jewish people
2. To rouse the Christian church to a sense of her obligation and responsibility toward the Jews and to encourage the proclamation of the whole counsel of God concerning His chosen people
3. To create a sympathetic attitude toward the Jewish people suffering through anti-Semitism or at the hand of agencies hostile to them
4. To present a united front on behalf of gospel witness to the Jewish people[11]

An annual meeting is held at the Gull Lake (Michigan) Bible and Missionary Conference grounds in late August to help fulfill the above objectives.

Missionary work among Jews is primarily a one-on-one ministry. Whether the ministry takes the form of door-to-door visitation, home Bible studies, correspondence courses, or telephone ministry, it requires patience and understanding. Radio ministry is effective because it provides a private atmosphere for personal study. A radio program of classical music can be useful since Jewish people often enjoy the classics.

Festive occasions are important to the Jews; therefore, missions have discovered that Jews may accept an invitation to a banquet in which a Jewish festival is being commemorated. Education is given a high priority in Jewish life-style, which means that quality Christian literature should be produced with a Jewish mind-set. It also suggests the need for a broad campus ministry. Statistics indicate that a higher percentage of Jewish college-aged youth are in college than the national average. Significantly, of the five largest evangelical campus ministries, the fourth and fifth are Jewish.

11. "The Fellowship of Christian Testimonies to the Jews," in *A Handbook of Jewish Mission Agencies*, ed. Harold A. Sevener (Englewood Cliffs, New Jersey: The American Board of Missions to the Jews, n.d.), p. 3. (Information gathered by the Fellowship of Christian Testimonies to the Jews.)

Jews are very much involved in social issues and cultural events. Matters affecting Israel receive their utmost attention. In some ways that interest can be capitalized on and used to the glory of the Lord.

Jews are not unaware of Christian terminology, but they probably have an incomplete or distorted understanding of its true meaning. It is essential that the missionary be aware of what Jews understand when certain terms are used such as *Jesus, Messiah, Christian, convert,* or *salvation.* The converse will also be true, for the Christian will need to understand Jewish theology to know what is meant by Jewish usage of certain terms.

There is widespread optimism that now is the day of Jewish evangelism. One mission leader says, "Never was there a more opportune time to present the claims of the Messiah. Jews are coming to know Jesus as the Messiah."[12] This presents a dilemma for both the missionary and the convert. The problem simply stated is, where will the Hebrew Christian go to church?

There are at least two options. First, the Hebrew Christian may join a Gentile Christian church. However, Huisjen notes that most churches are not prepared to receive the Hebrew Christian. Second, he may attend one of seventy messianic congregations. Manny Brotman, director of Messianic Jewish Movement, International, indicates that in this atmosphere the Jew can worship in a traditional manner centered around the Messiah who has brought new abundant life to Judaism. In the former option, it is suggested that the Hebrew Christian will of necessity need to lose something of his Jewishness, whereas in the latter option he may be less alienated from the Jewish community. Dr. Louis Goldberg of Moody Bible Institute summarizes succinctly:

> Cultural identification with the Jewish community is vital if we are to communicate the gospel properly and that attention must be given to ethnic, territorial, and historical forms. This will be incumbent upon the church of Gentile believers if they seek to adequately understand and communicate the message to Jewish people. When it is not possible for a non-Jewish congregation to be that kind of witness, it then may become necessary to have a Messianic Jewish congregational-type worship which will be able to witness more effectively to the Jewish community.[13]

---

12. "Pray for the Peace of Jerusalem," tract published by American Board of Missions to the Jews, p. 2.
13. Louis Goldberg, "Sharing with Jewish People," *Trinity World Forum,* Spring 1981, p. 2.

Moishe Rosen, founder of the Jews for Jesus Mission, second in size after the American Board of Missions to the Jews, popularized that approach in 1973. Several messianic synagogues have formed the Union of Messianic Jewish Congregations to give visibility to the Jewish community that there are other Jews who believe in the Messiah and to provide a place where they can take their relatives and friends who would not enter a Gentile church.[14]

On the other hand, there are those like Marvin Rosenthal, international director of the Friends of Israel Gospel Ministry, who believe that messianic Judaism is not messianic, Jewish, or biblical.[15] Any reasoned approach to the issue will at least raise the question as verbalized by Paul Feinberg of Trinity Evangelical Divinity School, "Does the Messianic Jewish approach make the Christian witness more credible in the Jewish community?"[16]

In answer, Richard Quebedeaux suggests that it does not when he says, "Because the established Jewish community feels that these Messianic Jews are really Christian evangelists masquerading as Jews to gain converts, it is extremely upset by their actions."[17] The controversy will not be settled without taking into account serious theological and missiological reasons for the new and effective approach.

If American Jews are to be reached for Christ, a twofold thrust must be developed. First, Jewish home missions must enlarge their work force and expand geographically. They must reach into the cities where there are Jews and no missionary presence. They must deploy their missionaries proportionately where there are concentrations of Jews, thus correcting such inequities as are manifest in the State of California, where only 21 percent of the missionary staff of Jewish missions working in California minister in Los Angeles, where 69 percent of the Jewish population resides.

Second, and perhaps more critical, the church will need to recognize its privilege and responsibility to include evangelization of the Jews in its own evangelistic program and support missionary efforts to reach the Jews. For nearly fifty years the leaders of Jewish

---

14. Union of Messianic Jewish Congregations, Beth Messiah Synagogue, 2208 Rockland, Rockville, MD 20851.
15. Marvin Rosenthal, "Half Truths Are Whole Lies," *Speak Tenderly to Jerusalem*, n.d., p. 6.
16. Goldberg, "A Response to Contextualized Jewish Evangelism," *Trinity World Forum*, p. 7.
17. Richard Quebedeaux, *Those Worldly Evangelicals* (San Francisco: Harper & Row, 1980), p. 161.

mission organizations have been offering training programs to local churches. All of the larger missions conduct seminars to train laymen to reach their Jewish neighbors, but the response has been meager. Perhaps an attitudinal problem needs to be addressed, for

> a number of years ago a survey revealed that the attitude of nearly two-thirds of rank and file church members is unbefitting a Christian, and therefore, a hindrance to the cause instead of a help. Further, it is one thing to assume a friendly attitude towards a Jew as we meet him, but, quite another to favor inviting him to attend one's own church and possibly having him into one's own church circle.[18]

From all indications, the Jew is more responsive to the gospel now than ever before. One study reveals that between 18,000 and 33,000 Jews have been converted to Christianity since 1965. Jack Heintz wrote in the *Prophecy News Bulletin*, "Many Jewish people are now more open to the Gospel than at any time since the first century."[19] To provide a national and international basis for fellowship for Jewish Christians, the Messianic Jewish Alliance was formed. It is also aligned with the International Hebrew Christian Alliance. These Alliances are intended to encompass all Jewish believers.

Jewish evangelism must now also include concern for 100,000 Russian Jewish emigres and the 10,000 who emigrate annually. In 1981, 80 percent settled in the United States. Mikhail Morgules of Slavic Gospel Association in New York City estimates that up to one-half of Russian-speaking Jews are locating in New York City. Jim Melnich, field director for Russian Emigre Ministries of the Slavic Gospel Association indicates that the mission has set up an Emigre Office in Chicago to assist the 10,000 Chicagoland emigres. The Friends of Israel Gospel Ministry began a work in 1980 among 10,000 Soviet Jews in the Dallas-Fort Worth area of Texas. Other groups of equal number have settled in Los Angeles, Detroit, and Cleveland.

It is necessary then that the church awake to her responsibility, for in the words of Marvin Rosenthal, "The church has yet to come to grips with its responsibility to evangelize the Jews as part of its present mandate."[20] It is true that the church has commissioned several missions to evangelize Jews, but it will take the combined

18. Huisjen, p. 168.
19. Jack Heintz, "God's Final Instructions Before 'Jacob's Trouble,'" *Prophecy News Bulletin*, n.d., p. 1.
20. Rosenthal, Introduction.

efforts of both missionaries and church laymen to accomplish the task. It needs to be remembered that "Jewish people are not uniquely difficult to reach with the gospel, but they must be reached uniquely."[21] There is a growing interest in Jewish evangelism. Bible schools, such as Moody Bible Institute, have developed a program of Jewish mission studies, and Jewish mission boards stand ready to assist any church interested in starting a Jewish evangelistic program.

MISSION BOARDS SERVING JEWS

1. American Association for Jewish Evangelism
2. American Board of Missions to the Jews
3. American Messianic Fellowship
4. Baptist Mid-Missions, Jewish Department
    Baptist Friends of Israel
    Baptist Friends of Israel of Pennsylvania
    Christian Information Service
    Columbus Hebrew and Christian Fellowship
    Hebrew and Baptist Fellowship
    Hebrew and Christian Society
    Los Angeles Hebrew Mission
    Twin-Cities Baptist Messianic Witness
5. Beth Emmanuel Fellowship
6. Beth Yeshua
7. Biblical Research Society
8. Buffalo Hebrew Christian Union
9. Catskill Messianic Fellowship
10. Christian Approach to the Jews
11. Christian Jew Foundation
12. Cleveland Hebrew Mission
13. Evangelism Missions, Inc.
14. Evangelization Society of Philadelphia
15. Friends of Israel Gospel Ministry (Israel's Remnant)
16. Hear O Israel
17. Hebrew Christian Fellowship
18. Hebrew Christians of Bridgeport
19. Hebrew Christian Witness
20. International Board of Jewish Missions
21. International Messianic Outreach
22. Israel's Evangelistic Missions

21. Ibid.

23. Israel's Hope, Inc.
24. Israel's Remnant Messianic Center
25. Jews for Jesus
26. Lederer Foundation
27. Los Angeles Messianic Witness
28. Message to Israel, Inc. (National Jewish Missions)
29. Messengers of the New Covenant
30. Messianic Fellowship Center
31. Messianic Jewish Alliance
32. Messianic Jewish Center
33. Messianic Jewish Movement, Int'l
34. Messianic Witness of Kansas City
35. Midwest Hebrew Mission
36. Mid-West Messianic Center
37. North American Jewish Ministries of the Christian and Missionary Alliance
38. Open Door Messianic Fellowship
39. Pacific Garden Mission
40. Peace for Israel, Inc.
41. Rock of Israel
42. Shalom Scripture Studies
43. Shofar
44. Slavic Gospel Association (Russian Jews)
45. World Messianic Fellowship, Inc.
46. World Missionary Outreach Ministries, Inc.

8

Non-Christian Religions

INTRODUCTION

At one time non-Christian religions were thought of as existing overseas in faraway countries where the religions developed. The only practitioners of these world religions in America were to be found among foreigners or perhaps some mavericks connected with a university campus. These people gathered in small groups in secret places and certainly not in foreign-looking temples. Obviously no educated non-ethnic would become a member.

The advent of modern mass movements of the world's peoples has radically altered the religious mosaic of American life. All of the non-Christian religions have been transplanted here, complete with temples, idols, and intricate ritual. A Gallup survey indicates that more than one-fourth of Americans believe in the reincarnation or transmigration of Eastern religions. Among teenagers, more likely to follow rock music stars, the figure rises to 30 percent.

Another factor to be noted is that thousands of nonemigre Americans are also enthusiastically involved in the practice of non-Christian religions. Not only has the foreign mission field come to America, it is also making converts.

AMERICAN MUSLIMS

In the United States there are 3,000,000 followers of Allah, the Muslim god, to whom they submit. For many American Muslims it is important to be an integral part of the worldwide family of Islam, encompassing 800,000,000, making it the world's largest non-Christian religion.

The growth of Islam in the world is nothing short of phenomenal. It began in A.D. 622 when Mohammed, the founder, fled from Mecca and conquered Medina, Arabia. Ten years later the Prophet was dead, but Islam's khalifs mounted campaigns that by 732 brought Islam to the door of Paris. The leaders demanded allegiance of all people in their path. They either saluted the green banner and crescent, the color and symbol of Islam, or died. Two exceptions were made, however, for Jews and Christians were protected, although taxed, because they were "people of the Book."

Islam in America, known as the American Muslim Mission or a splinter group called the Nation of Islam, is a recent phenomenon. (The first mosque was built about the turn of the century in Cedar Rapids, Iowa, complete with exclusive Muslim cemetery oriented toward Mecca.) It was brought by Muslim emigres from Arab countries and other lands where Islam rules. Muslims in America are to be found primarily in the larger cities, but "Muslims are found in nearly every American town."[1]

The largest Muslim concentration in the United States is in New York City and northern New Jersey, where 128,000 from twenty-five ethnic backgrounds live. In Detroit, Michigan's Arab Village, there are 100,000 Arabs with 40,000 alone from Chaldea, making it the second largest Chaldean population after Baghdad. Los Angeles (200,000 Muslims) is the third largest with a total of 30,000 to 40,000 Syrians, Lebanese, Pakistanis (10,000), Indians (5,000), Yugoslavians (5,000), Turks (5,000), and Afghanis.[2]

Funded with Arabian and Libyan petroleum dollars, Islam is "on the move in a manner unmatched since its conquests of North Africa and Europe in the seventh and eighth centuries."[3] In America the number of Muslims has multiplied by six in fifteen years. This growth, as reported by the Islamic Center in Washington, D.C., includes 300 Islamic centers in forty-one states across the country, including eighty-four mosques. A few mosques, such as the head mosque in Washington, D.C., are ornate structures costing millions

1. Constant Jacquet, ed., *Yearbook of American and Canadian Churches* (Nashville: Abingdon, 1979), p. 69.
2. Carol Glasser, "Prayer of the Hidden People," *Zwemer Institute Prayer Letter,* November 1980, n.p.
3. Fellowship of Isa, 1981.

of dollars. Islamic concern to gain the attention of students is indicated by the 133 student organizations planted on college campuses. Students from Islamic countries now form the largest group of internatioal students in North American universities and colleges (1984). No American has been a greater promoter of Islam than former heavyweight boxing champion Muhammed Ali, who has been called by many "Islam's most loquacious supporter."

Numerous sects have developed within the Muslim fold. Leo Rosten suggests there are seventy in the United States.[4] Our concern is to note three of those sects.

First, Bahaism began in Persia in 1844. The largest Bahai temple is located in Evanston, Illinois, but 900 groups totaling 100,000 members flourish across the country. Bahaism appeals to the educated; therefore, it has established 230 chapters on campuses. One of Bahai's eclectic roots is Islam. The name *Bahai* means "brother" in Arabic and indicates the desire of the group to be inclusive.

A second sect is the Ahmadiya Movement. It began in 1908 in India. It, too, is eclectic and is very evangelistic in America.

The third sect is the Black Muslim Movement, once known as the World Community of Islam in the West. Although the movement was denounced as unorthodox in the 1950s because of its alleged use of Islam to gain social and political ends, today its 100,000 adherents are generally accepted. In fact, Islam is making a concerted effort to win the blacks. That effort is most successful in converting black ex-convicts. "Parole officers and the police say that the Black Muslims are the best rehabilitation agency at work among Negro criminals today. They arrange parole for their converts and then carefully watch over them."[5] It has been suggested that "it is highly probable that Islam will become eventually the religion of the Negro in America if present trends continue."[6] In 1983 it was determined that 80 percent of Muslims living in Philadelphia were black. Perhaps that is an unrealistic prediction, but it should be a sobering warning to Christians that Islam is militant.

One large block of Muslims is from Iran. Unsettled conditions there in 1980 caused the number of Iranians migrating to the United States to escalate to 450,000 by 1984. Many are students, business people, tourists, and immigrants. Perhaps one-half of one percent are Christians, but most Iranians are Muslim.

---

4. Leo Rosten, *Religions of America* (New York: Simon and Schuster, 1975), p. 382.
5. William Peterson, *Those Curious New Cults* (New Canaan: Keats, 1975), p. 125.
6. Caesar E. Farah, *Islam* (Woodbury: Barron's Educational Series, 1968), p. 275.

Fifty percent of Iranians in America live in California, with other concentrations in New York, Boston, Chicago, and Texas. Working among Iranian Christians in southern California is Shahrokh Afshar. He established the Fellowship of Iranian Christians in 1979 with the vision to establish as many Bible studies in southern California as the Lord leads.

Another fellowship, Iranian Christians International, Inc., includes missionaries from Iran and other individuals interested in church planting among Iranian believers and directing evangelism towards winning Iranian Muslims to Christ. Ministries include staffing ten regional centers where Bible study, prayer, and worship are conducted in Persian; underwriting the printing of study materials in Persian and initiating national conferences for Iranian Christians.[7]

Another Muslim group is composed of many of the Palestinians who have been migrating to America since Israel occupied the land they considered theirs by right of lengthy occupancy. Discussion of the Palestinians is included in chapter 6.

Church planting is the primary missionary activity of mission boards working among Arabs. (See Figure 8.3.) Several missions provide Bible correspondence courses that have proved to be effective in Muslim work. (See Figure 8.1.) According to Bassam Madany, producer of the "Back to God Hour" aired in Chicago in Arabic, radio broadcasts in Arabic are useful in areas where large concentrations of Arab Muslims exist.

The largest ministry among Arab Muslims is that of the Home Mission Board of the Southern Baptist Convention. They work in eight states. Several missions such as International Students, Inc., work among 4,000 Muslim students on college campuses. This is a great opportunity to send the gospel back into Muslim countries where the missionary cannot go.

Mr. and Mrs. Victor Khalil, Arab Christians from Egypt, have found that a coffee house ministry near a mosque and home Bible studies are effective ministries in Detroit. He has further learned that Iranian Muslims love to hear the Bible read to them in Arabic; therefore, he has recorded the entire Bible on cassette tapes. Arabic language classes have been initiated for those who wish to learn Arabic to witness to their Arab neighbors.

International Missions established a summer ministry to train missionaries and laymen to witness to Muslim and Hindu people in Flushing, New York, where 200,000 aliens live, speaking fifty lan-

7. *Mojdeh,* September 1981, p. 9.

guages. In 1984, fifty students enrolled in the Muslim program and twelve enrolled in the Hindu curriculum through which they could earn college credit. The Samuel Zwemer Institute offers a six-week summer intensive training program called "Orientation to Ministry Among Muslims." Don McCurry, the director says, "The time for harvest and church planting among Muslims has come. The Zwemer Institute is helping to make this happen by awakening men and women in local churches to reach Muslims in their neighborhoods."[8] The Institute is publishing McCurry's doctoral dissertation pinpointing the Muslim communities and how to reach them for Christ. Concerned individuals are forming into groups such as the Philadelphia Area Ministry to Muslims (PAMM) to think through ways to reach Muslims for Christ.

Interest in reaching Muslims is growing. Evangelical Baptist Mission sponsors an Arabic Bible Conference. The Fellowship of Faith for Muslims prepares a monthly prayer bulletin and, among others, supplies materials necessary for Muslim evangelism. Materials are ready, training programs are available, and missions are prepared to lead the way, but according to Raymond Joyce, long-time Muslim missionary and executive director of the Fellowship of Faith for Muslims, among the churches of North America,

> there is a tragic and almost total ignorance of what Islam really is. Where there is an attitude expressed, it is usually one of apathetic dismissal of the task of reaching the Muslim for Christ as being too hard and unproductive. So naturally there is little or no involvement.[9]

A Moroccan Christian who visited America said,

> North American Christians have a unique opportunity to share Christ with Muslims at their doorstep. Thousands of students, visitors, temporary residents and workers from Muslim countries are scattered throughout the United States and Canada. You will find them in your neighborhood, in your shopping centers, in the work force.[10]

AMERICAN BUDDHISTS

Seven hundred thousand Japanese reside in the United States; one-third in Hawaii where there are 100 Buddhist temples in

8. *The Zwemer Institute Newsletter,* Summer 1981, p. 4.
9. Raymond H. Joyce, "Islam Is Here in North America," *Interlit,* December 1977, p. 7.
10. *Gospel Message,* October-December 1981, p. 6.

ASIAN PEOPLE IN UNITED STATES

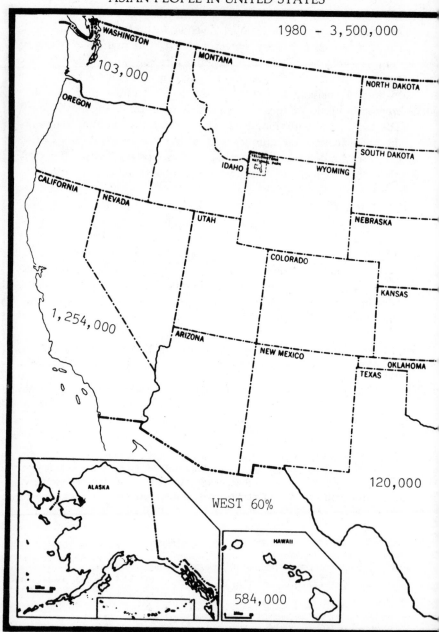

Figure 8.1

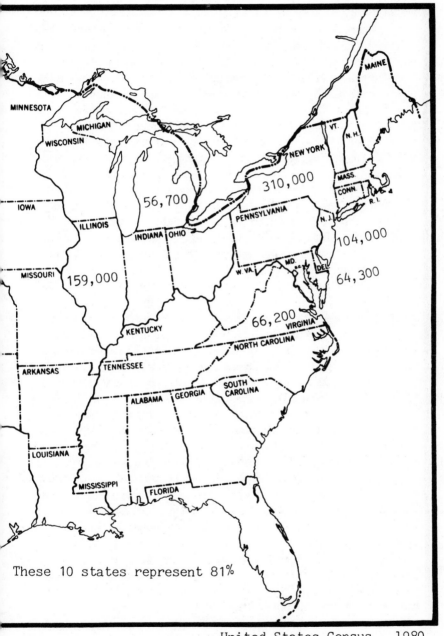

MINNESOTA

MICHIGAN

WISCONSIN

MAINE

VT.

N. H.

NEW YORK

MASS.

CONN.

R. I.

IOWA

56,700

310,000

PENNSYLVANIA

ILLINOIS

INDIANA OHIO

N. J.

104,000

MISSOURI

159,000

W. VA.

MD.

DEL.

64,300

KENTUCKY

66,200

VIRGINIA

NORTH CAROLINA

ARKANSAS

TENNESSEE

SOUTH
CAROLINA

ALABAMA

GEORGIA

LOUISIANA

MISSISSIPPI

FLORIDA

These 10 states represent 81%

United States Census - 1980

Honolulu. Three hundred thousand Buddhists in the United States are primarily of Japanese ancestry.

Japanese migration began after 1885 when Japan permitted her people to leave the islands. The West Coast was the logical port of entry and remains the most popular place for Japanese to reside.

With the outbreak of the Second World War and the bombing of Pearl Harbor by Japan, American racial discrimination fell to a new nadir. One hundred thousand Japanese American citizens were, without provocation, removed from their homes to concentration camps as far away as New Jersey. After the war many returned to the West Coast, but pockets of Japanese remained in coastal and mid-American cities where they had been interned. (See Figure 8.2.)

This ethnic group is one of the highest achievers of all the minorities. In education, Japanese adults have more schooling than whites. The penchant for learning was brought with them, for Japan has the highest literacy rate in the world. The average income of the Japanese American is greater than the national average. Yet, discrimination remains present today.[11]

Buddhism as practiced in America may be divided into two broad categories. The oldest and largest groups are called non-meditative. They attend churches that very much resemble any denominational church. The Buddhist Churches of America began in 1899 when two Japanese missionaries of the Pure Land Sect came to America to work among the Japanese immigrants. The denomination now numbers 100,000 members and includes the largest number of Oriental-born citizens. There are 100 member churches divided into eight districts. Only two districts are not on the West Coast. The eastern district, which includes Cleveland, Chicago, New York, Seabrook (New Jersey), Detroit, the Twin Cities, and Washington D.C., indicates how widespread the Buddhist churches are.

(I attended the dedication of a Buddhist church in Seabrook near my home. Other than the use of the Japanese language, incense, and occasional sounding of percussion instruments, the rest of the service was not radically different, nor was the architecture of the building particularly foreign.)

The largest and fastest growing non-meditative group is called Nichiren Shoshu of America. It is of the Sokagakkai Sect and includes 200 chapters. By effective conversion drives, 200,000 Americans have become members since 1960.

---

11. Leon F. Bouvier and Everett S. Lee, eds., *Population Profiles, The Nation's Minorities* (Washington, Conn.: The Center for Information on America, 1978), p. 6.

The second kind of Buddhism practiced in the United States is meditative. Membership statistics are not available, but many thousands of non-Orientals have become Zen enthusiasts within the last two decades. Meditative Buddhism tends to draw individuals instead of families. Many of the non-Orientals who have become Buddhists have come from the counterculture of the 1960s. Charles Prebish notes, "In the social domain, the most significant development for Buddhism in America was the emergence of a considerable counterculture, from which Buddhism was to recruit some of its most ardent supporters."[12]

American Buddhism also was enhanced by the Death of God and Human Potential Movements of the 1960s. With attendant secularization and growing pluralism in America, a religion that postulated nontheism and a do-it-yourself kind of mysticism appealed to the bifurcated, under 35, religious searcher who was deeply disenchanted with his urban treadmill-like existence.

Although there is no generic association between the religions of Buddhism and Confucianism, Shintoism, and Taoism, it is not uncommon to find Buddhists who also consider themselves to be followers of a second religion. Buddhists of China may also hold to Taoist or Confucianist beliefs. Those in Japan frequently are not only Buddhist but also Shintoist. In Hawaii I visited temples where homage was paid to several religions in the same sanctuary.

In the United States there are 90,000 Confucianists, 25,000 Shintoists, and 15,000 Taoists.

The refugees from Southeast Asia are frequently of a Buddhist heritage. They are treated in chapter 6.

As far as is known, the only missionary work among American Buddhists is being done in Hawaii (see chapter 17) on college campuses among international students and among the refugees.

AMERICAN HINDUS

Most of the world's 700,000,000 Hindus live in India, but at least 100,000 East Indians are included in the 3.5 million Asians living in the United States at the time of the 1980 census. The number of Hindus is estimated to be 100,000. Accurate figures are not available because there is no central agency recording statistics of American Hindus.

12. Charles S. Prebish, *American Buddhism* (North Scituate, Mass.: Duxbury, 1980), p. 29.

Many of the East Indians in the United States are professional people who migrated here for improved educational and job opportunities. Southern West Virginia provides jobs in the mining industry and medical field. Each year in the city of Beckley several hundred East Indians gather for an Indian festival called Duwali. They share Indian dishes and enjoy cultural events.

In the home of the Indian family an altar or shrine may be located in some prominent place. Offerings and homage are paid to the god or idols selected from the Hindu pantheon of thirty-three crores (estimated to be 330,000,000) of gods for personal involvement.

In the Pittsburgh area several hundred Indian families have settled. A one-half-million-dollar shimmering white Hindu temple stands off the Parkway east of Pittsburgh near Monroeville.[13] It is covered with carvings outside like the Tirupaths in South India. Hindus from all over the United States make pilgrimage to this shrine to venerate its idols and commemorate some anniversary. I visited this temple and attended the private services that were conducted by a Hindu priest who wore native garments and performed the ritual in an Indian language.

Numerous idols imported from India have been dutifully installed in the Sri Venkatesware temple. Photographing the statuary is forbidden with the explanation that the essence of the idols might be diminished.

Two other Hindu temples have been constructed in the borough of Queens, New York City, for the convenience of several thousand Hindus in the area. In Flushing alone an estimated 21,000 East Indians live. The First Baptist Church of Flushing is reaching out to its international community with ministries in eight languages. International Missions, Inc., is using the church facilities as a base of operations for its intensive summer training programs called Friendship International. Veteran missionaries teach classes for those who want to learn how to evangelize Hindu and Muslim people. One missionary said, "There may be some difficulty getting into India to do missionary work, but there is no such difficulty getting into Queens, New York City."

One of the many sects of Hinduism is the Hare Krishna movement. Thousands of disenchanted youth or college students give

13. Hindu Venkateswara Temple (Penn Hills), Muccully Drive, Monroeville, Pennsylvania. (It is open daily 9:00 to 7:00, Monday through Friday. No charge for admission.)

months of their lives to this cult as "an emphatic rejection of conventional affluent America."[14]

The Hare Krishna cult, founded in 1944, as the International Society for Krishna Consciousness (ISKCON) maintains thirty centers and seven self-sustaining farms in the United States. The purposes of the movement are to explore the ideas presented in ancient India's Vedic literature, especially the Bhagavad-Gita, and to teach Krishna consciousness throughout the English-speaking world. The founder, A. C. Bhaktivedanta Swami Prahubapada, died leaving eleven disciples as spiritual masters in the United States. The master for the central zone, Maharaja, is leading the group in founding the new Vrindaban community on Hare Krishna Ridge in Moundsville, West Virginia. The leader for all of America is the son of a Baptist minister, Srila Bhaktipada.

The devotees live in a literal barn in rooms constructed in a loft over the sacred cows that they venerate. They eat a vegetarian diet, wear rustic clothes, and repeat "Hare Krishna" 2,000 times each day. Many hours are spent chanting over sacred mantras 1,728 times and then performing duties as prescribed by the leader. In Moundsville the work built a $500,000 palace for the founder whose life-sized statues adorn prominent places.

The palace is but one of a community of seven temples and gardens being built on the 3,000-acre property. A restaurant and motel offer accommodations for the visitors who come to see what George Clark of Ohio State University says could turn into one of the most important and informative tourist attractions in the country. That is exactly the purpose of the buildings—to bring Prahubapada to the world. The leader of the community says that "Prahubapada should be as prominent as Jesus Christ."[15] The leader is not unwilling to receive adoration either, for when I was visiting the palace, the leader came to the site, and all the devotees got down on their hands and knees before him.

The name of the organization is taken from a "mantra," or saying, believed to be made up of mind-freeing transcendental sounds addressed to Krishna, who is one of Hinduism's many gods. The mission of the movement is to reach the people of every town and village in America so their minds can remain fixed on Krishna

14. Gregory Johnson, "The Hare Krishna in San Francisco" in *The New Religious Consciousness*, ed. by C. Glock and H. Bellah (Berkeley: U. of California, 1976), p. 39.

15. Bhaktivedanta Swami Prahubapada, ed., *Back to Godhead*, n.d., p. 1.

all day. They are eminently successful for "Hare Krishna, Hare Rama" is now as familiar a sound on the streets of most major American cities as the noise of passing traffic; no one even turns to stare at the saffron robes and shaved heads of devotees anymore.[16]

To many Americans, the act of meditating on a simple word or thought seems like such a harmless way of obtaining peace in a hectic world. They ask, What is wrong with putting the mind in neutral and allowing it to attain its natural state of bliss? Any school child can do it, and many are being taught how at the taxpayer's expense.

Three hundred thousand Americans are members of the Spiritual Regeneration Foundation of America or the Student International Meditation Society (SIMS) as followers of Transcendental Meditation. They see no reason why tax dollars should not be spent in teaching Transcendental Meditation in the public schools. However, instant Nirvana, as it is called, must be known for what it is—a sect of Hinduism.

Its founder was a Hindu guru, or spiritual teacher, by the name of Maharishi Mahese Yogi. Born in India in 1911, he began teaching his doctrine in 1959 after studying under a Hindu swami for nine years. He moved to England where in 1967, after the Beatles accepted his teaching, he received instant fame. American show business people also became his disciples, and the United States welcomed Transcendental Meditation (TM). Time magazine reported in 1972 that TM may well be the fastest growing cult in the West.

The guru's method of attaining peace involves a daily fifteen-minute meditation on his own personal Sanskrit mantra, which is given by the guru to fit the personality. By means of this exercise, it is alleged that suffering can be eliminated. TM becomes "a vague mixture of self-therapy, Hindu teaching, and flower power."[17]

The assasination of Indira Ghandi of India in 1984 by a Sikh made Americans aware that 150,000 Sikhs have emigrated to the United States. They can be recognized by their well-kept black beards and turbaned heads. Under the turban is packed their uncut hair held in place by a special comb. On the arm they wear steel bangles or bracelets and somewhere under their garments will be hidden a small dagger.

Sikhism is a syncretistic religion that drew its monotheism from

16. Donald Light, Jr., and Suzanne Keller, *Sociology* (New York: Alfred Knopf, 1979), p. 442.
17. Peterson, *Curious Cults*, p. 194.

Islam and the rest of its beliefs from Hinduism.[18] Although they have no active missionary program, their well-known soup kitchens provide free meals for any and all who may come to their temples to be found in Washington, D.C., New York City (8,000), Los Angeles, Espanola, New Mexico, and Oregon.

The earliest Sikhs came from the Punjab, India, in the early 1900s. Yogi Bhajan founded the Sikh movement in the United States called Health, Happy, Holy Organization, or the 3 HO Foundation.

The evangelical church must awaken and prepare literature and missionaries to reach these zealous but lost souls. International Missions has begun a work among Hindus with its Friendship International ministry in New York City. Christians across America should be aware that some of the professionals in their community may be Hindus or from a Hindu background. They can be befriended and won to Christ.

The non-Christian religions are growing in America. The church is just beginning to recognize its responsibility to reach the foreign mission field here at home. The greatest challenge of all the non-Christian religions may be Islam. "The spreading, militant evangelism of Islam from the Near East, which has already converted large segments of the world, will pose a serious challenge to Christianity as well as religion in general in America."[19]

MISSION BOARDS SERVING NON-CHRISTIAN RELIGIONS

1. Assemblies of God
2. Baptist Mid-Missions
3. Christian and Missionary Alliance
4. Evangelical Baptist Missions
5. Home Mission Board of the Southern Baptist Convention
6. International Missions
7. International Students, Inc.
8. Inter-Varsity Christian Fellowship
9. Navigators
10. Operation Mobilization
11. WEC/Muslim Ministries
12. WEF Ministries

18. John B. Noss, *Man's Religions* (New York: Macmillan, 1967), p. 130.
19. James Bjornstad, "America's Spiritual, Sometimes Satanic, Smorgasbord," *Christianity Today*, October 1981, pp. 28-29.

Figure 7.2

SERVICES AVAILABLE FOR MINISTRIES AMONG NON-CHRISTIAN RELIGIONS

I. Bible Conferences
1. Evangelical Baptist Missions—Arabic Bible Conference
2. Reformed Bible College-Annual Conference on Christian Witness to Muslims, 1869 Robison Road, S.E., Grand Rapids, MI 49506
3. Urbana—Scholarship for Iranian Christians from Muslim background, Allayhar Estaidi, O.R.U. Box 1776, Tulsa, OK 74717

II. Radio Ministry
"Back to God Hour" in Arabic, Bassam Madany, 6555 W. College Drive, Palos Heights, IL 60643 (Also has literature available)

III. Training
1. American Messianic Fellowship—Muslim training sessions
2. International Missions—Hindu and Muslim training, Flushing, New York
3. Samuel Zwemer Institute—Muslim training, Altadena, California
4. Joel Slaughter—Hawthorne Bible Church, Hawthorne, New Jersey

IV. 1. American Bible Society
2. American Missionary Fellowship—correspondence course
3. Fellowship of Faith for Missions—prayer list, range of materials
4. Fellowship of Isa—seminars, materials
5. Rev. Jadalla Ghrayyeb—Arabic books, cassettes, P.O. Box 442, Colorado Springs, CO 80901
6. Gospel Missionary Union—correspondence courses in Arabic, French, and Spanish
7. Institute in Public Evangelism—Arabic scriptures, tapes, and film: *Man from Tarsus* in Arabic or English, P.O. Box 495, Kansas City, MO 64141
8. International Missions—correspondence courses
9. *Life of Jesus the Messiah* by Dennis Clark—for Muslims in English (David C. Cook Publishing Company)

10. New Testament in Arabic on cassettes—Victor Khalil, Assembly of God Division of Home Missions, 1445 Boonville Avenue, Springfield, MO 65802

11. WEC Ministries—literature in Persian and English

Figure 8.3

9

American Cults

One of the most frustrating and confusing series of mission fields in America is the maze of unconventional religious movements, or new religious movements that are grouped under the rubric *cults*. Just about any religious organization that is not included under the title of Christian or non-Christian religion could be considered a cult.

The dictionary definition of *cult* includes the following concepts: (1) a system of religious ritual; (2) a group of followers; and (3) devoted attachment or extravagant admiration for a person, idea, or thing.[1] All of those ideas coalesce in the following definition. A cult is a religious organization that demands unquestioned commitment to its leaders and system of belief as portrayed in its scriptures as well as extravagant involvement in its projects.

It is easier to chronicle common characteristics of cults than it is to define a cult. Walter Martin, an authority on United States based cults, suggests the following characteristics of American cults.

1. Dynamic, self-selected and self-styled leader
2. Rigid membership standards including total dedication to the cause
3. Own scriptures or reinterpreted recognized scriptures, usually involving new and/or continuing revelation

1. *Webster's New World Dictionary of the American Language*, College ed., 1968, p. 358.

4. Special vocabulary
5. Activity fulfilling some special need in the life of the cult member
6. Devotess often isolated from friends and relatives[2]

For our purposes, a definition of a cult is needed to help identify groups of people who are effectively isolated from the evangelical church. The cultist is isolated if the church has not targeted the cult for evangelism, or the church members have not recognized their responsibility to witness to cult members.

EXTENT OF THE PHENOMENON

Many cults began as religious fallout from the frustration of the 1960s. An ABC-TV special in 1978 declared that 6,000,000 Americans were involved in a thousand cults. Dave Hunt, author of *The Cult Explosion*, reports "estimates of five thousand religious and pseudo-religious cults in the US."[3] Walter Martin, after years of research, concludes that "cults are multiplying faster than we can imagine. Collectively, cult membership in the United States may reach close to 20,000,000."[4] Bill Warner of Christian Apologetics Project suggests the figure should be 60,000,000 to 80,000,000. A Gallup poll in 1979 indicated that the "religious cult" population of the United States is 54 percent of the total population. That would mean that over 118,000,000 persons are cultists.[5] In attempting to verify the above figures, I compiled a list of less than 25 cults and found a total of 27,000,000 persons involved. (See Figure 9.1.)

It will be difficult to determine how widespread cultism is in the United States until an exhaustive list of cults is compiled. That compilation will vary depending on the definition used to decide which groups are cults. Christian Apologetics Research and Information Service (CARIS) defines a cult as "a group teaching a false gospel with a message contrary to Biblical Scripture."[6] Using this definition they have compiled a list of 1,300 groups and indicate that it is only a fraction of what exists in America today.

It would appear that evangelical Americans have little idea how widespread or how dangerous the cult phenomenon really is. Numerous organizations are now doing research about the cults and

2. Walter Martin, *The New Cults* (Santa Ana: Vision House, 1980), pp. 11-34.
3. Dave Hunt, *The Cult Explosion* (Irvine, California: Harvest, 1980), p. 18.
4. Martin, p. 17.
5. *Reaching the Unreached: San Francisco Bay Area,* May 1980, p. 13.
6. Jack Roper, *America: A Mission Field,* n.d., p. 1.

publishing their findings so that the church can be forewarned. Spiritual Counterfeits Project is one example. (See Figure 9.2.) The mission has compiled a library of 2,500 volumes for research on more than 1,000 spiritual trends, groups, gurus, and leaders. The purposes of the organization are:

1. To research and biblically critique current religious groups and individuals
2. To equip Christians with the knowledge, analysis and discernment that will enable them to understand the significance of today's spiritual explosion
3. To suggest a comprehensive Christian response that engages the church with all aspects of the problem (The church needs to repent of its compromises with the world and issue a strong prophetic warning to the secular culture.)
4. To bring the good news of Jesus Christ and extend a hand of rescue to those in psychological and spiritual bondage[7]

The cults are a particular problem on college and university campuses; therefore, student organizations frequently make packets of informational materials available. For instance, on the University of California campus, the University Religious Council makes available a list of organizations where students can get information about nontraditional religious groups and counseling services. They have found that the most vulnerable students are upper middle class youth, moderately depressed, with no major social affilations, and with no solid grounding in their faith.

Research reveals that those who become involved in the cults were brought up in a denominational church but knew little about their "faith." They were very much involved in life but had not realized just how shallow that life was until a persuasive cultist invited them to an intensive seminar, where in a short period of time their whole lives were reorganized around the cult that smothered them with attention and kindness. Without the persons realizing it, the cult had seduced them.[8]

Churches and their leaders should take note of the extent to which their members are conversant with the doctrines of their faith. Further, the church should take advantage of the information now available about cults and their teachings by subscribing to newslet-

7. *Spiritual Counterfeits Project Newsletter*, August 1981, p. 2.
8. Ronald Enroth, *The Lure of the Cults* (Chappaqua: Christian Herald Books, 1979), p. 116.

ters, buying books for the church library, and renting films. Then, the church should initiate classes with the junior high, senior high, and college age to inform their members about the dangers of cults.

Churches should also begin programs to teach their members how to witness to the cultists in their areas. Various organizations are available to assist the local church with seminars and materials. Some missions also offer internship programs for the serious Christian who is concerned to learn from those who are actively involved in evangelizing a particular cult. The church should learn about mission organizations that have targeted cults as their mission field and support them as it seeks to work in areas where cult movement is strong.

Finally, the church should survey its area and initiate programs to evangelize any cult group beyond its present programs. Missionary organizations have developed programs and are actively evangelizing members of two cults.

MORMONISM

The Church of Jesus Christ of Latter Day Saints is one of the oldest (1830) and is the largest (5,000,000) cult in America. According to one author, the Mormon church wields more economic power than any other organized religion. Mormons attend 7,500 churches that are divided into organized communities. Perhaps the best-known program of the Mormon church is the everpresent (30,000), black-suited, clean-cut pair of Mormon youth who spend two years of their lives knocking on doors as missionaries of the church. The success of the eager, well-trained young missionaries need not be chronicled, for the 600 baptisms per day are an impressive fact.

It is that kind of enthusiastic ministry that needs to be generated within the evangelical church generally and toward Mormons in particular. John L. Smith, seasoned minister of twenty years of service in Utah, believes that Mormons can be won to Christ. From his experience he has written a book, *Witnessing Effectively to Mormons.* He has a cassette tape ministry that includes studies on Mormonism, how to witness to Mormons, and a tape specifically for Mormons. His experience has revealed that in witnessing to a Mormon it is good to begin with the Mormon's doctrine of God. The more he learns about Mormonism, the more he feels, "I cannot wait; I dare not rest. I know Mormonism's error and I must make it known to all who will hear.[9]

The Mormons must be evangelized because they are lost. Although the church is highly organized and there is great emphasis on the home, the fact remains the people are adrift in a sea of humanism without the unadulterated Bible and the Christ who saves. The state of Utah has the highest divorce rate in the nation, which is 25 percent.

At least eleven mission organizations sustain various kinds of effective ministries among Mormons. (See Figure 9.3.) Programs include campus ministries as well as church planting. Several Christian radio stations carry programming that targets Mormon populations. Research and writing that expose the errors of Mormonism are a major concern for several missions and service organizations. Cassette tape ministries are available and have proved very effective in Mormon evangelism. Tracts and books prepared for the Mormon reader are available from several sources. (See Figure 9.2.)

Ministries to the Mormons are effective, and many are turning to Christ. Those who are saved out of Mormonism need special discipling to help them correct wrong understanding of doctrine. It is helpful if the ex-Mormon can find fellowship with others who have also come out of the cult. Edward Decker, an ex-Mormon, founded a mission organization called Ex-Mormons for Jesus (EMFJ). There are four national directors in regional offices located in Washington, D.C., California, Illinois, and Florida, who supervise local chapters of Ex-Mormons. A goal of Ex-Mormons for Jesus is to increase the current 20 chapters to 100 chapters across the country. The objectives of the mission are to enlarge the "ministry of Christ's love to ex-Mormons, by sharing the gospel of Jesus Christ with the Mormon people, and training the Christian body to reach out in love to those who are 'led to err and destruction.' "[10] The same organization is known in Utah as Saints Alive in Jesus.

JEHOVAH'S WITNESSES

The Jehovah's Witnesses began in 1874 under the ministry of Pastor Charles Russell, who was greatly concerned about Christ's second coming. Those who followed his teaching were known as

9. *Utah Evangel,* August 1980, n.p.
10. *Saints Alive in Jesus,* July-August 1981, n.p.

Millennial Dawnists and International Bible Students or Russellites. In 1931 the group split and the name *Jehovah's Witnesses* was taken. Each of the 600,000 members is considered a minister and gives 15 hours a month as "Publishers of the Kingdom." Pioneers give 100 hours a month, and missionaries give a minimum of 150 hours per month. Members congregate in "Kingdom Halls," which are located in twenty-six districts of the United States.

The Jehovah's Witnesses are a mission field because

> they are the deadliest and most fierce enemies of the Christian religion extant today. Their zeal is in keeping with their hatred of all the evangelical doctrines, such as the Trinity, the Deity of Christ, and the true Biblical teaching concerning atonement, and they do not hesitate to denounce all others as enemies of Jehovah's kingdom on earth, grouping and labeling them the organization of "Satan the Devil."[11]

The Jehovah's Witnesses are not generally targeted by the evangelical church for evangelism; however, several research organizations and missions are concerned about reaching them for Christ. Several years ago a worldwide tract ministry was begun in England called Help Jesus Ministry. In the United States the national representative is Christian Apologetic Research and Information Service (CARIS). Forty-three consultants are scattered throughout the country providing tracts in quantity at near cost to those willing to aggressively seek to bring Jehovah's Witnesses to Christ. CARIS also ministers in the church by providing seminars, a newsletter, and producing literature to help equip church members to evangelize the cults. (See Figure 9.2.)

At least nine missions are seeking to evangelize Jehovah's Witnesses. (See Figure 9.4.) Some provide literature, tapes, and seminars to equip and encourage Christians to evangelize the Jehovah's Witnesses. Two organizations have extensive telephone ministries in several states. They provide counsel and witness to Jehovah's Witnesses and encouragement to ex-Jehovah's Witnesses.

In 1979 the first National Convention of Ex-Jehovah's Witnesses gathered together many who had been saved out of the cult. The convention was addressed by Pastor Joe Hewitt, author of the book *I Was Raised a Jehovah's Witness.*[12]

11. Jan Karel Van Baalen, *The Chaos of Cults* (Grand Rapids: Eerdmans, 1958), p. 231.
12. *CAP News*, December 1979, pp. 4-5.

Conclusion

Millions of people in America are involved in thousands of cults. Two of the cults are being evangelized. Church planting is taking place primarily among only one—the Mormons.

Numerous organizations are researching and publishing information about many cults. They are also prepared to help churches equip their people to evangelize the cults.

Cultists can and are being won to Christ. Groups of ex-cultists are meeting across the nation. Not only are there former Mormons and ex-Jehovah's Witnesses, but also ex-Christian Scientists.

Churches need to alert their young people to the dangers of the cults and train them in biblical truth. The church library should be equipped with materials about cults. Seminars should be held to equip the saints. Yet, "the average American is spiritually naive, and vulnerable," and churches are evincing an "incredible degree of apathy."[13] Christians should be concerned about cult growth because 70 percent of those who inquire about a cult actually join. Most of those who join cults (82 percent) are churched, and 35 percent are Protestant.[14] William Schnell, author of *Thirty Years a Watch Tower Slave*, testifies, "They brainwash the personal religion of Jesus from all those who have become its slaves."[15]

Partial List of Cult Membership

This list supplies the membership of each cult, the number of known churches within the cult, and the date of its founding.

	No. of Churches	Membership
1. Armstrongism or Worldwide Church of God	250	75,000
2. Astrology (16,000 in the West)		2,000,000
3. Bahai (1912)	837	100,000
4. Christian Science (1866)		500,000
5. Hare Krishna (see chapter 8)		2,000,000

13. Ronald Enroth, "Dimensions of Cult Conspiracy," *Christianity Today*, October 1981, p. 27.
14. John Blackwell, *20th Century New Religions: Help or Hindrance* (New York: United Church of Christ, n.d.), p. 15.
15. William J. Schness, *Thirty Years a Watch Tower Slave* (Grand Rapids: Baker, 1965), p. 203.

6. Jehovah's Witnesses (1874, name taken in 1931)	7,000	600,000
7. Maharaji Ji (Divine Light Mission)	480	35,000
8. Mormons (The Church of the Latter Day Saints, 1830)	7,500	5,000,000
Reorganized	1,000	156,000
9. Satanism		100,000
10. Scientology		3,500,000
11. Spiritualists (1875)		150,000
12. Seventh Day Adventists (1830s)		450,000
13. Sun Myung Moon (Unification Church, 1959)		500,000
14. Transcendental Meditation (see chapter 8)		1,000,000
15. Witchcraft		10,000,000

Some of the above figures are from William Peterson, *Those Curious Cults* (New Canaan: Keats, 1975).

Figure 9.1

SERVICES AND MATERIALS AVAILABLE FOR MINISTRY TO THE CULTS

1. The American Family Foundation, Inc., P.O. Box 343, Lexington, MA 02173. *The Advisor,* a newspaper exposing cults, giving the latest on legislation.
2. Association of Former Christian Scientists, 1550 S. Anaheim Blvd., Anaheim, CA 92805.
3. B'Nai B'Rith International, Adult Education Department, 1640 Rhode Island Avenue, N.W., Washington, D.C. 20036. Cult information.
4. Center for Study of New Religions on the campus of Graduate Theological Union, 2465 LeConte Avenue, Berkeley, CA 94709. *New Religious Movements Newsletter.*
5. Citizens Freedom Foundation, P.O. Box 7000-89, 1719 Via El Prado, Redondo, CA 90277. Produces a newsletter; local chapters in each state give current information on cults.
6. Christian Apologetics Research and Information Service (CARIS), P.O. Box 1783, Santa Ana, CA 92702. Home of the Help Jesus tract ministry to Jehovah's Witnesses. Maintains a catalog of materials on cults.
7. Christian Information Network Referral Service, P.O. Box 421, Pine Lake, GA 30072. A computer readout called CULTS gives lists of countercult agencies and material sources.

8. Christian Ministry to Cults, P.O. Box 507-M, Hoboken, N.J. 07030. Seminars and literature.
9. Christian Research Institute, P.O. Box 500, San Juan Capistrano, CA 92675. Offers a newsletter and information.
10. *Cult Explosion*, a fifty-five-minute film distributed by New Liberty Enterprises, 1805 W. Magnolia Blvd., Burbank, CA 91506.
11. Ex-Mormons for Jesus. Offers literature.
12. "Gospel Truth" (Radio Free Utah), Johnny Yount, P.O. Box O, El Toro, CA 92630. Uses radio station KBBX, Salt Lake City, Utah.
13. Home Mission Board, Southern Baptist Convention. Offers literature and list of Sun Myung Moon organizations.
14. Institute of Contemporary Christianity, P.O. Box A, Oakland, NJ 07436.
15. Modern Microfilm Company, P.O. Box 1884, Salt Lake City, UT 84110. Mormon literature.
16. Personal Freedom Outreach, P.O. Box 26062, St. Louis, MO 63136.
17. Philippian Fellowship, Inc., P.O. Box 164, North Syracuse, NY Offers tracts.
18. Radio station KANN, 2222 Washington Street, Ogden, UT 84401.
19. Saints Alive in Jesus, P.O. Box 1076, Issaquah, WA 98027. Tapes, literature.
20. Spiritual Counterfeits Projects, P.O. Box 4308, Berkeley, CA 94704. *SCP Newsletter*; catalogs of tapes and literature.
21. Utah Christian Mission, P.O. Box 511, Oren, UT 84057. Offers literature.
22. Utah Christian Tract Society, P.O. Box 725, La Mesa, CA 92041.
23. Utah Mission, Inc., P.O. Box 348, Marlow, OK 73055. Produces the *UTAH EVANGEL* paper.

Figure 9.2

MISSION BOARDS SERVING MORMONS

1. Baptist Mid-Missions
2. Conservative Baptist Home Mission Society
3. Ex-Mormons for Jesus (EMFJ)
4. Inter-Varsity Christian Fellowship (IVCF)
5. Mission to Mormons
6. New Life
7. Rural Home Missionary Association
8. Saints Alive in Jesus

9. United Missionary Fellowship
10. Utah Bible Mission
11. Utah Missions, Inc.

Figure 9.3

MISSION BOARDS SERVING JEHOVAH'S WITNESSES

1. Christian Apologetics Project (CAP)
2. Christian Apologetics Research and Information Service (CARIS)
3. Cult Exodus for Christ (JWs/LDS)
4. Ex-Jehovah's Witnesses
5. Frontline (JWs/LDS; tract)
6. Help Jesus (a ministry of CARIS to Jehovah's Witnesses); the parent organization: World Crusade in England
7. New Life (JWs/LDS)
8. Watchman Fellowship (JWs/LDS); maintains telephone ministry in nine cities
9. Witness, Inc.; maintains national telephone ministry in twenty cities

Figure 9.4

Part 4

Institutional Ministries

Introduction

In 1982 most Americans lived in one of 83.5 million households; however, millions of others were not so fortunate. America, as a highly developed society, has created institutions where certain segments of society are given constant care under circumstances that basically isolate them from the rest of society. This isolation may be involuntary as in the case of those who are incarcerated in penal institutions.

Others are resident in facilities that may be called institutions of mercy because they were created for those who cannot help themselves. These institutions include children's homes for the orphaned, abused or abandoned children, and other facilities for the severely handicapped. Then there are the rest homes and geriatric wards for those advanced in age or incapacitated by illness.

A third kind of institution is the military establishment. In it are men and women who have committed themselves to a term of service or to a military career. They are effectively removed from family, friends, and church.

Finally, there is the educational community. America offers extensive opportunities for advancement in knowledge both in the public and private sectors. Americans become members of educational groups very early in life. They progress through various facilities from kindergarten through graduate schools. With the secularization of education, students are progressively separated and alienated from the teachings of the evangelical church.

The church has responded in two ways. First, it has created parochial schools to provide an alternative educational opportunity. Second, it has established missions that have sought various ways to provide Christian teaching in the educational community, whether by released-time classes on the elementary level, Bible clubs in the secondary schools, or missionaries on the college campus.

Institutional ministries are necessary for several reasons. In most instances the residents of the institutions cannot go to church or have not been exposed to the teachings of the evangelical church. Second, institutions run by the state are reluctant to provide religious teaching using public funds or facilities lest they violate the principle of separation of church and state. Therefore, only a minimal number of chaplains are engaged for service, and they are required to minister to members of more than their own faith.

Third, the church cannot provide regular, specialized spiritual ministry to the residents of institutions with its in-house programs. At best it ministers evangelistically and inspirationally to these hidden groups, but seldom pastorally. Finally, the average Christian is unprepared to cope with the problems of the institutional resident nor is he experienced in communicating his faith in that context.

10

Prison/Jail Ministries

INTRODUCTION

The prison population of the United States is a mission field because most inmates are unchurched,[1] and churches and active Christians often have not responded with the gospel to those who are incarcerated within their community.[2] Perhaps the church is unaware of the prisoners or, worse yet, does not want the Christian criminal or his family in the church. Such disregard is reprehensible in the light of specific scriptural injunctions such as, "Remember those in prison as if you were their fellow prisoners" (Hebrews 13:3, *New International Version*). Imprisonment is also a general theme of the Bible, for prisons and prisoners are mentioned in both Testaments 130 times. The evangelical church must again take a look at the total community, for ignorance of those locked up in prisons and jails within reach of the church cannot be offered as an excuse for apathy.

HISTORY OF CHURCH INVOLVEMENT

Widespread use of prisons as a primary means of criminal punishment was originally an eighteenth-century phenomenon.

---

1. Dale K. Pace, *A Christian's Guide to Effective Jail and Prison Ministries* (Old Tappan: Revell, 1976), p. 97.
2. Duane Pederson, *How to Establish a Jail and Prison Ministry* (Nashville: Thomas Nelson, 1979), p. 32.

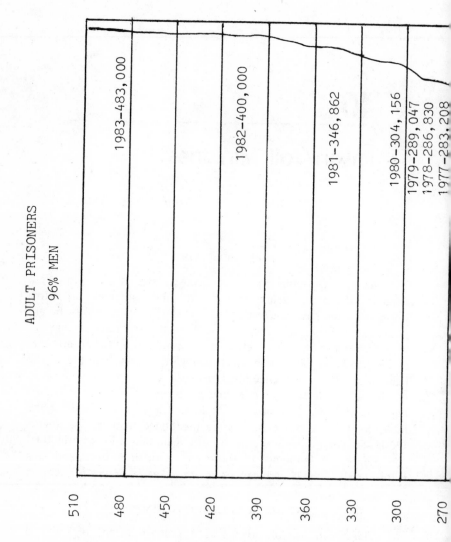

ADULT PRISONERS
96% MEN

1983—483,000
1982—400,000
1981—346,862
1980—304,156
1979—289,047
1978—286,830
1977—283,208

510 480 450 420 390 360 330 300 270

Figure 10.1

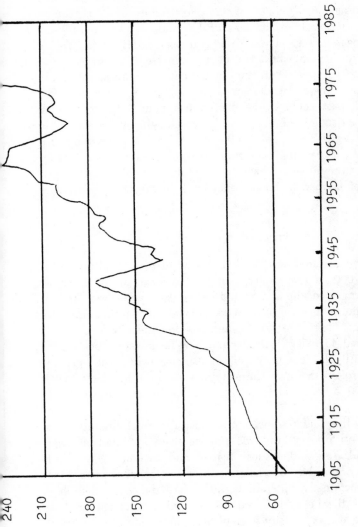

In state and federal institutions from 1904 through 1983.
Data was obtained from U.S. Department of Justice.

Before that time, various forms of personal and family humiliation, such as public flogging and execution, were effective social control.

The roots of prison ministries go back to a time when John and Charles Wesley and others of the Holy Club of 1730 sought permission to preach in the jails of England. In this country the Quakers began the Pennsylvania Prison Society (1787) to provide volunteers for prison work. During the nineteenth-century, prison reform was given greater attention by the church. Spiritual interest in inmates was shown by denominations providing chaplains, but during "the past century, the church has done little more than provide for prisoners the religious services sought by the state."[3] In recent years a growing interest in the inmate has been shown by such serving churches as the Salvation Army and the Volunteers of America. Faith missions have also multiplied and encouraged thousands of laymen to do personal work in the jails. (See Figure 10.1.)

EXTENT OF THE PROBLEM

All larger communities have some kind of penal institutions for there are 6,000 in the United States. The local jail is the most common form of lockup and should be the easiest for the church to evangelize, but 40 percent of the 4,000 jails have no spiritual ministry of any kind. There are 400 institutions for juveniles, 950 adult programs, and 45 federal prisons, and new facilities are being built each year. All of these institutions are overcrowded with persons who have broken the law. The state of California calculates that it costs $25,000 a year for each inmate, but what does it "cost" spiritually?

Inmates live under some of the most abnormal circumstances. They have no privacy (in 1983 prisons were 100 percent over-crowded) and are bored, restless, fearful, and uncertain. Two-thirds are under age 35. Over one-half are drug or alcohol abusers. One-fifth are functionally illiterate because they did not finish high school. Since the better behaved are paroled, 66 percent of those remaining have a propensity to fight. It is no wonder, then, that 80 percent of those paroled recidivate or are rearrested. Most of them recidivate within 90 days. Under those conditions many are tempted to backslide as Christians.

Altogether, 483,000 inmates are locked up in our state and

3. Pace, p. 19.

federal prisons, the third largest total in the world. That is an increase of 75 percent in the last decade. (See Figure 10.2.) On a given day 500,000 prisoners are confined, and in a year 1,000,000 to 4,000,000 pass through the penal system. Ten million juveniles and young adults are involved with the criminal justice system. Those who are convicted of a crime, and their families, are in spiritual need because the overwhelming majority are unchurched.

CHAPLAINCY

The spiritual welfare of inmates is delegated by the states to 500 chaplains—about 25 percent of the 2,000 needed to staff the prisons. In 30 percent of the institutions there are no chapels in which the chaplain can conduct services. The chaplain's work load is so heavy that he can have meaningful contact with no more than 25 percent of the inmates. He can work in depth with 100 and see another 400, but that does not make provision for all those who would like to counsel with him. Yet, "the need for religious and spiritual guidance is far more acute in prison than in free society."[4] The role of the chaplain has evolved over the years. At first he was responsible for providing personal pastoral care for the inmates. Then counseling the total person became his primary responsibility. Now he is essentially a "broker of religious programming," for the state permits various outside religious groups to provide services for the institution. The chaplain at San Quentin Prison, Nick Neufeld, arranges schedules for services to be conducted by Christians as well as Christian Science practitioners, Mormons, Seventh Day Adventists, Black Muslims, Jehovah's Witnesses, and Jews.[5]

MISSIONS ACTIVITY

Since 1950 there has been a rapid growth of mission organizations targeting penal institutions as a mission field. One directory lists 100 organizations.[6] Many of those societies are small, providing missionaries (chaplains) for some of the local institutions (23 percent) as well as those throughout the state (23 percent). Other missions (25

---

4. U.S. Department of Justice, Bureau of Prisons, *Report on U.S. Penitentiary in Lewisburg, Pennsylvania,* n.d., p. 11.

5. Letter from Chaplain Nick Neufeld, California State Prison, San Quentin, California 94964, Garden Chapel, 4 November 1972.

6. Carol Heimbach, ed., *The Logos Guide to Prison Ministries* (Plainfield, New Jersey: Logos International Fellowship, n.d.). (Now defunct, 1981.)

percent) are working in several states across the nation whereas 29 percent have expanded to an international ministry. (See Figure 10.1.)

International Prison Ministry, under the direction of Ray Hoekstra (Chaplain Ray), reaches into the prison world with extensive radio broadcasts, free Bibles, literature, book racks, and a bimonthly magazine called *Prison Evangelism*. The magazine reports stirring testimonies of inmates who have found Christ as Savior.

Charles Colson, made famous by the Watergate scandal and his subsequent conversion to Christ, established the Prison Fellowship to provide Christian seminars for prisoners. In 1971 the first in-prison seminar was given. During 1981, 230 in-prison seminars involved 4,000 inmates. *Jubilee* newsletter reports that 100 workers under the Prison Fellowship (PF) are giving seminars.[7] Colson's activities are newsworthy; therefore, he has probably done more than any other to alert the church about prison ministries and the authorities about needed prison reforms. PF's ministries are now international because they found that out of 100 missions surveyed, only two had an overseas prison ministry.

Christian Prison Volunteers initiated a "Visit by Mail" ministry. Recognizing that 25 percent of all inmates have no visitors and five percent never receive a letter and have no one to whom to write, names of prisoners are given to pen pals who will write and send a little "paper sunshine" to an inmate.

In 1955 Yokefellows International Prison Ministry was founded in response to the message of Matthew 25:36: "For I was . . . in prison and you visited me." The Yokefellows ministry yokes three or four outsiders with one dozen insiders who meet together in weekly meetings. The outsiders visit the groups of the population and share the Word of God. On the outside they can also have a ministry with the family of the inmate. The Yokefellow volunteer commits himself to seven "disciplines." He agrees (1) to pray every day for the inmates, (2) to read the Bible daily, (3) to attend church weekly, (4) to tithe his income, (5) to tithe his time, (6) to witness in daily life, work and words, and (7) to study Christian books.

With increased spiritual activity in the prisons, numerous inmates are being saved. It is the purpose of Good News Mission to establish converts in indigenous churches behind bars. The Christian inmates are living in "warehouses of fear" and need Christian fellowship and support within the walls, where they are in Satan's stronghold. The inmates with leadership potential are given special

7. *Jubilee*, July 1981, p. 4.

training as church leaders. A National Fellowship of Congregations Behind Bars is sponsored by the Association of Evangelical Institutional Chaplains.[8]

Good News Mission is the largest civilian supplier of chaplains (72) and offers a graduate level course for chaplains. The philosophy of the mission is to seek the salvation of every inmate, releasee, and each family member. Their follow-up ministry includes 30,000 who are enrolled in the mission's Bible correspondence courses.

In Chicago the Light Bearers Association of America is a mission organization that trains young men as institutional chaplains by on-the-job training with chaplains working in penal institutions within the city.

Recognizing that a host of volunteers will be needed to service the many penal institutions and their large populations, the Association of Christian Prison Workers holds seminars to train volunteers to work in prison ministries. Men are needed who "have an infinite capacity for disappointment."[9]

Many volunteers are needed in this "island of isolation" from the rest of society. The Christian inmate will need help with his crippled personality. The volunteer can support the Christian inmate in his alien culture. He can help him to reenter society and his family. He can be the friend or spiritual buddy the inmate never had. He can model social and Christian ideals before the new Christian as one who is currently experiencing a daily walk with the Lord.

It is important to realize that the volunteer is an unusual person who must play a number of roles. He is "a citizen doing a very complex, frustrating and at times demanding job. His reward is the knowledge that he has walked with the inmate on the road leading to Calvary."[10]

A number of service organizations offer materials that are prepared for inmates. (See Figure 10.3.) Special literature is available from several sources. Bible correspondence courses are very important. An 850-word New Testament is available for the functionally illiterate. Cassette-loaning libraries are also helpful. An adult *Power for Living* paper is available.

Concern for the prison population of the United States is

8. *Volunteer*, July-August 1979, p. 1.
9. Pace, p. 164.
10. Paul R. Markstrom, "Volunteers in Corrections," cited in Reference Library (n.p.: Evangelism and Home Missions Association of the National Association of Evangelicals, n.d.), p. 2.

growing. God has prepared mission societies to lead the way. Many more professional chaplains are needed to work within the penal institutions and direct the work of others who are allowed to go in for ministry. Missionaries are needed to help with the work within and to train the volunteers who are playing a key role in discipleship and the reentry of the inmates into the community.

The volunteers might be likened to the short-term foreign missionaries so popular in recent years. Without question, in "many ways the mission field behind bars is the most 'foreign' of mission fields."[11] Dr. William Simmer asks, "Why is it that we have become preoccupied with sending missionaries far away when our own communities are about to explode with frustrated and neglected peoples? Many churches and Christians either have not yet recognized or wish to ignore the fact that there are prisoners in their own community who require a response from the church."[12]

Finally, the Christian believes in inmate rehabilitation and is concerned to help the Christian ex-con return to society as a responsible citizen and active Christian in the local church. Prison Fellowship is working to establish in every major city and community near a prison facility Care Committees of Christians ready to help Christian inmates upon release to find jobs, fellowship in a church, and to readjust to society. In 1982, 157 Care Committees were functional.

MISSION BOARDS SERVING PRISONERS

1. American Institute for Evangelism (International)
2. The Association of Christian Prison Workers
3. Christian Jail Workers, Los Angeles, Calif.
4. Christian Prison Volunteers (International)
5. Cons for Christ (International)
6. Florida Chaplain Service
7. Forgotten Man Mission, Grand Rapids, Michigan
8. Golden Key Ministry, New York
9. Good News Mission (International)
10. Go Ye Mission, Los Angeles
11. Home Mission Board, Southern Baptist Convention
12. Hope Aglow Ministries

---

11. Pace, p. 199.
12. William Simmer, *Why Bother with Prisoners?* (Arlington, Virginia: Good News Mission, n.d.), p. 4.

13. International Prison Ministries, Chaplain Ray
14. Light Bearers
15. Lester Roloff Ministries
16. Missionary Gospel Fellowship
17. Outreach to Troubled Teens, Inc., Delaware
18. Pals for Christ (International)
19. Prison Bible Fellowship, Baptist Mid-Missions
20. Prison Fellowship, Inc. (National)
21. Prison Mission Association (Servicemen's Division of PMA Bible Correspondence Fellowship)
22. Prisoners for Christ (International)
23. P. S. Ministries, Campus Crusade
24. Rock Bottom Evangelistic Association
25. Salvation Army Correctional Services Department (National)
26. Tarrant County Baptist Association, Fort Worth, Texas
27. Tom Skinner
28. Volunteers in Correction, Oklahoma
29. Yokefellows International Prison Ministry

Figure 10.2

SERVICES AVAILABLE FOR PRISON MINISTRIES

1. American Bible Society, P.O. Box 5656, Grand Central Station, New York, NY 10017
2. American Indian Missions, Inc., P.O. Box 2800, Rapid City, SD 57701 (offers the 850-word New Testament)
3. Assemblies of God Prison Division, 1445 Boonville Avenue, Springfield, MO 65802 (provides correspondence courses and *The Living Bible for Inmates*)
4. Bible Believer's Cassettes, Inc., 130 N. Spring Street, Springdale, AK 72764 (2,500 tapes available)
5. Bible Portions League, Route 3, P.O. Box 12, Coushatta, LA 71019
6. Crusaders Club, Winona Lake, IN 46590 (offers free correspondence courses)
7. Fellowship of Christian Peace Officers, P.O. Box 30179, Los Angeles, CA 90030
8. Gideons (provides services and Scriptures)
9. Logos International Fellowship, Inc. Prison Ministry, P.O. Box 191, Plainfield, NJ 07060 (offers literature and correspondence courses)

10. Moody Bible Institute Correspondence School, 820 N. LaSalle Drive, Chicago, IL 60610 (offers free courses, literature, and films)
11. Scripture and Christian Literature Mission, 1818 S. Summerlin Avenue, Orlando, FL 32806 (offers literature and Bible courses; maintains correspondence with inmates)
12. Scripture Press Ministries, P.O. Box 513, Glen Ellyn, IL 60137 (Produces *Free Way, Power for Living,* and books)
13. Source of Light Mission, P.O. Box 8, Madison, GA 30650 (offers Bible courses)
14. World Home Bible League, P.O. Box 11, South Holland, IL 60473 (Offers Scriptures and correspondence courses)

Figure 10.3

11

Institutions of Mercy

Within every community are those who cannot care for themselves. Whether they are abused or abandoned children, severely handicapped, abusers of alcohol or other drugs, the aged or infirmed, American society responds by creating institutions of mercy where specialized and extended care can be provided.

It is necessary that total care be made available for those who cannot help themselves. The best in facilities, trained personnel, and medical attention are the results of a biblical ethic that postulates the inestimable value of the individual regardless of his ability to care for himself. However, it is ironic that provision is made for all of man's needs except the most important—his spiritual needs.

Seldom is a resident chaplain available in such facilities. Their residents are virtually isolated from the larger community of Christians in general and the church specifically. Few churches have prepared either evangelistic programs or pastoral care on a continuing basis to meet the special spiritual needs of the residents; therefore, the church has commissioned home mission societies to minister in institutions of mercy primarily by creating Christian facilities. The missions are now providing programs to train laymen in the church to assist them in institutional ministries. They are also assisting the local church in establishing programs within the church ministry to reach certain neglected segments of the community.

MINISTRIES TO ABANDONED AND ABUSED CHILDREN

God ordained that families should be fruitful and multiply and that they should "train up a child in the way he should go" (Proverbs 11:6). It is a great tragedy for the child, the family, and the community when parents do not fulfill their privilege and responsibility. If that happens, the child becomes a ward of the state.

In 1981, 600,000 children were in need of out-of-home care. The state's first concern is to provide permanent placement for those wards by adoption, but for the older child or for the child who has been in trouble, adoptive parents are seldom available. Therefore, two-thirds of state children are placed in state schools, reform schools, or in foster homes where surrogate parents are paid to rear the child for the state. The other 200,000 children are remanded by the courts to public or private facilities known as children's homes.

Children's homes were once known as orphanages because most of the residents had lost one or both parents, usually by some incapacitating tragedy or by death. Orphanages were begun by churches in the early 1900s to provide care for orphans. The number of orphanages multiplied to 400 by 1920 following serious outbreaks of influenza that orphaned up to 3 percent of the populace.[1] Even then, only one in ten orphans could find refuge.

Following the decade of the 1950s, the orphan population declined because of improved health care in the country. However, the population of childcare facilities did not decline as rapidly because it was offset by residents whose parents were living. The children were now psychologically orphaned by parents who either could not or would not care for them. The dereliction of parental responsibility was often the result of alcoholism, prostitution, child abuse, or serial monogamy. The National Center of Child Abuse and Neglect estimates that 10 percent of all children are severely abused or neglected. In 1981 that represented 625,000 children.[2]

Historically, denominations provided children's homes for their constituency. By 1973 Social Security was providing funds for the maintenance of children who needed out-of-home care. As public funds became available, privately-chartered children's homes declined to 400 units, and government sponsored facilities nearly quadrupled to 1,500 units.

Perhaps 100 of the 1,900 child-care facilities in 1981 were

1. *World Survey,* 2 vols. (New York City: Interchurch, 1920), 1:252.
2. *Youthletter,* November 1981, p. 83.

considered missionary enterprises. (See Figure 11.2.) Virtually nothing is being done for children spiritually in most childcare facilities that are not Christian. In the mission-run childcare homes, every effort is made to provide Christian surrogate parents and a Christian homelike atmosphere. For instance, the stated purpose of the Dessie Scott Children's Home is

> to give love and care to needy, neglected, dependent children. It is the aim of this home to see boys and girls truly born again and become established in the Word. Devotions are held regularly at breakfast and bed times. The children are taught to memorize the Scriptures. The family attends the Community Church regularly and some have been baptized.[3]

Children's homes maintain a variety of ministries including day care, summer conferences, family counseling, alcohol and drug counseling, and psychological counseling for abused children.

Resident population in children's homes changes rapidly because current philosophy maintains that a child should be permanently placed. Gerald Lehman, Director of Miracle Hill Children's Home in Greenville, South Carolina, indicates that most of their residents stay less than two years.

Sometimes a children's home is a branch of a rescue mission. It is perceived that the home is a ministry for rescuing children. Brookside Children's Home, for instance, is a branch of the Union Gospel Mission in Charleston, West Virginia.

Financing the children's home as a mission is a growing problem. Arch Cammeron, formerly of Eliada Homes, founded in 1906 in North Carolina, indicates that 60 percent of their funding has come from individuals and 30 percent from state funds, but only 10 percent derives from the church.

Bethel Bible Village is a unique children's home, for it provides shelter for children whose parent or parents are in prison. The children are often emotionally neglected, abused, or abandoned because of incompetent or immature parents. These parents often will not allow the children to be adopted. To call attention to abandoned children, the home has prepared a film, *Crime's Forgotten Children.*

3. Brochure of Dessie Scott Children's Home, n.d.

MINISTRIES TO YOUTH IN TROUBLE

Not only are children in need of spiritual help, but so also are the 25,000,000 teenagers of America in serious trouble. A half million youths under the age of 18 are jailed annually, 5 to 10 percent for serious crimes, the others for running away. A recent survey indicates that 15 percent of high schoolers are routinely unhappy and not doing well in school. There are 3,000,000 teenagers who have few friends and many psychosomatic complaints. Their lack of direction in life is a reflection of the troubled conditions at home.

The Reader's Digest (January 1984) reported that one million teenagers run away each year. (In 1982 the figure was 1.6 million.) Their median age is 15. Thirty percent were pushed out of their homes as children nobody wanted. They are called "throwaways." Many of the girls become prostitutes (25 percent of America's prostitutes are under 18). Baptist Mission to Forgotten People has ministries to those children in New York City and Dallas.

For many girls such circumstances lead to teenage pregnancy and early dropout from school. The National Institute of Education reports that 80 percent of pregnant teenagers drop out of school. Pastor Ronald Williams, sensing the need of these girls, led his church (Believer's Chapel at Winona Lake, Indiana) to establish Hephzibah House as a live-in rehabilitation and discipleship center for girls. The name of the mission is taken from Isaiah 62:4: "Thou shalt no more be termed Forsaken . . . but thou shalt be called Hephzibah," which means "my delight is in her."

New Horizons Group Home was established in Marion, Indiana, for boys who get into trouble. It is a specialized residence experience for teenaged boys in trouble at home, in school, or in a foster home. It is called a home away from home where Christian love, guidance, and male role models are everpresent.

The parent organization, New Horizons Youth Ministries, was founded by Gordon Blossom and with a goal of ministering to troubled teenagers in unique ways. He developed the Wilderness Survival Academy in northern Canada and Carribe-Vista in the Dominican Republic. The latter program, which provides strong Christian training and experience in a missionary setting, is a Christian coeducational school for troubled American teens. The latest ministry is the New Horizons Christian Academy. It is a boarding high school in Villa Park, Illinois, offering intense, personalized instruction in a sheltered setting.

His Mansion, located in New Hampshire, is a "place of healing for troubled youth." The one year live-in residential care facility provides help for junkies, dropouts, pregnant teenagers, prostitutes, and those with severe emotional problems. The ministry is summarized in the acronym CHRIST, which means Christians Helping Rehabilitate Individuals by Scriptural Therapy. The ministry was inspired by reading the life story of George Mueller of Bristol, famous founder of orphanages. Following Mueller's lead, there are no charges levied or funds solicited.

Another ministry includes a Christian Counselor Training Program, which is a course designed to prepare dedicated Christian young people for greater usefulness in their home assembly.

MINISTRIES TO HANDICAPPED

All American communities include an invisible group of special people who are handicapped. Every fifth home has a handicapped person. One in every ten persons in the world is handicapped. In America there are up to 35,000,000 disabled persons who all have significant spiritual needs, but especially the 80 percent who are unchurched. In fact, "the handicapped and their families are one of the most neglected mission fields that exist."[4]

Joni Erickson, a Christian who was disabled in a diving accident, indicates that only 5 percent of churches have programs for the handicapped. Another handicapped person says, "For the most part, the body of Christ, hindered perhaps by fear and lack of love has failed to reach out to individuals who are handicapped. As a result, the church is indeed handicapped."[5] Harold Wilke, handicapped from birth and now founder of the Healing Community, says that the church has a unique opportunity to respond to persons with handicaps.[6]

A special person may be handicapped physically, mentally, or both. A physical handicap restricts a person's mobility. A mental handicap hinders a person's ability to learn in conventional ways. Some physical handicaps such as deafness and blindness may lead to learning problems. Handicapped person have differing degrees of incapacitation.

The church should recognize two areas of ministry with the handicapped. First, institutions of mercy could be provided for the

4. *Evangelizing Today's Child,* November 1981, p. 10.
5. Ibid., p. 3.
6. Harold H. Wilke, *Creating the Caring Congregation: Guidelines for Ministering with the Handicapped* (Nashville: Abingdon, 1980), p. 16.

2,000,000 special people who are severely handicapped, disabled, or abandoned. Many are in the latter category because four out of five exceptional people are from broken homes. An already faltering marriage often is not able to survive the stress caused by the presence of a handicapped person. These institutions may take the form of residential homes where 200,000 mentally retarded live, or non-residential ministries such as camps for handicapped persons.

Second, the church should develop programs for the 6,000,000 handicapped persons who remain in the community, but who are often hidden away from the mainstream of life. For those who are less severely handicapped, personnel from the institutional ministries are prepared to help the local church develop ministries within the church. They will train laymen for this ministry and survey the community to discover the handicapped. They will help the church prepare their facilities to receive the handicapped and then teach the church how to aggressively evangelize these special persons and prepare programs that meet their spiritual and physical needs.

Shepherd's Home in Wisconsin is a residential home for 200 mentally retarded. In this Christian facility the total needs of the retarded person are provided on a level that he can comprehend. Most are capable of learning about the Lord Jesus Christ and memorizing Scripture.

Hope Town and Camp Hope are ministries of the Children's Bible Fellowship in New York City. Hope Town is a residence and school for physically handicapped. Camp Hope is a camping facility staffed with those who are highly trained to work with handicapped in a camping ministry. It is a most unforgettable experience to see wheelchairs parked around a swimming pool waiting for their occupants who are in the pool.

The Christian League for the Handicapped in Wisconsin has established an occupational community where the handicapped live either in the home for total care or in apartments for independent living. Opportunities for employment are provided on campus for those who can be gainfully employed. A Bible conference center is provided for the residents and for those who wish to drive in. It is a complete Christian community for the handicapped.

The Bill Rice Ranch in Tennessee is a Christian conference center and camp for the deaf. It is the world's largest camp for the deaf and the South's largest independent conference ground.[7]

---

7. Pete Rice, *The Story of the Bill Rice Ranch* (Murfreesboro, Tennessee: The Branding Iron, 1970), p. 119.

Through the ministry of evangelist and Mrs. Bill Rice, Cumberland has become the most renowned missionary work for the deaf in the world. It all began because their daughter became deaf as an infant because of the ravages of a high fever. Having effectively trained their own deaf daughter, they were asked by others to help train their deaf children.

The Rices then became aware of 19,000,000 in the United States who need special help because they live in a world of silence and loneliness. They also discovered that only a few Bible-believing churches have ministries to the deaf.

The Christian Deaf Fellowship sponsors an annual World Bible and Missionary Conference in Norfolk, Virginia.[8] It is held on the campus of Virginia Wesleyan College.

Cecil Etheridge, consultant for the visually handicapped, indicates that there are 6,400,000 persons with some visual impairment. Statistics in 1981 revealed that 1,700,000 have 80 percent loss of their vision and 600,000 are totally blind. Seventeen thousand of the blind are also deaf. He also concedes that few churches have a visible ministry to the blind, largely because they do not know how. He says, "We've treated the blind as we have the blacks; we've overlooked them because they were out of sight."[9]

Dr. Ralph Montanus, America's blind evangelist, is founder of the Gospel Association for the Blind, Incorporated. It sustains several ministries including a free circulating library of braille books, records, cassettes, Thanksgiving dinners for the blind at different locations in the country, and a week of Bible conferences in Jaffrey Center, New Hampshire. It publishes the Gospel Messenger, a fifty-page monthly magazine in braille and sends it without cost to the blind worldwide. The association also publishes tracts, a Bible study course, Christian books, and commentaries. The largest outreach of the ministry is the weekly national broadcast "That They Might See." Montanus is burdened for the 25,000,000 sightless in the world of whom fewer than 600,000 or 2.4 percent are Christians.

Christian Fellowship for the Blind, by means of an extensive printing ministry, provides free braille literature to blind ministers and laymen. They print Decision magazine, Power for Living, Bible study books, and commentaries. The cost per braille book is fifteen times that of a conventional book.

Christian institutional ministries to the handicapped are effectively ministering to the small percentage of severely handicapped who are resident in their facilities, but little or nothing is being done for those in non-Christian facilities.

The handicapped are resident in every American Community. They are hidden away in homes where families are trying to cope with their special problems. The Christian church and community can have a very effective ministry, not only to the handicapped, but also to the family.

Melvin Howell, pastor of the First Evangelical Free Church of Fullerton, California, appointed a special education staff and developed a ministry to the handicapped. They discovered that an effective ministry to the handicapped must first include an aggressive search for the special people. Second, the church must demonstrate compassion for the exceptional people. Third, it must be recognized that the gospel is for everyone, including the handicapped, for most of them can understand the message of the gospel.[10]

A ministry to the blind can be very effective. But it must have the support of the whole church, not just a few of its members. The ministry must not only be *with* the blind, but also *to* the blind. The program should develop slowly to allow time for the training of staff. Sufficient staff must be trained so that they can be rotated. Materials are available from several missions specializing in ministries to the blind. (See Figure 11.3.)

Assistance in starting a ministry to the deaf can be found by reading Edgar Lawrence's book *Ministering to the Silent Minority*, with the subtitle, "How to Develop a Church Ministry for the Deaf."[11] Bill Rice Ranch personnel are available to come to the church to hold a two-week seminar to train church members for ministry to the deaf. They will be taught to interpret and to understand the problems faced by the deaf. Several other ministries to the deaf are available. (See Figure 11.5.)

Ministry in the church to the mentally retarded is also needed. Dr. Andrew Wood, executive director of Shepherd's, has prepared a manual for reaching retarded children for Christ in the church. In the introduction he says:

> Today, the mentally retarded and their families represent a vast mission field scarcely touched for Jesus Christ. Many of these families are looking for help and hope, yet, all too frequently they find little more

10. Lippy, *Today's Child*, p. 8.
11. Edgar Lawrence, *Ministering to the Silent Minority* (Springfield: Gospel, 1978), n.p.

than scorn or indifference. As more and more programs are developed on the community level to meet the physical, emotional, educational and social needs of the mentally retarded, fundamental Bible believing churches should make provision for the most important need of all—the spiritual. Thus, it is not only the responsibility of these churches to reach this segment of the population for Jesus Christ, but it is their glorious privilege to show the way!

Sunday School for the mentally retarded in the local church is one concrete way of meeting a pressing need. Pastor and people working together can be a real force in reaching these children and their families for the Savior.[12]

Handi-Vangelism, a ministry of the Bible Club Movement, helps establish Sunday school departments for handicapped in local churches. They offer six training sessions in the church for laymen as well as seminars and workshops on how to deal with the handicapped. Literature and resource people are available from numerous missions and other sources. (See Figure 11.1.) Concordia Publishers provides a curriculum for the mentally retarded.

The United Nations proclaimed 1981 as the International Year of Disabled Persons. The Christian church should take the lead in providing ministry to the invisible minority in the community—the handicapped.

MINISTRIES TO ADDICTS AND ALCOHOLICS

The National Institute of Drug Abuse estimates that 120 billion dollars a year is spent by Americans on controlled substances and their consequences. A survey in 1982 revealed that 22.5 million persons had used cocaine. Another 500,000 are heroin addicts. While gold sold for $435 per ounce, heroin cost $10,000. In New York City, 70 percent of those arrested for robberies had prior narcotics arrests. Sixty percent of all accidents are alcohol related.

About one-half of all Americans drink the social lubricant, ethel alcohol, a habit-forming drug. Twelve percent drink heavily, 10 percent have a problem, and 5 percent are addicted. Notice what happens to the odds that a person will develop a drinking problem or become addicted when the figures are compared with those who drink as revealed in the following chart:

50% of Americans drink	—	100 million
10% have a problem	—	20 million (1 in 5 drinkers)

12. Andrew Wood, *Guidebook for Ministries in the Local Church* (Union Grove, Wis.: Shepherd's Inc., n.d.), n.p.

5% are alcoholics	—	10 million (1 in 10 drinkers)
10% of alcoholics are on skid row	—	1 million (1 in 100 drinkers)

It is important to note that although only 10 percent of Americans are problem drinkers, of those who do drink, one in five will develop a problem. The median age to start drinking is now 11 years, for the drug is available in the family liquor cabinet. Studies show that the younger the age at which a person starts to ingest alcohol, the greater the probability that he will develop into a chronic alcoholic. Three-fourths of all teenagers will drink before graduation and one-third with regularity.

Five percent of Americans are addicted to alcohol. But notice that one in ten drinkers becomes addicted. The addicts are equally divided between the sexes. Nearly 1,000,000 addicts are hardcore juveniles under the age of 20. Fifty percent of all alcoholics have at least one alcoholic parent. The problem is likely to continue because it is estimated that 32,000,000 youngsters are living with an alcoholic parent. The risk of a child becoming an alcoholic is four times greater if the parents are alcoholics.[13]

The typical alcoholic now has a respectable source of income for his habit. He is probably on welfare. But no amount of money can satisfy the progressively debilitating disease that is destroying him. Alcoholism is a total sickness. He is sick physically, emotionally, mentally, socially, and spiritually.[14]

Christians who have been saved from drug addiction know better than others the total enslavement from which the Holy Spirit has delivered them. (See Figure 11.6.) They know that "once drinking has passed a certain point it becomes alcoholism, an affliction which cannot be met effectively by the unaided efforts of the victims."[15]

The greatest concern for the alcoholic has been shown by the redeemed alcoholic who founded missions to rescue his fellow alcoholic. Rescue missions began in the 1870s with the founding of McAuley Water Street Mission in New York City (1872), Bethel society for Men in Duluth, and the Pacific Garden Mission (1877) in Chicago. The Pacific Garden Mission is perhaps the best known because of its famous radio program "Unshackled," in which stirring

13. Cathlene Brooks, *The Secret Everyone Knows* (San Diego: Kroc Foundation 1981), p. 4.
14. John E. Keller, *Ministering to Alcoholics* (Minneapolis: Augsburg, 1966), pp. 32-33.
15. Joseph L. Kellerman, *Alcoholism: A Guide for the Clergy* (New York: National Council on Alcoholism, 1965), Introduction.

testimonies of saved alcoholics are professionally presented. Among the mission's famous converts are Billy Sunday, who became an evangelist, and Mel Trotter, who founded sixty rescue missions. New York City also had its Bowery Mission and Los Angeles its Union Rescue Mission, which has now become the nation's largest rescue mission.

More than a century later (1981) 230 rescue missions, representing 1,000 missionaries hold membership in the International Union of Gospel Missions.[16] This fellowship of missions was founded in 1913.

Over the years the program of rescue missions has evolved from a less complicated offering of "soup, soap, and salvation" (which meant that at the mission a meal, a change of clothes, and the gospel were available) to a ministry that has been greatly enlarged to meet the alcoholic's total needs and those of his family.

The plant and personnel of the mission also changed from a storefront and a saved alcoholic with a vision to a multidepartment complex and a highly trained staff that is skilled in many services. Programs that once served only men now minister to women and children.

A rescue mission is defined as a home mission organized for the evangelization, the physical relief, and the rehabilitation of the whole person in areas where local churches are unable to minister, and to people not ordinarily reached by the church. The primary aim of the mission is the whole, new person in Christ.[17]

The programs of the rescue mission may include an industrial division for salvage operation of usable clothing, furniture and appliances, a sheltered workshop, a store to sell used items repaired by the men, welfare for the family, rehabilitation and counseling, and evangelism to the "least, last, and lost." Seventy percent of those helped by the rescue missions have a problem with alcoholism. It is a discouraging work, for fewer than 25 percent of the men remain recovered from their problem.

Rescue missions listed in the IUGM Directory are located in 190 cities and in all but five states. Twenty-five states do not have missions in more than three cities. California has the largest number of missions with at least one mission in twenty-four cities.

Missionary activity in alcoholic rehabilitation began with Wil-

16. *1980-'81 Directory*, published by International Union of Gospel Missions.
17. Charles E. Morey, *Rescue Mission Dynamics—Regeneration Rehabilitation* (Kansas City: International Union of Gospel Missions, 1963), p. 5.

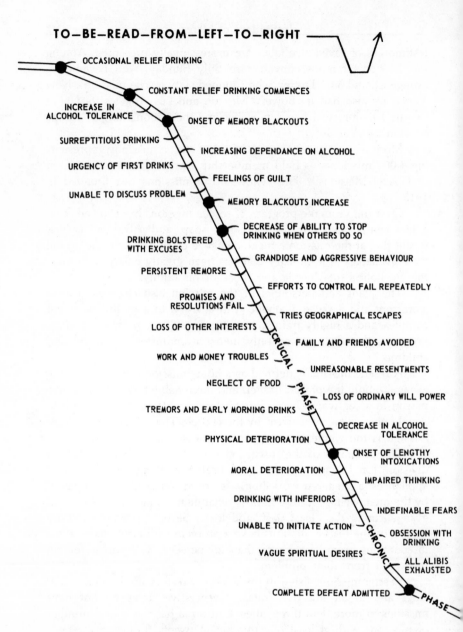

TO−BE−READ−FROM−LEFT−TO−RIGHT

OCCASIONAL RELIEF DRINKING

CONSTANT RELIEF DRINKING COMMENCES

INCREASE IN ALCOHOL TOLERANCE

ONSET OF MEMORY BLACKOUTS

SURREPTITIOUS DRINKING

INCREASING DEPENDANCE ON ALCOHOL

URGENCY OF FIRST DRINKS

FEELINGS OF GUILT

UNABLE TO DISCUSS PROBLEM

MEMORY BLACKOUTS INCREASE

DECREASE OF ABILITY TO STOP DRINKING WHEN OTHERS DO SO

DRINKING BOLSTERED WITH EXCUSES

GRANDIOSE AND AGGRESSIVE BEHAVIOUR

PERSISTENT REMORSE

EFFORTS TO CONTROL FAIL REPEATEDLY

PROMISES AND RESOLUTIONS FAIL

TRIES GEOGRAPHICAL ESCAPES

LOSS OF OTHER INTERESTS

FAMILY AND FRIENDS AVOIDED

WORK AND MONEY TROUBLES

UNREASONABLE RESENTMENTS

NEGLECT OF FOOD

LOSS OF ORDINARY WILL POWER

TREMORS AND EARLY MORNING DRINKS

DECREASE IN ALCOHOL TOLERANCE

PHYSICAL DETERIORATION

ONSET OF LENGTHY INTOXICATIONS

MORAL DETERIORATION

IMPAIRED THINKING

DRINKING WITH INFERIORS

INDEFINABLE FEARS

UNABLE TO INITIATE ACTION

OBSESSION WITH DRINKING

VAGUE SPIRITUAL DESIRES

ALL ALIBIS EXHAUSTED

COMPLETE DEFEAT ADMITTED

CRUCIAL PHASE

CHRONIC PHASE

OBSESSIVE DRINKING IN VICIOUS

M. M. Glatt, M. D., D.P.M.
THE BRITISH JOURNAL OF ADDICTION,
Vol. 54, No. 2

Figure 11.1

A CHART OF ALCOHOL ADDICTION AND RECOVERY

ENLIGHTENED AND INTERESTING WAY OF
LIFE OPENS UP WITH ROAD AHEAD TO
HIGHER LEVELS THAN EVER BEFORE

GROUP THERAPY AND
MUTUAL HELP CONTINUE

INCREASING TOLERANCE

RATIONALISATIONS RECOGNISED

CONTENTMENT IN SOBRIETY

CARE OF PERSONAL APPEARANCE

CONFIDENCE OF EMPLOYERS

FIRST STEPS TOWARDS
ECONOMIC STABILITY

INCREASE OF EMOTIONAL CONTROL

APPRECIATION OF REAL VALUES

FACTS FACED WITH COURAGE

RE-BIRTH OF IDEALS

NEW CIRCLE OF STABLE FRIENDS

NEW INTERESTS DEVELOP

FAMILY AND FRIENDS
APPRECIATE EFFORTS

ADJUSTMENT TO FAMILY NEEDS

NATURAL REST AND SLEEP

REHABILITATION

DESIRE TO ESCAPE GOES

REALISTIC THINKING

RETURN OF SELF ESTEEM

REGULAR NOURISHMENT
TAKEN

DIMINISHING FEARS
OF THE UNKNOWN
FUTURE

APPRECIATION OF POSSIBILITIES
OF NEW WAY OF LIFE

START OF GROUP THERAPY

ONSET OF NEW HOPE

PHYSICAL OVERHAUL BY DOCTOR

SPIRITUAL NEEDS EXAMINED

RIGHT THINKING BEGINS

ASSISTED IN MAKING
PERSONAL STOCKTAKING

STOPS
TAKING ALCOHOL

MEETS FORMER ADDICTS NORMAL AND HAPPY

LEARNS
ALCOHOLISM
IS AN ILLNESS

TOLD ADDICTION CAN BE ARRESTED

HONEST DESIRE FOR HELP

CONTINUES
CIRCLES

NATIONAL COUNCIL OF ALCOHOLISM
2 East 103rd St., New York, NY 10029

Published in Joseph Kellerman, *Alcoholism: A guide
for the Clergy* (New York: National Council of
Churches), pp. 40-41.

liam Raws at Keswick Colony of Mercy in 1897. Raws recognized that the alcoholic who accepts Christ as Savior in a gospel rescue mission has little chance of living a successful Christian life without help. One survey indicates that less than one-tenth of one percent of alcoholics remain committed to the Lord because they have not been discipled and have no church home.

Raws established the "colony approach" to rehabilitation to overcome this problem. To enter the colony the alcoholic must personally want to be shown a completely new kind of life, be willing to cooperate with the efforts of the mission, and stay for at least three months. During that time he will work for the colony and learn how to live the Christian life.

The colony is usually located in a remote place away from the temptations of the world. It is completely free to the resident, although he is expected to help in the colony. While resident he will receive

> the equivalent in Bible teaching to several years of training in the average church. Thus the alcoholic can return to his home environment with hope—hope established upon a foundation of Biblical principles that he can resist temptation and function normally in an acceptable Christian fashion.[18]

About twenty Keswick-type organizations in the eastern United States meet annually for fellowship under the auspices of the Christian Alcoholic Rehabilitation Association.[19]

During the decade of the 1970s, eighty rescue missions developed rehabilitation programs to maintain a longer contact with the saved alcoholic. Forty of those rescue missions with such programs also maintain membership in CARA.

It should be noted that some of the missions maintaining membership in CARA also hold membership in IUGM. The IUGM lists 230 member missions; CARA lists sixty missions. Those missions with rehabilitation programs (80) and the Keswick-type (20) total 100 organizations with an estimated membership of 600 missionaries.

Alcoholics Anonymous (AA) began as a Christian organization in 1934 to give encouragement to the dry alcoholic. In fact, "the

---

18. William Wooley, *Alcoholic Rehabilitation as Related to the Colony Approach* (Albany, Georgia: The Ambrose, n.d.), p. 2.
19. Richard Barth, *Directory of Christian Alcoholic Rehabilitation Association* (Pocahontas, Miss.: Friends of Alcoholics, n.d.), n.p.

greatest number of recovered alcoholics have been restored to
sobriety within the fellowship of AA."[20] However, AA "is a way of
salvation for alcoholics, [which] they have experienced and believe
that there is a valid spiritual awakening, not necessarily Christian, in
which alcoholics receive from God what they need to stay sober."[21]
ALANON is AA for the alcoholic's family and ALATEEN is AA for
the alcoholic's teenagers. Alcoholic's Victorious (1948) is a Christian
AA, designed to assist the local church in more effectively meeting
the needs of alcoholics that look to it for guidance.

The Salvation Army has an extensive work with alcoholics;
however, it is not a mission, but is recognized by the government as
a church. The Volunteers of America is an outgrowth from the
Salvation Army. It, too, has a large network of rescue works
scattered over the country. The government recognized it as a church
in 1958.

Ministries to Senior Citizens in Rest Homes

A unique subculture of citizens over 65 years of age has been
growing in the United States over the last several decades. Americans
are now living longer, and senior citizens are capturing a larger
percentage of the total population because America has one of the
world's lowest birthrates. Some of this minority group gravitates to
retirement villages. Others retire in their own homes or go to live
with their children, but 8 percent of the 25.5 million citizens over 65
have been forced to enter one of the thousands of rest homes that
have been described as "half-way houses somewhere between society and the cemetery."[22] The over-65 age group is growing in
number, from 11.4 percent (present) to a projected 12.4 percent of
the populace in 1994.

Prior to 1935, older persons who could no longer care for
themselves had to retire to poorhouses, county homes, or infirmaries,
because there were only 300 rest homes in this country.[23] With the
advent of social security, some could afford to pay for limited care in
private homes called "Mom and Dad Operations," which catered to
semi-invalids.

By 1965 Medicare and Medicaid funds revolutionized the industry. Some seventy chains of homes emerged as developers recognized

20. Keller, p. 35.
21. Ibid., p. 41.
22. Robert Butler, *Why Survive?* (New York: Harper & Row, 1975), p. 263.
23. *World Survey*, p. 256.

that there was gold to be had in geriatrics. Eighty percent of those living in rest homes reside in facilities developed to make a profit. Many of those residents are poor; therefore, public funds pay three-fourths of the bill.

Only 1,500 rest homes (6 percent) are religious in nature. Within those homes reside 117,000 whose spiritual needs are being addressed. Paul Sweeney, president of Nursing Home Ministries, observes that most of the 2,000,000 residents in non-Christian nursing homes have never heard the plan of salvation.[24] Nursing Home Ministries was developed in 1975 to recruit and train volunteers to visit care centers and to appoint chaplains for service in the 24,000 rest homes in the United States.

There is a great need to minister to this hidden subculture where 85 percent never have a visitor and 90 percent receive no mail. One-half of the residents have no living relatives and 85 percent will die in the home. One-third will live only one year in the facility, and another one-third will remain only three years. Many (37 percent) need not be in the home except they have no other place to go. Even though 87 percent have some amount of brain damage, an effective ministry is possible. One of the most important ministries is to prepare these forgotten souls to meet their Maker and assure them of a proper burial.

Mission societies are on the cutting edge of spiritual ministry to those who, because they cannot help themselves, are institutionalized. Much more needs to be done for these minorities; therefore, missions are developing training programs to equip laymen to assist them in ministry. (See Figure 11.4.)

Missions are also helping the evangelical church to visit handicapped minorities in the community and develop ministries for them within the context of the local church.

Finally, missions are reminding the church about the growing community of the elderly. Churches need to be planted in retirement villages and pastoral programs developed for those living out their years in rest homes.

It is a great task, for ministries of mercy face a mission field of 50,000,000 souls.

24. Paul Sweeney, "An Introduction to Nursing Home Ministries," *Roundtable*, January-March 1981, n.p.

CHILDREN'S HOMES

1. Bethany Children's Home, Kentucky
2. Bethel Bible School, Tennessee
3. Dessie Scott Children's Home, Kentucky
4. Edwin Denby Memorial Children's Home, Michigan
5. Eliada Homes, North Carolina
6. Grace Children's Homes, Nebraska
7. Hephzibah House, Indiana (live-in rehabilitation for girls)
8. Joy Ranch, Virginia
9. Lazy Mountain Children's Home, Alaska
10. Lester Roloff, Texas
11. Miracle Hill Children's Home, South Carolina
12. New Horizons Youth Ministries, Wisconsin (group home for boys)
13. Oneida Baptist Institute, Kentucky
14. Youth Guidance, Inc., Pennsylvania (for abused children)

Figure 11.2

MISSION BOARDS SERVING THE BLIND

1. Christian Fellowship for the Blind
2. Gospel Association for the Blind (Ralph Montanus, radio, magazine, circulating library, camping)
3. John Milton Society for the Blind (service providing braille publications)
4. National Church Conference for the Blind
5. Oakley Kimble Gospel Tape Ministry
6. United Missionary Fellowship

Figure 11.3

MISSION BOARDS SERVING THE DEAF

1. American Mission to the Deaf
2. Baptist International Mission, Inc. (helps to establish deaf ministries)
3. Bill Rice Ranch, Tennessee (conducts seminars; distributes tracts, newspapers, Bible correspondence courses, and tapes)
4. Christian Deaf Fellowship
5. Deaf Missions, R.R. 2, P.O. Box 26, Council Bluffs, IA 51501

(provides daily devotions for the deaf, color films, Bible visuals, and Christian newspapers)

6. Home Mission Board, Southern Baptist Convention (consultant on deaf ministries)
7. National Association of Deaf, 5125 Radnor Road, Indianapolis, Indiana 46226 (monthly publication: *The Deaf American*, 814 Thayer Avenue, Silver Springs, Maryland 10910)
8. World Bible Translation Center, Inc., Arlington, TX 76010. (*The New Testament: English Version for the Deaf*, 1978; distributed by Baker Book House, Grand Rapids, Michigan.)
9. First Assembly of God Deaf Ministries, 8825 Airline Highway, New Orleans, LA 70118 (tracts for the deaf)
10. United Missionary Fellowship

Figure 11.4

MISSION BOARDS SERVING THE HANDICAPPED

1. American Rescue Workers, Pennsylvania (serves socially and physically handicapped men; a breakoff of the Salvation Army)
2. Baptist Mid-Missions
3. Child Evangelism Fellowship (workers often work with the handicapped)
4. Children's Bible Fellowship, New York
5. Christian League for the Handicapped (occupational home)
6. Echoing Hills, Inc., Route 2, Warsaw, OH 43844
7. Handi-Vangelism (Bible Club Movement), Pennsylvania
8. Joni and Friends, P.O. Box 3225, Woodland Hills, CA 91365 (fellowship to serve handicapped and assist the church in reaching the handicapped and his family)
9. Joy Ranch, Virginia
10. Martin Luther Home, 804 S. 12th Street, Beatrice, NB 68310
11. Shepherd's Home (resident home; college of special education; Sunday school curriculum; *Guidebook for Ministries in Local Church*; Andrew Wood, director)
12. Teens, Inc. (camp for disadvantaged children)
13. Youth Guidance, Inc. (abused children)

MATERIALS FOR SERVING THE HANDICAPPED

1. Abingdon Press, 201 Eighth Avenue, S., Nashville, TN 37202 (resources for exceptional persons)

2. Concordia prints a curriculum for the mentally retarded: Welborn, Terry. *Leading the Mentally Retarded in Worship*. 1973.
3. Clark, Dorothy. *Teach Me, Please, Teach Me*. Elgin, Ill.: David C. Cook, 1974.
4. Towns, Elmer. *Successful Ministry to the Retarded*. Chicago: Moody, 1972.

Figure 11.5

SERVICES AVAILABLE FOR REST HOME MINISTRIES

1. American Missionary Fellowship
2. Nurses Christian Fellowship
3. Nursing Home Ministries
4. The Oakley Kimble Gospel Tape Ministry, 407 Somerset Street, N., Plainfield, NJ 07060

Figure 11.6

12

The Military Establishment

Because its personnel are removed from normal community life, where the local church functions, the United States military establishment is a mission field. Life in the military is often temporary, unusual, and impersonal. There is loss of identity and privacy with resultant loneliness. Irregular duty hours make involvement in church and community life difficult, and boredom makes it easy to participate in drinking, drugs, gambling, and prostitution. Defense Department surveys indicate that 7 percent of those in the army regularly use marijuana. A greater number use and abuse alcohol as a form of cheap entertainment.[1]

Gaylord Chizum, director of Servicemen's New Life Center, observes that the military is a most neglected mission field. Even with godly chaplains and sound local pastors, most servicemen go through military service and the nearby community without encountering a definite, personal witness for the Lord Jesus Christ.[2]

EXTENT OF OPPORTUNITY

American military personnel in 1981 numbered 2,050,000, including 150,000 women. Around the bases other thousands of

1. "The Better Alternative," prayer letter of Overseas Christian Servicemen's Centers, December 1981.
2. Gaylord Chizum, in a tract published by Servicemen's New Life Center.

military families live temporarily, thereby creating a potential mission field of 5,000,000.

Military installations are to be found in every state. Some of the bases were originally forts established during the early founding years of the nation. The army, navy, and marines were created by the Continental Congress in 1775. The Air Force was added in 1926.

Every state has a National Guard. The guardsmen are reservists that trace their history back to the militia of 1636; therefore, they are the oldest military force. They can be activated by the governor of the state or in national emergency by the president. The Guard includes both the Army and Air National Guard.

In addition to the regulars of each branch of the service, there are reservists. It is necessary to add to those the Coast Guard, which was inaugurated in 1790. In a disaster, even the Civil Air Patrol can be activated. Most American military personnel are stationed on bases stateside, for only 500,000 are assigned overseas and 50,000 are at sea on one of the Navy's 400 active combatant vessels. The opportunity for missionary activity is large and widespread in every state.

CHRISTIAN SERVICE OPPORTUNITIES

The United States government provides 3,000 chaplains for its servicemen stationed on several hundred bases. If the chaplains were evenly distributed, each would have a parish of 700 military personnel, in addition to 1,000 military dependents living nearby. But some chaplains are responsible for as many as 3,000 men and their dependents.

The government recruits chaplains from 100 (1983) active religious groups out of a list of 120 groups that have been recognized by the Armed Forces Chaplains' Board. The board was assisted by the General Commission on Chaplains and Armed Forces Personnel, which was a consortium of forty sponsoring Protestant denominations. But as of January 1982 this commission was replaced by the National Conference on Ministry to the Armed Forces, which represents all 120 recognized religious groups, including Catholics, Jews, Buddhists, Hindus, Moslems, and cults. Each representative group can recommend a number of chaplains commensurate with the percentage of the general populace the group holds.[3]

---

3. Edward Swanson, Director of General Commission on Chaplain and Armed Forces Personnel, in a telephone interview, December 1981, before it was disbanded.

Chaplains work under serious limitations. They must minister to men of different faiths. Facilities are often limited. Work schedules are hectic. They are often rotated every two years and usually move with the outfit wherever it goes.

Some local churches near military bases have developed visitation programs on the bases and provide transportation from the base to the church. Church families often invite personnel home for Sunday dinner and fellowship in the afternoon.

Christian Servicemen's Centers began in 1941 in Illinois as a Christian counterpart of the United Service Organization (USO) centers. The USO organization is a federation of six volunteer agencies that mobilizes civilians to serve the needs of servicemen. The Christian Servicemen's Centers are established by missionaries who are concerned to win servicemen to Christ and train them as witnesses to win their buddies. The centers also function as homes away from home by providing a place for servicemen to go when they have free time.

There are sixty centers in the United States listed in the *World-Wide Directory of Christian Servicemen's Centers*.[4] The centers are located in twenty-two states and function under different names, such as the Salt Cellar and Fisherman's Wharf. In some instances there is a chain of centers with the same name, such as Christian Servicemen's Centers and Missions to the Military. (See Figure 12.1.) Keith Davey of Missions to the Military observes that a servicemen's center affords today's military man the best opportunity available for the help and encouragement he needs.

In 1933 Dawson Trotman, stationed aboard the battleship *West Virginia*, began a ministry known as the Navigators. He led servicemen to Christ and then trained them in the Word of God to disciple others after the admonition of 2 Timothy 2:2. By the time of World War II, there were 1,000 Navigators serving on ships and on shore. In 1949 the ministry became international in scope. Today, in the United States alone, 153 Navigator staffs serve on 111 military bases as well as on 141 college campuses and 75 cities in various community ministries.

Within the services are two fellowships of Christian servicemen. The Officer's Christian Fellowship is an organization of 3,300 Christian officers who are concerned to present the gospel to 250,000 men in the officers corp. The sister organization is the Christian

---

4. *World-Wide Directory of Christian Servicemen's Centers* (Denver: Overseas Christian Servicemen's Centers, 1977).

Military Fellowship, which promotes Christian outreach to military personnel who are not officers.

Within the U.S. Navy a group of concerned Christian men collect the names and addresses of Christian personnel and distribute them in a publication entitled *Link-Up*. By means of this information Christians can find others in their command. Information can be obtained from Navy Christian Link-Up, P.O. Box 9635, Norfolk, VA 23505.

Some ministries to the military are one among many programs of the ministering organization. Baptist Mid-Missions sustains a military ministry. The Prison Mission Association has a servicemen's division. Pacific Garden Mission caters to the military as well as to alcoholics. The Gideons, although not a mission organization, presents free Bibles to members of the military. The Christian Businessmen's Committee, along with its many ministries, sponsors servicemen's centers.

The missionary to the military will face several challenging circumstances. If there is a chaplain on the base he may not welcome the ministry or the missionary. The missionary may have difficulty gaining access to the base. He will have to adjust to constantly changing military schedules. He will face the unique problems experienced by uprooted singles and families constantly in transition.

The average age of all military personnel is 26. Fourteen percent of service persons are black, which is three percentage points above the national average. Women now constitute 8 percent of the military. All of those factors influence the ministry of a missionary.

The American military services are a responsive mission field according to Charles Cassety, a veteran now serving as a regional representative of Philadelphia College of the Bible. Their unique circumstances provide the alert believer with unlimited opportunities for witness and discipleship.

MISSION BOARDS SERVING THE AMERICAN MILITARY

1. Baptist International Missions, Inc.
2. Baptist Mid-Missions
3. Campus Crusade for Christ
4. CBMC Servicemen's Center
5. Christian Servicemen's Centers, Inc., 113 Sangamon Street, Rantoul, Illinois 61866 (13 centers)
6. GI's for Christ, Illinois
7. The Living Word Ministries, Inc.

8. Maranatha Baptist Mission
9. Missions to the Military, Inc. (3 locations)
10. Navigators (111 installations)
11. Overseas Christian Servicemen's Centers, 1955 (4 U.S. centers)
12. Pacific Garden Mission
13. Prison Mission Association, Servicemen's Division (Bible correspondence courses)
14. Seamen's International Christian Association (U.S. ports)
15. Servicemen for Christ, Baptist Mission (2 locations)

Directory of Christian Servicemen's Centers available from:

> Overseas Christian Servicemen's Centers
> P.O. Box 10308
> Denver, Colorado 80210

Figure 12.1

13

The Educational Community

The evangelical church has a growing concern for American youth who are being reared in homes that are floundering, who are growing up in a hedonistic and selfish society that is morally deteriorating, and who are being educated in a system that is based on a philosophy of secular humanism.

Thirty percent of school-aged children live with parents who have been divorced at least once. In 1983, one in eight children lived in one of 35 million single parent homes. A majority of youth have mothers who work outside the home; therefore, guidance at home is at a minimum much of the time or transferred to day care operators (22,000 professional and 25,000 sponsored by churches). Few parents realize that 69 percent of their teenagers consult horoscopes for decision making, and 90 percent are concerned about their zodiac sign. It is estimated that children spend at least forty hours per week watching television and witness 13,000 killings before they are 15 years old.

By age 11 many begin to drink and by age 16, 84 percent of boys and 78 percent of girls use alcohol, making it the number one drug problem. Between the ages of 10 and 15, 50 percent of American youth experiment with drugs. At least 75 percent of our teenagers are sexually active and 40 percent of teenaged girls will become pregnant. In 1982 that represented one million teenaged girls, one-third of them under 15. During the decade of the 1980s, premarital pregnancies doubled to 14 percent for 15-to 19-year olds and accounted for half of all illegitimate births and one-third of all abortions. The suicide rate for white males of the same age increased by 66 percent, so that suicide is the number one cause of death among adolescents. It is probably the highest suicide rate of any age group. In 1981 juveniles accounted for 20 percent of all serious crime and 40 percent of all criminal arrests. Living in this milieu, America's youth are in trouble; no wonder one-fourth will never graduate from high school.

The church should be concerned because 67 percent of those under 14 never go to church and 83 percent of children raised in the church leave it by age 16. Three out of four teenagers do not read the Bible. In fact, only 6 percent of all teenagers use the Bible regularly and 20 percent by churched teens, according to a 1980 Gallup survey. School age youth, then, have become a major mission opportunity in the United States. Because the prime years for accepting Christ as Savior and surrendering to Christ for service are between the ages of 16 and 25, the church should be especially concerned to reach the academic community.

One problem to be faced is that 60 percent of teenagers work at least part-time and spend 35 billion dollars. A second problem concerns the 2.5 million (and growing) number of children aged 5 to 15 who have a limited English proficiency because their mother tongue is one of eighty different languages.

The church must also face an internal problem involving their own youth leaving the church. One survey shows that when both parents attend church, 72 percent of their children remain faithful to the church. When the father alone attends, 50 percent of the children remain attenders, but when mother takes the children to church, only 15 percent remain faithful to the church.

PUBLIC SCHOOL MINISTRIES

The church is desirous of evangelizing America's youth not only because they are lost, but also because they are in their prime years for being saved. According to Child Evangelism Fellowship estimates, statistics show that 60 percent of church members and 85 percent of those serving as missionaries were saved as children. Furthermore, it is estimated that 90 percent of all who are born again made that decision before they were 20 years old. But only 33 percent of America's youth go to church; therefore, it is necessary to look for them elsewhere. The one place most youth gather daily and spend one-fourth of their time is in school. The school, then, is the logical place to expose America's youth to biblical truth. However, there are problems to be faced in presenting the Bible in the public schools.

In a pluralistic and democratic society, the rights of all religious groups must be protected. In countries where a particular religion is in the majority and the constitution does not preclude it, the beliefs of the predominant religious group may be taught exclusively in the school system. Pakistan is an example. In that country, Islam is taught in the public schools as mandated by law. That kind of religious exposure cannot be practiced in America because the first amendment forbids it.

In Protestant America, by 1913 twelve states required daily Bible reading and prayers during homeroom exercises or assembly programs. The Bible was also included as a subject taught in the standard curriculum. Many of the teachers and administrators were Christians, and school boards, elected from primarily Christian communities, sensed that they had community approval for Christian instruction at public expense.

During the 1940s religious minorities became vocal about their rights and complained about unwelcome religious indoctrination of their children in the local schoolroom. School officials were responsive and began to modify the religious programming in the schools. Where the Bible was read, out of deference to the Jewish students, only passages from the Old Testament were used. Bible classes were offered on a voluntary basis and those who attended had to obtain written permission from their parents indicating that they had no objection to their children's attending. Those children who did not have permission for this instruction were permitted to move to the back of the room or to go to another room.

By 1948 the Supreme Court determined, in the McCullam case, that religious teaching could not take place on school premises because that violated the First Amendment. After that date, most Bible teaching was removed from the public schools. However, justice Arthur Goldberg clearly stated that teaching *about* the Bible should be included in literature or history courses. Justice Tom Clark noted that education without the study of religion is incomplete and that such study is not prohibited by the First Amendment. In certain communities that are overwhelmingly Christianized, found primarily in Appalachia, the Bible is still taught in schools during school hours.

The Supreme Court further decided in 1962 that Bible reading and prayers could no longer be mandated by law. That decision has been challenged by different groups of students who wished to conduct their own prayer meetings on school premises before school began. As late as December of 1981, the Supreme Court has upheld the 1962 decision for public elementary and secondary schools. However, in December 1981, in a separate ruling, the same Court determined that state colleges and universities must allow all student groups to worship and hold religious discussions in campus buildings.

Although the Supreme Court decision effectively removed the Bible from the public schools, there continued to be widespread interest in religious instruction being given students during school hours but off school premises. By 1952 it was determined that school officials could release the students to go to a nearby church or other facility for instruction in the faith of their choice.[1] All costs for such instruction are borne by the church or mission providing the teaching.

Approximately twelve mission organizations seek to conduct released-time Bible classes for 37,000,000 school children in thousands of grade schools and high schools across the United States. Most of this activity seems to be taking place in states east of the Mississippi. Among many ministries, Rural Bible Mission is located in Michigan; Scripture Memory Mountain Mission holds classes in Kentucky; Bible to Youth Crusade ministers in Pennsylvania; and Southern Highland Evangel has a ministry in Virginia. (See Figure 13.1.)

One innovative approach to providing a facility for released-time classes involves a chapel-on-wheels, which may be a trailer or self-propelled vehicle specially prepared as a classroom. Among others, Children's Bible Mission, which conducts ministries in eight states from Pennsylvania to Florida, sends the missionary to the public school in a mobile chapel. This moveable classroom is parked near the school property so that the students can walk to the facility during their released-time. Various classes frequent the chapel throughout the day, and then the chapel is moved to another school in a regular circuit.

Christian students can be found in most schools. The number, however, is declining. By 1981 the Christian day school movement claimed 3,000,000 students attending nearly 15,000 schools. Three additional schools open every day. The exodus of Christian students is making the public school more of a mission field than ever.[2] In

---

1. *World Book Encyclopedia,* 1970 ed., s.v. "Religious Education," by William Nault.
2. Thomas C. Hunt and Marilyn M. Maxson, eds., *Religion and Morality in American Schooling* (Washington, D.C.: University Press of America, 1981), p. 88.

addition the Supreme Court decided (June 1982) that 20,000 to 30,000 children of illegal aliens are entitled to a free public education. In response to this opportunity, several groups send missionaries to the public schools to seek out the Christian students and organize Bible clubs. Brandt Reed, general director of High School Evangelism Fellowship, states that the purpose of their Hi-BA clubs (High School Born-Againers) is to stimulate fellowship, Bible study, Scripture memorization, and personal witness to fellow students.

Youth For Christ establishes 2,000 clubs each year in grade schools and high schools across the country. They send 1,000 missionaries into the public schools to discover Christian students or lead students to Christ, and establish clubs for their encouragement through local chapters in 500 communities and 1250 cities.

Oscar Hirt, Director of the Bible Club Movement (BCM), says that they prepare many of the materials their missionaries use. The objective of BCM, as that of other club ministries, is to direct the students into local churches for involvement in Sunday schools, youth programs, and all the church activities.

The place and time of club meetings varies. Clubs meet at the school before classes begin, during the noon lunch hour, or right after school. It is usually necessary to have a teacher sponsor the club if it meets on the premises. Other clubs meet off campus, most often in a nearby home and just after school hours.

A national fellowship of youth ministries, Youth Evangelism Association, maintains a membership directory of thirty-four organizations whose purposes are:

> to promote aggressive Biblical Evangelism through mass meetings, personal witness, the media, printed page and every legitimate means possible . . . and to be a fellowship of men and women (and organizations) helping each other in the cause of youth evangelism, holding high standards of Christian separation, teaching the Bible, emphasizing consecrated, victorious Christian living, and providing leadership training.[3]

It should be noted, however, according to Jay Kessler, president of Youth For Christ, that even with this activity, all nondenominational youth organizations put together are active in only 15 percent of the nation's high schools. Some youth organizations are constituted as a mission, but their primary ministry consists of assisting the

3. Youth Evangelistic Association brochure, Dick Snavely, executive vice-president, 1981.

local church in beginning a ministry or expanding its current ministry by training church people to minister to youth.

Child Evangelism Fellowship (CEF), founded in 1937, establishes Good News Clubs in schools and homes. The hostess in the home is often a member of the sponsoring church. She opens her home for the club, which is conducted by someone who has been trained in special sessions held in the local church by the area CEF director. The director is a missionary who trains local church members to function not as "missionaries" but as effective Christians. CEF has 600 missionaries in the United States and many overseas, who marshal the help of thousands of laymen to win young people to Christ and to encourage them to become active church members. CEF maintains a number of different ministries. It designs and publishes its own materials, including visuals. In the summer, Five-Day Clubs are conducted in the out-of-doors. High school and college young people are recruited and trained at one of the CEF area headquarters. The recruits then spend their summer teaching the clubs as summer missionaries. By faith they trust the Lord to provide some stipend for their work. The children who make salvation decisions are encouraged to join the Mailbox Club, which is a follow-up Bible correspondence course. They are also encouraged to tune in to the television program "Tree House Club." In addition CEF sponsors a telephone ministry called "Tell-A-Story," and a radio program, "Kids Bible Club."

Word of Life Clubs were developed as a ministry of Jack Wyrtzen's Word of Life Fellowship. These clubs are established in local churches by Word of Life missionaries who train local church members to administer the program. Club members are encouraged to recruit their unsaved friends at school to attend the club with them. The area missionary sponsors numerous youth-oriented programs throughout the year to train and involve the members in Christian activities. Other organizations of a similar nature are Pro-Teens, a program of Positive Action for Christ; Boys Brigade and Pioneer Girls; and Awana Youth Association, which maintains approximately 11,000 clubs.

Materials and uniforms are available for purchase from their headquarters. Challenging programs encourage the members to earn advancement in rank. Points are earned by reading the Bible, memorizing Scripture, attending church, bringing guests, and participating in the various programs.

Another related youth ministry is Christian camping. Camping programs are an integral part of many youth ministries conducted in local schools or churches. A week at camp may be earned as a reward for memorizing Scripture or some other special service rendered. There are probably 10,000 camps in the United States, 40 percent of which are religiously oriented. Some local churches own and run their own camps. Others maintain a cooperative camp with several churches. Some rent the facilities of a professional camp and provide their own staff and program. Perhaps 5 percent of camps are profit-making businesses.

Several hundred camps have developed as home mission organizations. Frequently, the camp ministry is one of several ministries conducted by the parent organization. Alpine Bible Camp, for instance, is a ministry of the Appalachian Bible Fellowship (ABF). The ABF is a mission agency maintaining three ministries including the Appalachian Bible College, Appalachian Bible Conference, and Alpine Bible Camp.

In Pounding Mill, Virginia, the Southern Highland Evangel conducts Camp Evangel, a public school and church-planting ministry in rural Virginia. Camp Nathanael is administered by Scripture Memory Mountain Mission that also sponsors the teaching of the Bible in the public schools and church planting in eastern Kentucky (see chapter 14).

The membership directory of Christian Camping International (CCI) lists 750 member organizations, representing 4,000 staff members. Camps are listed for all but four states. CCI has divided the United States into five regions, with the western region having the largest number of camps.

COLLEGE MINISTRIES

Collegians are a mission field because at least 60 percent do not attend church even once a week (according to a Gallup poll). There are 3,400 college campuses in the United States and less than 1 percent have any valid on-campus representation of the gospel. A total enrollment of 12,000,000 indicates that one in every 2.5 persons between the ages of 18 and 24 is in college. That compares with one in six in West Germany and one in eight in Great Britain.[4] As of 1980 there were more women than men enrolled, and an increasing number are part-time students. By 1983 nearly a million were blacks.

The college campus as a mission field is being neglected

4. *Evangelical Newsletter*, November 1981, p. 2.

according to Edmund Lidell, dean of the University of Denver. He says:

> If there's any one segment of society of Christian life that's bankrupt, it's the campus ministry.... It's my particular point of view right now that the church has dramatically, drastically and I think sometimes thoughtlessly, abandoned the basic precepts that gave it the vitality for life it once had. [5]

A member of Campus Bible Fellowship comments, "One of North America's greatest mission fields today is the college and university campus. But, the local church, which should provide leadership, doctrinal stability, and continuity is conspicuous by its absence."[6]

Because the church is not normally near the college campus, it has responded by commissioning numerous campus ministries to minister in its behalf.

InterVarsity Christian Fellowship, founded in 1941 in the United States and maintaining work on 850 campuses representing 30,000 students and servicing 400 staff members, notes that ministry on the college campus is essential because college years are often years of crisis. Tragically, many are not able to cope with the stress of life. The suicide rate, increasing for those between the ages of 20 and 24 by 86 percent since 1978, is now the leading killer of collegians.

InterVarsity ministries include small group Bible studies, daily prayer meetings, and weekend retreats. The InterVarsity Press publishes materials designed to challenge the collegian about the Christian life. In fact, *Welcome to America* by Lawson Lou seeks to not only help international students feel at home, but also encourages concerned Christians to help internationals find Christ. On Christian campuses IVCF sponsors Student Foreign Missions Fellowships (SFMF) to encourage prayer for foreign missions and to challenge students to consider foreign missionary service. It is to be hoped that the SFMF would drop the foreign emphasis and recognize that home and world missions are one and indivisible.

Perhaps the best-known IVCF-sponsored event is the Urbana Missionary Conference, held on the campus of the University of Illinois every three years. In December 1981, 14,000 collegians gathered during the Christmas break to learn about world mission

5. *Rocky Mountain News*, April 1971, p. 4.
6. *The Challenge of the Secular Campus* (Cleveland: Baptist Mid-Missions, 1981), n.p.

opportunities and experience a few days together in Christian fellowship. There are numerous follow-up workshops held around the country called "Urbana Onward."

InterVarsity also sponsors a Nurses Christian Fellowship and Christian Faculty Fellowship on secular campuses. Each year various projects are proposed to involve students and faculty in opportunities for witness to non-Christian colleagues. (See Figure 13.2.)

The Forever Generation, under the direction of Terry Herbert, has a ministry on twelve campuses in six states. Mr. Herbert states that approximately 1,000,000 college students receive undergraduate degrees each year, but only a small number are fundamental Christians. Yet, those graduates are the future leaders of our country, who will help determine the course of events in days to come. The Forever Generation is burdened to present the gospel to today's generation. Strong emphasis is placed on fellowship on campus and membership in a local church.

Baptist Mid-Missions reports that one of its most fruitful ministries is the Campus Bible Fellowship. The Conservative Baptist Home Mission Society campus ministry is called "Campus Ambassadors."

One hundred thirty-nine Navigator staff members are serving on 141 college campuses. Navigators on campuses use the same effective programs developed by Dawson Trotman fifty years ago in his ministry with servicemen. He called his ministry "dynamic multiplication," and based it on 2 Timothy 2:2. Simply stated, the ministry is one person helping another, who in turn helps someone else. The collegiate work is the largest segment of the Navigator's United States ministry. It provides most of the Navigator staff and disciplemakers sent overseas.[7]

Campus Crusade for Christ International, now thirty years old, maintains 16,000 staff worldwide in 150 countries. In the United States, they have 2,000 workers on college campuses including ministries to internationals, ethnics, the military, and Christian athletes. The Agape House ministry ministers to Japanese students on campus. Their film *Jesus* produced by Genesis Project, which is seeking to put the entire Bible on film, is being translated into fifty languages and being shown internationally. By 1981, 10.5 million people had viewed it.

International Students Incorporated (ISI) concentrates on minis-

7. *Navilog,* special edition, "Annual Report of the American Navigators," Fall 1980, p. 8.

tering to the international students who have come to the United States from 181 countries in unprecedented numbers. In 1984, 339,000 internationals were studying on hundreds of campuses. In fact, eighty-four colleges have more than 500 international students enrolled. Sixty percent of the foreigners are from Asia, 15 percent from Latin America, 13 percent from Africa, and 8 percent from Europe. California has the largest number of foreign students (47,000), with 3,300 enrolled at the University of California. Miami has 10,000.

One very important group of internationals is the 7,000 students from the People's Republic of China. It is predicted that the number will double by 1985, providing American Christians with perhaps one of the most unusual opportunities for Chinese evangelism in this decade.[8]

Mark Hanna of ISI suggests that international students are the greatest blind spot in missions today. He reports that fewer than one-half of 1 percent of all Protestant missionaries are working among international students, who constitute one of the greatest missionary opportunities of the century. These internationals in the next twenty-five years will be among the top leaders of the world. Many will be returning to closed countries and resistant cultures, yet less than one-fourth of 1 percent are being effectively reached for Christ.

ISI, founded in 1953, now has 150 missionaries working on American campuses. The mission's leaders plead with American Christians to recognize that:

> missions is not to be understood solely or primarily in terms of geography. That is one of the great misunderstandings of missions today. Rather, in the truly biblical sense, missions is to be understood in terms of persons. The location is a secondary concern.
> Can we consistently claim that we are concerned about world evangelism when we are largely ignoring the transplanted foreign mission field which God has brought to us?[9]

That is an excellent question, but it also raises another question. Why is ISI incorporated as a foreign mission organization when its ministry is in the United States? It might be suggested that ISI faces the same attitude from the churches in America that other home mission agencies face. That attitude suggests, improperly of course,

8. *Watchman on the Great Wall,* October 1981, p. 6.
9. *The Great Blind Spot in Missions Today* (Colorado Springs, Colo.: International Students, 1975), n.p.

that all groups in America could hear the gospel if they wanted to; therefore, missionary work is really overseas. It has always been easier to raise support for work overseas. Yet, will the church recognize her responsibility to reach all groups here in America? Missions is not a matter of geography; it is a matter of groups of people being beyond the message of salvation wherever they are. It is amazing, however, that the burden for a particular people seems to lessen when they come to America.

Other mission organizations have ministries to internationals including International Missions, which is primarily involved in overseas ministries. They also have a work among international students on American campuses. It is this attitude of missions that is truly international.

T. E. Koshy, a Christian from South India, became burdened for internationals while studying at Syracuse University. After he married a medical doctor, also from India, they together established International Friendship Evangelism to focus their ministry among internationals at Syracuse University. They open their home every weekend and serve international cuisine to their guests. Doctors Mr. and Mrs. Koshy cite the fact that:

> most foreigners, even after being in the U.S. for four years, return to their countries without having been invited into a Christian home or having met a born-again Christian. Christians in America have an unprecedented opportunity to reach these foreign leaders for Christ from our living room in practical ways. This is missions at our doorsteps.[10]

CONCLUSION

The public school is not a closed door for Christian ministries. Although the Supreme Court has ruled that Christianity cannot be taught to the exclusion of other religions, the First Amendment is not to be construed to mean that religion is to be removed from the schools. Mandated Bible reading and prayer have been ruled against as well as private gatherings that resemble a worship service. However, the Supreme Court is concerned that there should be teaching about the Bible and Christianity; therefore, churches and missions should be aggressive to seek out such opportunities.

The college or university campus is viewed in a different light

10. Bob and Georgia Hill, "Launching Pad at Syracuse," *Evangelical Review*, 1981, pp. 18-20.

by the Supreme Court. There is no mandate against Bible study and even worship services on campus; therefore, a concerted effort should be made to enlarge the ministry of presenting Christ on American campuses. Hunt and Maxson give an excellent understanding of such opportunities in their book *Religion and Morality in American Schooling.*[11]

MISSION BOARDS SERVING HIGH SCHOOL/YOUTH MINISTRIES

(Also listed are the various ministries of each mission or organization.)

1. Appalachian Bible Fellowship (1950): camp
2. Awana Youth Association (1950): kindergarten, high school clubs
3. Bible Christian Union: youth ministries
4. Bible Club Movement (1936): publishes materials for children, teenagers, adults, Bible clubs, camps, DVBS, 5-day clubs, rallies, released-time classes
5. Bible Mission of Southwest Virginia (1939): teach Bible in public schools, camps, retreats
6. Bible to Youth Crusade, Pennsylvania: schools, camps
7. Campus Crusade for Christ
8. *Campus Life* Magazine, P.O. Box 2721, Boulder, CO 80321
9. Campus Light of Life Fellowship
10. Campus Living Association (CLASS): evangelism
11. Child Evangelism Fellowship (1937): Good News Clubs, "Tree House Club" (TV), fairs, 5-day clubs, Tel-a-Story (telephone), camp, open air, CEF Press, Radio Kids Bible Club, leadership training
12. Children's Bible Fellowship, New York City
13. Children's Bible Mission, Florida (children and youth): Bible clubs, released-time classes, Rolling Chapel, camps, radio, telephone, correspondence courses, DVBS
14. Christian Service Brigade
15. Hi-BA: teach high schoolers how to witness
16. Pioneer Ministries (Pioneer Girls), 1939
17. Probe Ministries, *Student Survival Manual* (high school)
18. Pro-Teens
19. Rural Bible Mission, Michigan
20. Scripture Memory Mountain Mission, Kentucky: clubs, camp
21. Southern Highland Evangel, Virginia: schools, camp

11. Hunt and Maxson, n.p.

22. Teen Challenge
23. Teen Encounter
24. Word of Life Fellowship, Inc. (1960), Schroon Lake, New York 12870: teenagers' clubs, camp
25. World Home Bible League: correspondence courses
26. *Young Ambassador*
27. Young Life
28. Youth For Christ (1945): clubs, music teams, rallies

Figure 13.1

MISSION BOARDS SERVING COLLEGES

(Also listed are the various ministries and emphases of each mission.)

1. Agape House Ministries: Japanese students on campuses
2. Baptist Student Union
3. Campus Ambassadors (Conservative Baptist Home Mission Society): 40 campuses
4. Campus Bible Fellowship (Baptist Mid-Missions)
5. Campus Christian Fellowship
6. Campus Crusade for Christ (1951): trains staff for high school, college, ethnics, military, athletes
7. Campus Light of Life Fellowship, Inc. (1970)
8. Forever Generation (1970)
9. Inter-Varsity Christian Fellowship
10. International Missions: foreign students
11. International Students, Inc. (1953)
12. Navigators (1931): NavPress
13. Open Air Campaigners
14. Pocket Testament League and the Free Bible Literature Society: Distribution of free copies of the *New American Standard* New Testament to all students on campuses internationally through Operation Campus; now an arm of P.T.L.
15. Probe Ministries, International
16. Real Life Ministries
17. Teen Challenge: addicts
18. Young Life

Figure 13.2

Part 5

Geographic Ministries

Introduction

Most Americans tend to be rather provincial in their thinking about this great land, assuming that there is a mythical American, who is essentially just like himself, and that all parts of the country are much like the place where he lives. This assumption may seem logical at first, but it is far from the truth. This illusion persists because of television stereotyping, or the fact that the average American has never visited the distant parts of his country or areas that are different from his own familiar territory. Even though the people of the United States are very mobile and 25 percent move annually, the truth is that they do not move far. Many only move across town or to the next state. Although many Americans take holiday breaks, the vast differences in American culture are not perceived from the cursory contact provided by a vacation visit; nor are Americans aware that evangelicals are not evenly spread out over the fifty states. In some areas there are few or no churches. There is a dearth of the gospel in many geographical areas of the United States.

The chapters in this section discuss the spiritual needs of individuals living in different sections of North America. Many nostalgically think of living in the countryside with its quiet and peaceful context, but seldom do they consider the problems encountered in maintaining a church in an isolated or dying community. In fact, rural America may be the most unchurched section of our country.

Seventy-five percent of Americans now live in an urban context. Although the rate of urbanization has slowed, it has by no means stopped. For many urban-suburban folks there is no adequate gospel witness within reasonable distance. Also, many Americans who move do not look for a church in their new location.

Alaska, although located in the extreme Northwest, is still a part of the home missions scene. Whereas many Alaskans live in the few larger cities, countless others live in the vast hinterland, where their contact with the outside world and the gospel is limited and often dependent on radio. Here missions take on a distinctly foreign flavor.

The fiftieth state, Hawaii, is primarily thought of as the place for a great vacation. Most vacationers seldom look for a church while away from home; therefore, they have little idea that it is easier to find a Buddhist temple in Honolulu than an evangelical church. In many ways this Garden of Eden is also a graveyard for missionary services.

Then there are those groups of people who move about the country in their line of work. The spiritual needs of truckers, seamen, airline personnel, vacationers, taxi drivers, gypsies, and others also need to be considered. Their life-styles make them extremely difficult to reach and also may prevent them from being faithful in a local church. Yet, there are missionaries who are concerned for their souls.

14

Rural/Mountain Areas

RURAL/MOUNTAIN AREAS ARE A MISSION FIELD

To suggest that rural America is a mission field is clearly to be at odds with popular opinion and seems to contradict pollsters' findings. The polls suggest that 65 percent of small-town Americans are churched. This is five percentage points above the national average. However, averages totally ignore the hard fact that some areas must have a higher percentage of unchurched. The greatest ratio of unchurched Americans is found in rural areas of the Western states, the Ozark mountains, and the Appalachian mountain regions. (See Figure 14.1.) As the darkened areas indicate, in most of these counties 40 to 60 percent of the residents are unchurched. This observation led pollster Russell Hale to postulate that "the unchurched phenomenon in the United States may be primarily rural rather than urban."[1] Keep in mind that 80 percent of America's 3130 counties are rural.

Americans living in nonurban areas are a mission field for three reasons. First, many rural communities have no local church witness. That is true in 10 percent of the counties in the United States. It is also true for 15,000 villages scattered across the country. Some places have never had a church, and in other areas churches have closed. Maynard Matthewson of the Rural Home Missionary Association

---

1. J. Russell Hale, *The Unchurched* (San Francisco: Harper & Row, 1980), p. 173.

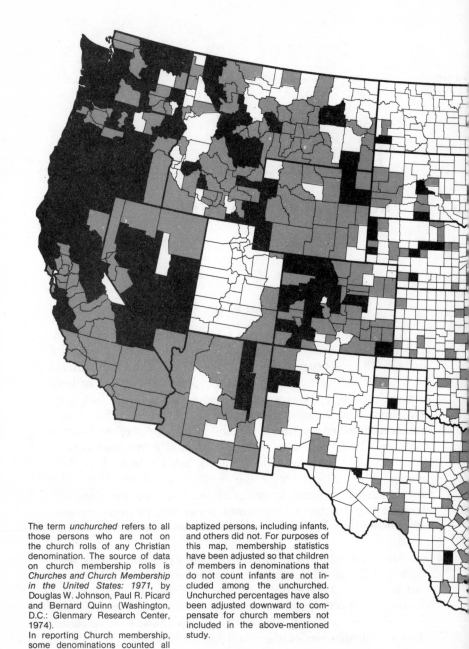

The term *unchurched* refers to all those persons who are not on the church rolls of any Christian denomination. The source of data on church membership rolls is *Churches and Church Membership in the United States: 1971*, by Douglas W. Johnson, Paul R. Picard and Bernard Quinn (Washington, D.C.: Glenmary Research Center, 1974).

In reporting Church membership, some denominations counted all baptized persons, including infants, and others did not. For purposes of this map, membership statistics have been adjusted so that children of members in denominations that do not count infants are not included among the unchurched. Unchurched percentages have also been adjusted downward to compensate for church members not included in the above-mentioned study.

Figure 14.1

PERCENT OF POPULATION UNCHURCHED

By Counties of the United States: 1971

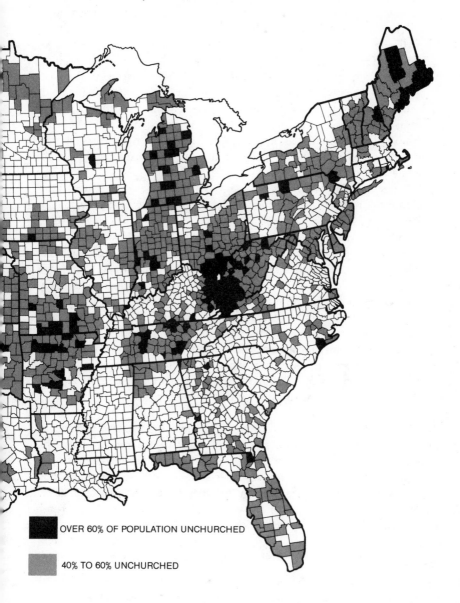

OVER 60% OF POPULATION UNCHURCHED

40% TO 60% UNCHURCHED

J. Russell Hale, *Who Are the Unchurched? An Exploratory Study* (Washington, D.C.: Glenmary Research Center), p. 5.

estimates that between 70,000 and 90,000 rural churches are closed. That amounts to 20 percent of America's 343,000 churches. He further speculates that 1,000 churches are closing each year. Bob Clark, director of the Rural Bible Crusade of Wisconsin, suggests that in the last fifty years, 90 percent of America's rural churches have closed. This is a colossal waste, but more important, it limits the spiritual help available to 57,000,000 people who live in rural areas.

The tragedy of closed rural churches is not the abandoned church buildings. It is the fact that more people now live in many rural areas than ever before, yet often there are no rural churches.[2] In many rural communities it is "only as the rural missionary comes into the area with the gospel that the people encounter an active witness for Christ."[3]

Second, rural America is a mission field because many rural churches are small, struggling, or dying institutions. One-half of all American churches have an attendance of fewer than seventy-five members. Clyde White of Operation Out-Reach says that many rural churches have an attendance of fewer than fifty. In many situations the churches cannot afford to give the pastor a living wage; therefore, they find it difficult to attract highly-skilled men unless those men are willing to be bivocational. As a result, at least 26,000 churches are without a pastor and other thousands of churches have itinerant clergy who minister to several congregations periodically. In such circumstances missions such as the American Mission for Opening Churches supply missionary-pastors. The missionary-pastor, having raised at least part of his support from concerned churches, is able to carry on an effective full-time ministry because his salary is subsidized.

Third, rural America is a mission field because 84 percent of rural church members do not attend church on a regular basis. In some instances there is no church to attend in the immediate area or within commuting distance. In other situations some people do not feel welcome in the rural church that may have a high percentage of interrelated members. For whatever reason, 32 percent of rural church members rarely attend church and another 43 percent never attend.

Kenneth Meyer, president of Trinity Evangelical Divinity

2. James Palmer, *The Vital Ministry of the Rural and Small Church* (Atlanta: Home Mission Board of Southern Baptist Convention, n.d.), p. 6.
3. C. J. Rediger, "The Rural People," in *The Fields at Home*, ed. Peter Gunther (Chicago: Moody, 1963), p. 149.

School, senses a need to strengthen the small churches of America. He cites two polls that indicate that more evangelicals live in small towns than in the suburbs where the masses of Americans live.[4] If the masses are to be evangelized it will be through the mobilization of American's evangelicals who live in small towns.

Forty mission societies recognize as a mission field rural Americans who are often isolated, overlooked, bypassed, or forgotten. (See Figure 14.4.) Walter Duff of Village Missions, which has fielded 450 missionaries, says North America also remains a great mission field. This is especially true in the rural areas where missionary activity is limited.

DEFINING RURAL AMERICA

American society for many years was predominantly a rural culture. In 1790, 95 percent of Americans lived on their own land and were basically self-sufficient. A hundred years later, three-fourths of all citizens still lived off the land. But during the next century, the industrial revolution stimulated 75 percent of all Americans to move off the farm and into the cities. From 1940 to 1960, 9 million people were involved in the rural exodus. Two hundred counties lost 50 percent of their population. Today 95 percent of the populace lives within commuting distance of a metropolitan area of 25,000 or more. Prior to the 1980 census, the federal government considered any area with less than 2,500 people to be rural. With the advent of urbanization, the government began to use a new base for measuring urban centers that they now call Standard Metropolitan Statistical Area (SMSA). An SMSA includes at least 50,000 people who are dependent on a central city industrial complex for their livelihood. It includes those who live in surrounding counties and commute to the city for jobs. Therefore, *rural* now refers to areas that are not included in an SMSA of 50,000. In 1980 there were 57,000,000 people who lived outside of 350 SMSAs.

In 1970, two-thirds of all counties were at least 50 percent rural. In fact, more than one-half of all counties had fewer than 25,000 population. Ten percent of all counties had fewer than 5,000 citizens.[5]

There are 18,500 municipalities in the United States. Fully 75

---

4. Kenneth M. Meyer, "Editorial," *Voices,* Fall 1980, p. 2.
5. Ben J. Wattenberg, *The U.S. Fact Book* (New York: Grosset and Dunlap, 1978), p. 298.

percent of all municipalities have a population of fewer than 5,000, and 50 percent have fewer than 1,000 residents. Many areas are barely large enough to incorporate. It is interesting to note that every state has at least 200 towns with fewer than 300 citizens.

Rural may still refer to an area that is relatively unpopulated, isolated, agricultural, and where limited higher educational and cultural opportunities exist; however, sociological differences are more important. There is a rural mind-set, for "the culture and work habits of the rural person are vastly different from those of the city."[6]

The rural person has several positive cultural characteristics. He lives at a slower pace and is much more concerned about other people. He is friendly and gets involved in the lives of his neighbors. He tends to be conservative in most areas of his thinking and takes an active part in town life. He tends to be more secure because there is less crime. Nine out of ten persons are satisfied with living in the country. In contrast, six out of ten urbanites would like to move away from crime, pollution, and anonymity.

Numerous negative characteristics are also inherent in rural life. The greatest problem is limited job opportunities and a 25 percent lower wage scale. With the advent of industrialization and the rising standard of living, small acreage farming became less and less feasible. Therefore, the farmer sought a job in the nearby town and tried to work the farm at night. He was called a city-farmer. His children went off to college and took jobs in the industrial centers. Ultimately the farmer sold his farm land for small building sites in the growing suburbs or sold out to wealthy farmers who were able to add to their acreage and to purchase expensive agricultural equipment to be more efficient. Others retired on the old homestead and grimaced as double-digit inflation eroded their economic base and slowly condemned them to rural poverty.

By 1979, 16 percent of rural Americans lived in poverty, as compared to 11 percent for urban centers. America's most persistent poverty exists in the country, and two-thirds of the nation's substandard living is to be found in rural areas.[7] Seventy percent of the rural poor are white. Not only are many rural Americans unable to afford proper medical care, but often there are no medical facilities, or the facility does not include the latest advances in medical technology.

6. Clyde White, *Operation Out-Reach* (North Platte, Neb.: Operation Out-Reach, n.d.), n.p.
7. Ernest F. Hollings, "The Rural Poor," *Current History*, Summer 1973, p. 258.

Fifty percent fewer doctors per 100,000 citizenry service rural areas. A higher percentage of infant mortality and chronic diseases exists in the countryside.

Other persistent problems in the country include poor and often unpaved roads and the distance between neighbors or to the nearest shopping center. In small towns prices may be higher and selectivity limited. It is difficult for rural areas to provide cultural centers or events.

Geography sometimes makes rural conditions inevitable. In the plains states of the West, rural conditions exist because thousands of acres are included in only a few ranches; therefore, population density is low, and industrial centers are few. Mountainous areas of the country also give rise to rural conditions. Rugged terrain has made the building of efficient roads difficult and expensive. Lack of waterways has prevented easy movement of raw materials and finished products; therefore, the creation of industrial centers was minimal. It was easy for people to be isolated in mining towns and to live with only the barest of life's essentials.

Life was often difficult, but mountain people were of a hardy stock. They were clannish for purposes of self-preservation and often fearful of outsiders, who all too often proved to be of an unsavory character or who came to exploit the people and the mountain resources. The people were also religious. Their religion was often as hard and demanding as the mountains in which they lived. Sometimes the religious fervor was carried to extremes and included proving one's religion by drinking poisonous substances and handling deadly snakes. Although those excesses may still exist, they are the exception and not the rule. Exodus from the mountain rural areas was inevitable, especially for the youth who could not find jobs. But times and circumstances have changed and continue to change in all of rural America.

Not only has the rural exodus slowed, but beginning in 1970 many of the younger and more educated began leaving the metropolitan areas and moving back to the countryside in a movement dubbed by sociologists as the "hayseed revolution." Within the next five years 400,000 had bypassed the suburbs and moved to small towns.[8] It is significant that rural areas are now growing at 5.5

8. *Information Please Almanac 1980* (New York: Simon and Schuster, 1980), p. 787. See also Larry Long and Diana Detre, "Migration to Non-metropolitan Areas," no. CDS80-2, Superintendent of Documents, U.S. Government Printing Office, Washington, D.C. 20402, November 1981, p. 21.

percent, which is twice the growth rate of the suburbs. Job opportunities are improving as interstate roads are built and industry moves out of the city. A fascinating "new frontier" is being discovered in non-metropolitan America by retired persons who are moving back to their natural homes and by suburbanites who are looking for a new place in which to escape the problems faced in the central city. It appears that the rural church has a new opportunity for service for, "the rural church can stand as a buttress of the kingdom and act as a spiritual vanguard to the migration of people back to the country. God is creating a new mission field in the shadow of many rural church steeples."[9]

THE RURAL CHURCH

The rural church is an essential ingredient in the evangelization of the United States. In communities where a local body can be sustained, a functioning church should be strengthened or a closed church opened. If there is no church, then one should be planted. All denominations and fellowships of churches have church extension agencies. Most church planters, except those of the mainline denominations, are commissioned as missionaries.

The rural church should be encouraged because it has a good track record. Most evangelicals today have their root in the small-town church. Edwin Hunter claims that 48 percent of all Christians come from communities of fewer than 1,000, and another 14 percent have emerged from communities of between 1,000 and 2,500.[10] Lloyd M. Perry of Trinity Evangelical Divinity School says that most evangelical pastors and missionaries come from small churches.[11] Village Missions personnel indicate that historically 85 percent of pastors and missionaries hail from rural America.

Historically, the colonial church was concerned for America's remote or rural areas. The church sent itinerant clergy as missionaries into the interior as the population moved west. Unfortunately, the weakness of this era was the lack of church planting to preserve the message and train new personnel in service. The American Sunday School Union was concerned by 1871 to establish Sunday schools in rural America. Many of those ultimately became local churches. But,

9. Palmer, p. 6.
10. Edwin Hunter, *Small Town and Country Church* (Nashville: Abingdon-Cokesbury, 1975), p. 34.
11. Richard Allen Bodey, "Dr. Lloyd M. Perry on the Small Church," *Voices*, Fall 1980, p. 9.

until the twentieth century, "the hinterlands of America were largely left in the shadows."[12]

Perhaps the Southern Baptist Convention has been the most active in planting churches in rural America, for 30,000 of their 36,000 churches are rural. It is also significant to note that the South has the highest number of churched Americans—66 percent. They further indicate that 24,000 of their churches have fewer than 300 members. Most other mainline denominations subsidize their rural churches, but today much of that subsidy is being withdrawn and their churches are closing.

The small, rural church has a number of advantages. More of its members have opportunity to serve in the church. The church often has a higher ratio of the number saved per membership. There is a greater opportunity for personal contact with members, and they become better acquainted. That encourages prayer and interdependence.

Serious disadvantages may also emerge. There may be not enough young people and too many senior citizens. In a small, struggling church a poor self-image may develop so that the group loses its vision, self-identity, and purpose. By becoming bitter, decimated by conflict and disillusioned, it loses its effectiveness. It is to be hoped this will not happen because the rural church can be more significant in its setting than the urban church. The rural church has the opportunity to become a major institution in community life, which seldom happens in an urban setting.

Rural churches may need to recognize new opportunities for service and seek to evangelize newcomers in the community, even if the new neighbors are ethnic or unaware of the local customs. For instance, studies indicate that most mobile home parks are in nonmetropolitan areas.

RURAL MINISTRIES

Missionary interest in rural America grew in earnest during the twenty years following 1930, when most of the thirty-eight organizations working in rural America were founded. Six of those missions each field over 100 missionaries for a grand total of 82 percent of the more than 1,800 missionaries working in nonmetropolitan areas. The largest, representing 450 missionaries, is Village Missions. The oldest, the American Missionary Fellowship, along with all of the

12. Gunther, p. 148.

American Missionary

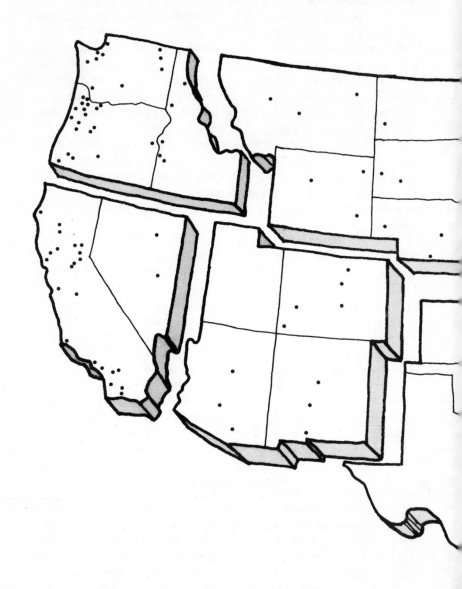

Figure 14.2

Fellowship

U.S. map showing AMF regions and missionaries

DISTRIBUTION OF RURAL/MOUNTAIN MISSIONS

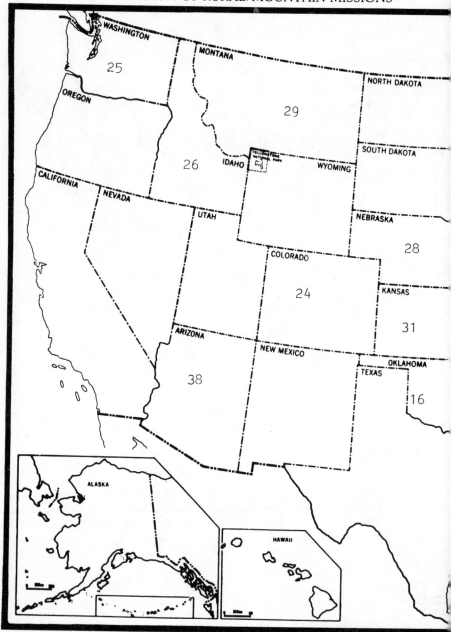

Figure 14.3

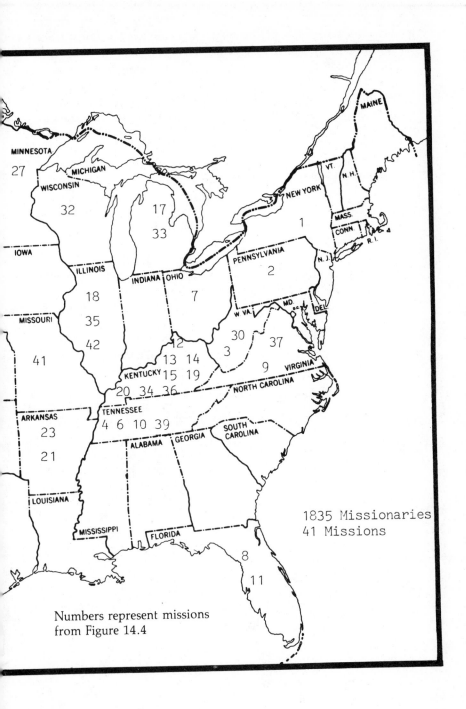

1835 Missionaries
41 Missions

Numbers represent missions
from Figure 14.4

larger and a few of the smaller missions, maintains a national work, but most rural missions work primarily in the state in which they were incorporated or in adjacent states. (See Figure 14.2.)

One-half of all rural missions work primarily in the Appalachian Mountains. (See Figure 14.3.) The state with the largest number of missions (eight) is Kentucky. The large number of missionaries working in Appalachia is to be expected because, according to pollster Hale, the eastern Appalachian strip contains one of the highest ratios of unchurched citizens.[13] In fact, some mission leaders believe that the southern Appalachian Mountains constitute one of the larger single home mission areas.[14] It was concern for the spiritual well-being of the people of Appalachia that motivated Robert Gulick to invite Lester Pipkin to found the Appalachian Bible Fellowship in 1950. This home mission organization fields sixty missionaries, sponsors the Alpine Camping Association, a summer Bible conference ministry, and the Appalachian Bible College. All are ministries in the southern Appalachian Mountains.

There is growing interest in church planting in New England, the northern end of the Appalachians. The American Missionary Fellowship has done the most complete survey work of the area and, along with the American Mission for Opening Churches and the Rural Home Missionary Association, is fielding the largest number of missionaries working in this area.

It should be of concern that the Northwest, which has the highest number of unchurched, be targeted for special prayer. The Northwest Independent Church Extension Mission sponsors 129 missionaries working in the area as church planters.

Missions in nonmetropolitan areas are seeking to reach the unchurched in smalltown U.S.A. The responsibility is formidable, for the field represents as many people as live in either England, France, Germany, or Italy. Most missions are involved in either church planting or church nurturing. As a source of contact some missions are working, where possible, with children in the public schools. In conjunction with this ministry, several missions have established camping programs and Bible conferences as their primary summer ministry. The children are encouraged throughout the school year to earn their way to camp by memorizing Scripture verses and to grow in grace by studying Bible correspondence courses the missions offer.

13. Hale, p. 44.
14. Gunther, p. 142.

Those contacts are used to open doors into the homes where adults can be led to Christ.

Village work usually involves pastoring a small country church. Missionary pastors are well received, and provide the people with spiritual leadership. Maynard Matthewson observes that rural America is indeed a valid and important part of the world missionary task. In some circumstances it is pioneer work. The American Mission for Opening Churches has entitled their prayer bulletin "AMOC Pioneer Fellowship Prayer Calendar." To establish strong rural churches is a valid burden all over the mission world. James Montgomery and Donald McGavran argue that the only way the Philippines will be churched is to create standard rural churches, "The churching of the pieces is the only way in which the churching of the nations can be achieved."[15] Perhaps that could also be said of America.

MISSION BOARDS SERVING RURAL/MOUNTAIN AREAS

The following list of rural/ mountain missions gives the state in which the mission is incorporated, the date the mission was established, the number of missionaries currently serving with the mission, and the area of the mission's ministry outreach. Although an effort was made to provide complete data, some entries are incomplete because of unavailable information.

	State Incorporated	Date	Number of Miss.	Area
1. American Mission for Opening Churches	New York	1943	40	N.Y.
2. American Missionary Fellowship	Pennsylvania	1817	147	U.S.
3. Appalachian Bible Fellowship	West Virginia	1950	60	
4. Bancroft Gospel Ministry	Tennessee			
5. Baptist Fellowship for Home Missions				

---

15. James H. Montgomery and Donald A. McGavran, "The Discipling of a Nation," *Global Church Growth Bulletin*, n.d., p. 144.

6. Baptist International Missions, Inc.	Tennessee	1960	223	U.S.
7. Baptist Mid-Missions	Ohio	1920	320	U.S.
8. Baptist Mission to Forgotten People	Florida	1980	7	U.S.
9. Bible Mission to Southwest Virginia	Virginia	1939	11	
10. Cedine Bible Mission	Tennessee	1946		
11. Children's Bible Mission	Florida	1935		
12. Cumberland Mountain Mission	Kentucky			
13. Cutshim Bible Mission	Kentucky	1936	6	
14. Emmanuel Bible Fellowship	Kentucky			
15. Faith Mountain Mission	Kentucky			
16. Go Ye Mission	Oklahoma	1943	2	Oklahoma
17. Hiawatha Baptist Mission	Michigan	1968	191	U.S.
18. Illinois Bible Church Mission	Illinois	1952	12	Illinois
19. Kentucky Mountain Evangelical Fellowship	Kentucky			
20. Kentucky Mountain Mission	Kentucky	1938	25	
21. Mid-America Mission	Arkansas	1958	26	
22. Mission to the Man Farthest Back				
23. North Arkansas Gospel Mission	Arkansas	1947	7	Arkansas
24. Northwest Baptist Mission	Colorado			
25. Northwest Independent Church Extension	Washington		129	Northwest
26. Northwest Mountain Mission	Idaho			
27. Oak Hills Fellowship	Minnesota	1926	13	Minnesota

28. Operation Out-Reach	Nebraska		8	Nebraska
29. Rocky Mountain Bible Mission	Montana		24	Montana
30. Rural American Mission Society	W. Virginia		2	W.V.
31. Rural Bible Crusade	Kansas	1937	4	Kansas
32. Rural Bible Crusade of Wisconsin	Wisconsin	1939	4	Wisconsin
33. R.B.M. Ministries	Michigan	1935	30	
34. Rural Evangel Mission	Kentucky			
35. Rural Home Missionary Association	Illinois	1943	25	U.S.
36. Scripture Memory Mountain Mission	Kentucky	1932	34	
37. Southern Highland Evangel	Virginia	1930	35	
38. Southwest Bible Church Mission	Arizona			
39. Tennessee Mountain Mission	Tennessee		4	
40. Videocassette Ministry of Evangelical Covenant Church/ Covenant Press Video				
41. Village Missions Affiliated with:	Missouri	1948	450	U.S.

Christian Business and
Professional Women's
Councils
Christian Women's Clubs
Business and Professional
Couples Clubs
Friendship Bible Coffees
Rural Missions (Single women)

42. World Home Bible League	Illinois			

15

Urban/Suburban Areas

Urban America as a Mission Field

Urban America is a mission field because most of the 75 percent of Americans who live in the city are unevangelized. The unevangelized are found in every economic level of the city and in all of the various residential areas. Urban America may be divided into two main divisions: the central city in which 30 percent of Americans live, and the suburbs containing 45 percent of the populace.

The central city includes the ghetto, high rises, and affluent residences. A high percentage of those living in the ghetto are poor and ethnic. More ethnics are urbanized than the general populace. The 1980 census reveals that 81 percent of blacks, 88 percent of Hispanics, and 90 percent of Asians are urban. Only Indians fall below the general populace with 48 percent urban. Merely 25 percent of whites live in the central city, but 58 percent of blacks, 51 percent of Hispanics, 46 percent of Asians, and 21 percent of Indians live there.[1]

And the central city is becoming more ethnic. Detroit has 110 ethnic groups. Each group is separated from the others by invisible boundaries. There are 58 million culturally distinct peoples living in America's cities. It is estimated that only 14 million (24 percent) are

1. U.S. Department of Commerce, Bureau of the Census, 1980 Census of Population, p. 3.

active Christians.[2] In some cities it is against the law to have a Bible study in a home.

The central city also includes shop owners and others who can afford to live in apartments in well-guarded high rises. These upwardly mobile people have insulated themselves from much of society including the church, which many consider to be an anachronism left over from the Middle Ages.[3]

The best residential areas have been purchased by the affluent who are the power brokers and decision makers of the city. They live in expensive, high-rise condominiums located in neighborhoods like Chicago's Gold Coast, which spans an area five blocks by eight blocks and includes 70,000 residents. The average salary of $53,000 permits them to enjoy the best of the city, but, according to one survey, for 99 percent that does not include the church.[4] The affluent constitute a needy mission field.

Surrounding the central city in concentric rings are the suburbs. In these bedroom communities, centered on shopping areas, have gathered half of America's urban population. Many suburbanites fled the central city as their affluency permitted. Although many were once church members, as empty inner city churches bear witness, a large percentage of those who moved did not continue membership in the churches that followed them to the suburbs. A Southern Baptist survey of greater Los Angeles estimates that of the 14 million residents living in 100 communities, 7 million are unchurched.[5] That may be typical of suburbanites across the United States.

Finally, urban America includes an area where city meets country called *exurbia*. Here the best of two worlds is sought, but, unfortunately for most people, distance from the church is a major factor in their not becoming actively involved in Christianity.

The 1980 census indicates that 75 percent of Americans live in urban population centers of 50,000 or more. This means that 175,000,000 people live in urban America. G. Paul Musselman suggests that most of America's 100 million unchurched reside in the

2. Jim Newton, "Keying on the Cities," *Missions USA*, January-February 1981, pp. 2-8, 25-32.
3. "The Cities," *Interlit*, June 1980, p. 20.
4. William H. Leslie, "The Importance of the Urban Church," cited in *Reference Library of Evangelism and Home Missions Association of Evangelicals* (Wheaton, Ill.: National Association of Evangelicals, n.d.), p. 3.
5. Newton, p. 6.

city[6]; therefore, at least one-half of all urbanites are unchurched. The number of unchurched in America approximates the population of Japan or Brazil. In fact, the number of unchurched Americans is surpassed by the population of only four countries in the world— China, India, Russia, and Indonesia. Indeed, America is a mission field, especially urban America.

It is naive to believe that urban America will be won to Christ by mass evangelism or any other in-house church programs. The complexities of the city require that the church galvanize her missionary vision and forces not only to see the masses congregating in the cities of the world but also here at home. But at present the urban church is in deep trouble.

BIBLICAL PRECEDENT FOR URBAN MINISTRY

The twentieth-century call for emphasis on urban evangelization in the United States and internationally is not without biblical precedent. The word *city* is mentioned over 1,200 times in the Bible, and at least 1,400 references to cities are made in both Testaments.

One hundred nineteen cities are mentioned by name in the Bible. Christianity began in a city and spread from city to city along the trade routes of the urbanized Roman world. The disciples saw the city as the key to the expansion of the Christian church, for their Teacher, the Lord Jesus Christ, ministered with them in the towns and villages of their day (Matthew 9:35-38).

The great New Testament missionary Paul was a metropolitan man, having been reared in Tarsus, an important city (Acts 21:39), and educated in Jerusalem. It was while on the way to Damascus that Paul was saved, and Antioch, the "Queen of the East," was where he began his missionary career. Paul traveled 6,000 miles as an urban missionary, establishing churches in important cities throughout the Mediterranean world.

One key to the successful spread of Christianity during the first three centuries of this era was the urban strategy established by Paul. That strategy, coupled with the message of the cross of Christ as proclaimed by discipled laymen, could be just as effective in evangelizing the twentieth-century urban world.

---

6. G. Paul Musselman, *The Church on the Urban Frontier* (Greenwich, Conn.: Seabury, n.d.), pp. 1, 16.

HISTORY OF URBAN DEVELOPMENT

In 1790 only two cities in the United States had a population of 25,000. They were New York City and Philadelphia. Within a century 200 cities with double that population had developed. By 1980, 75 percent of all Americans lived in what the government census takers call SMSAs. (See chapter 14.) The SMSA includes at least one large population nucleus or central city and surrounding outlying counties, or suburbs that maintain close commuting ties with the central city. The government lists 318 SMSAs, which include 429 central cities, 629 counties, and 566,000 square miles of land. This means that 75 percent of Americans live on 16 percent of the land.

Even more astounding, 28 percent of the populace has moved to 100 metropolitan areas with a population of over 100,000, and 10 percent have crowded into six supercities of over 1 million people. Metropolitan New York is the largest city, with a population of 16 million, or two-thirds the population of all of Canada or California (both 24 million), or more than live in the whole state of Texas (14 million).

Urban growth in the United States was encouraged by a series of historical events. First, European immigration peaked between 1860 and 1945 as 27 million emigres arrived and settled in metropolitan places. Second, an expanding economy gave rise to new industries, which provided jobs. Third, the development and mass production of the automobile between 1920 and 1940 made it possible for what was traditionally a walking city to expand into the suburbs.[7] (See Figure 15.1.) A fourth factor was the institution of the Federal Housing Authority (FHA) in 1934. The FHA made credit available for the purchase of suburban homes.

Finally, an upwardly mobile society provided movement within the social, political, economic, and religious sectors of society. Cities were established near transportation centers. Labor was available from the ethnic communities, which developed near the industries. Old World patriarchal family patterns persisted in these communities, which were run by an ethnic, political party boss. That assured a steady supply of cheap labor for industry and jobs for newcomers to this land.

Most European family members were raised to be hard workers.

---

7. Richard T. Geruson and Dennis McGrath, *Cities and Urbanization* (New York: Praeger, 1977), p. 101.

The older family members sacrificed for the younger members and encouraged them to get an education. By frugal living, careful management, sacrifice, hard work and education, economic advancement made it possible to move to the suburbs. This exodus made room for new immigrants.

The system worked efficiently until a new series of historic events radically altered the balance of life in the city. By the end of World War II (1945), the concept of an everexpanding economy was discovered to be more accurately described as an oscillating economy with serious recessions.

Second, there was a complete change in the source of manpower. European immigration gave way to black migration from the South and Asian and Latin emigres. Third, the system of ethnic political bosses in the city was replaced with a more democratic party system. At the same time the federal government began its welfare program. Finally, the civil rights movement manifested to the country that a vastly different attitude of life was altering the psyche of America's inner cities.

The work ethic of the Europeans was not shared by the new workers. The entrance of dark-skinned peoples into the cities of the North sparked latent racist attitudes of residents and employers. Ethnic composition of communities rapidly shifted. Industries moved out. Taxes escalated as leaders sought to maintain services even as the economic base eroded. The quality of education and services declined and housing deteriorated. Then, the churches closed their doors as the white middle class abandoned the elderly and the new ethnics by moving to the suburbs.

The cycle of upward mobility, albeit more slowly, continues to function in urban America. Blacks and Hispanics are gaining better education and jobs. They, too, are moving to the suburbs. Refugees and Latin Hispanics are the new source of cheap labor. Racist attitudes are diminishing. Immigration to the inner city was down by 3 percent during the 1970s. In the same period the suburbs received a 14 percent in-migration, so that now 45 percent of all Americans are suburbanites.

A new trend has developed called *gentrification*. In recent years, suburban whites have been moving back to the central city and purchasing old property. After renovating it, they are taking up personal residence in the inner city once again. The trend is not strong, for central city population numbers are basically stable.

Urbanization continues at a much slower rate since it peaked in the decade of the 1950s at 18.5 percent. During the 1960s it slowed to

THE GROWTH OF AMERICAN CITIES
DEPENDS ON TRANSPORTATION

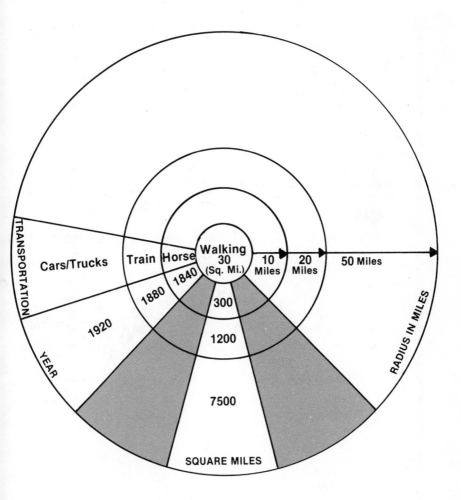

Information adapted from Richard Geruson and Dennis McMath,
Cities and Urbanization (New York: Praeger, 1977), p. 101.

Figure 15.1

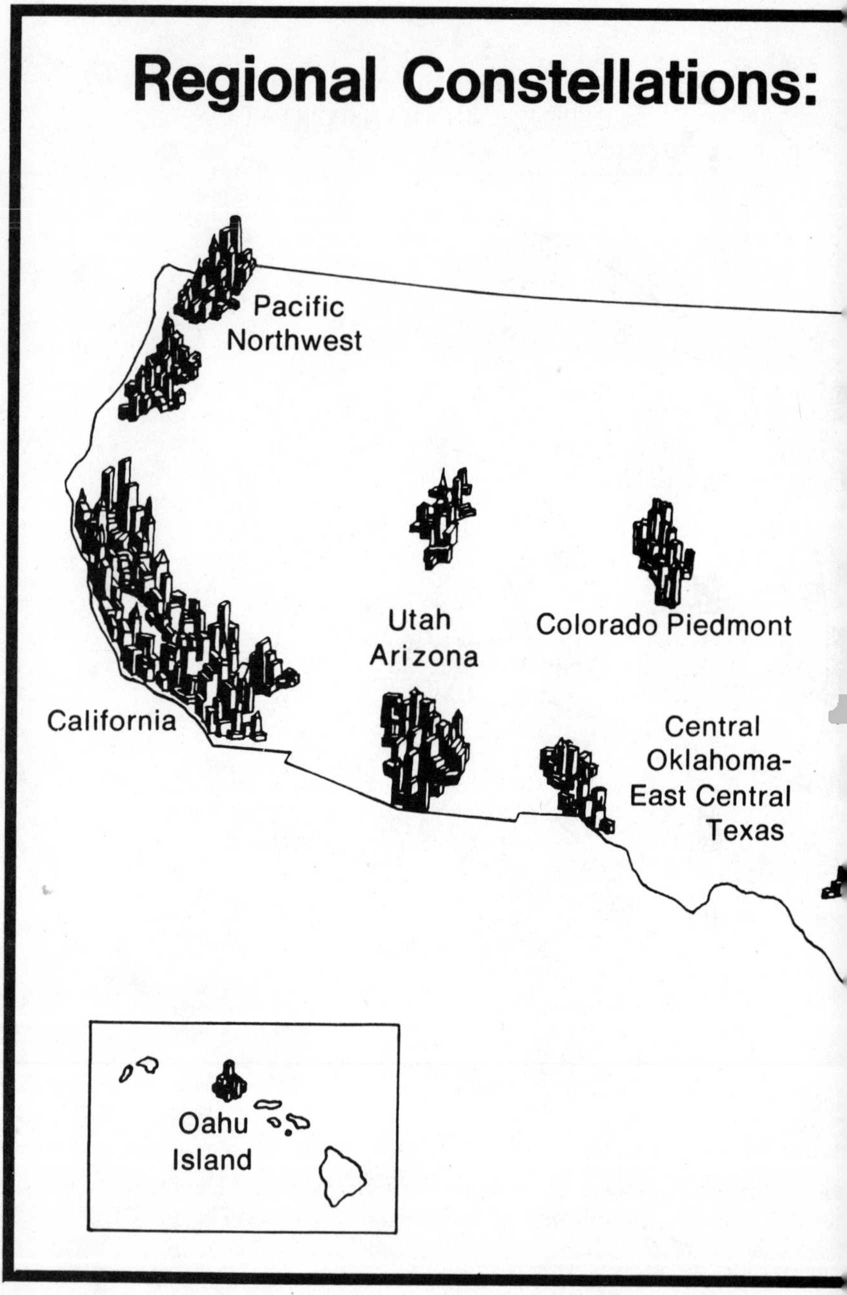

Regional Constellations:

Pacific
Northwest

Utah
Arizona

Colorado Piedmont

California

Central
Oklahoma-
East Central
Texas

Oahu
Island

Figure 15.2

Urban Sprawl In The Year 2000

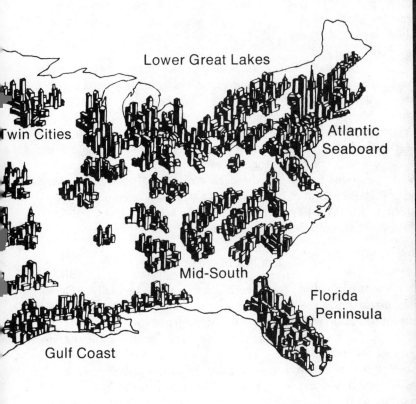

Lower Great Lakes

Twin Cities

Atlantic Seaboard

Mid-South

Florida Peninsula

Gulf Coast

13.3 percent and has now fallen to 11.4 percent. However, American metroplexes are expected to continue to grow as urban sprawl follows the interstate road system. (See Figure 15.2.) With fast, efficient transportation and communication, industry is able to move to areas with cheaper taxes and nonunion labor markets. As this takes place, strip-cities develop called *megalopolises*. These are areas where one city merges into another. The 1980 census revealed the presence of seventeen such areas. They are called Standard Consolidated Statistical Areas (SCSA) and are defined as adjoining and integrated SMSA's.[8]

Metropolitan Los Angeles is designated SCSA #49. It is the most widespread city in the country. It seeks to maintain 600 miles of streets. It has seventy communities that, someone has said, are looking for a city. According to the census, this SCSA contains two SMSA's. One is SMSA #4480 and is designated Los Angeles-Long Beach. The other is SMSA #360 and is designated Anaheim-Santa Ana-Garden Grove.[9] Los Angeles, as all but twenty-nine American cities, continued to grow in the decade of the 1970s. One thousand people, mostly ethnics, are added daily to this city of 9 million, which is already 74 percent nonwhite. America is now a nation of cities that are growing more complex.

THE URBAN CHURCH

The urban church from the beginning was essentially a church that ministered to the more affluent of society.[10] Denominations were careful to build large, pointed edifices, which at first dominated the cityscape.[11] Downtown churches were established in the heavily commercial areas and ministered to the leadership of the city. By the dawn of the twentieth century, steam hammers drowned out church bells, church steeples were dwarfed by skyscrapers, and business became more important than belief. The Protestant city was in transition.[12]

Ethnic language churches were slowly established by those who preferred their Old World language and had been brought up to be

8. U.S. Department of Commerce, *1980 Census*, p. 6.
9. Ibid., p. 66.
10. Allen M. Wakstein, ed., *The Urbanization of America: An Historical Anthology* (Boston: Houghton Mifflin, 1970), pp. 334-35.
11. Gaylord B. Noyce, *Survival and Mission for the City Church* (Philadelphia: Westminster, 1975), p. 13.
12. Philip C. Dolce, ed., *Suburbia* (New York: Anchor, 1976), p. 3.

God-fearers. These churches were exclusively for those who lived in prescribed areas and maintained their cultural identity, because people have difficulty fellowshiping with persons having different social and cultural life-styles. Most churches were not able to become culturally heterogeneous even in a multicultural society. That characteristic led to the ultimate failure of the urban church when the ethnic character of the community changed. With urbanization and secularization, the church was faced with its most serious challenge.[13]

Black churches were established, but they were often of a storefront variety and lacked a trained clergy. Jewish missions have always been an urban ministry, but affluent Jews were among the earliest to move to the suburbs. Missions moved also, and the elderly Jews who were fearfully living out their days in guarded high rises were forgotten. The skid row ministries are the mainstay of early urban church outreach. They have remained and are doing an effective ministry among those who are down and out.

Some churches remained and designed effective ministries to minister in the changing urban setting, but most "liberal and evangelical Christians were quick to surrender their witness and mission."[14]

The Keystone Baptist Church in Chicago is one church that did remain. Among its innovative new ministries is the West Side Family Center, which is a Christian social service agency. Many inner city people have special needs for services they cannot afford. This agency helps provide medical, legal, and counseling service.[15]

Calvary Baptist Church in New York City, founded in 1847, is another inner city church that has remained. Stephen Olford, when asked how Calvary has managed to do so, replied, "The secret is primarily preaching."[16]

Urban Americans are essentially unevangelized because the central city church moved. It failed to see its total community and ministered in a clublike manner only to its own kind of people.[17] It

13. Larry Krause, "Lessons from an Urban Church in Transition," in *The Urban Mission,* ed. Craig Ellison (Grand Rapids: Eerdmans, 1974), p. 137.
14. Arthur L. Whitaker, "Urban Church in Urban Community," in *Urban Mission* (Grand Rapids: Eerdmans, 1974) ed. Craig Ellison, p. 154.
15. Jack Estep, ed., *Challenge* (Wheaton, Ill.: Conservative Baptist Home Mission Society), May 1980.
16. William R. DePlata, *Tell It from Calvary* (New York: Calvary Baptist Church, n.d.), p. 116.
17. William Leslie, "The Ministering Church," in *Metro Ministry,* eds. David Frenchak and Sharrel Keys (Elgin: David C. Cook, 1979), p. 127.

neglected the spiritual needs of numerous others in the community and then failed to notice the changing character of the neighborhood. As church members moved away and the congregation became essentially a commuting body, a dwindling congregation failed to bring in new members from the community. As early as 1920 it was reported that "efforts put forth by Protestant churches to reach alien immigrants have been feeble. The church is not appealing to the working man in the city."[18] Finally, the church admitted its failure and fled to the suburbs, leaving the central city as mission territory.

Not only did the central city church fail, but the suburban church is also failing. Most suburbanites, happy to be in the promised land halfway between nature's beauty and civilization's conveniences,[19] feel little responsibility toward those who live in the inner city. One suburban pastor confesses, "My members just don't feel the need to reach the city of Detroit."[20] However, clergy and laity alike in American Protestantism seem to suffer from an "anti-urban animus."[21] It is reported that "inner city people are unwanted by society, which includes most Christians."[22] Even ministers, including Protestant ministers, have negative attitudes toward the city.

The suburban church has also failed to reach its own community. Quietly and steadily over the last decade particularly, suburbia has received an everincreasing number of ethnics. The census reveals that not only do 48 percent of white Americans live in the suburbs, but that 44 percent of Asians, 37 percent of Hispanics, 27 percent of Indians, and 23 percent of blacks live there also. Suburbia is, therefore, culturally diverse.

It would appear that the problem of urban evangelism is larger than merely the failure of the urban church. It is a problem that needs to be faced by the evangelical church at large, which has sought to evangelize the city by means of mass media including radio, television, and literature, and mass campaigns. Although evangelistic campaigns can attract huge crowds, at least 25 percent of city dwellers will not attend a church or campaign. Some who labor in urban ministries are convinced that the city will most effectively be won by the personal witness of born-again believers who commit

18. *World Survey*, 2 vols. (New York: Interchurch, 1920), 1:28, 30.
19. Dolce, p. vii.
20. Newton, p. 3.
21. Noyce, p. 27.
22. George Sheffer, Jr., "Young Life in Metropolis," *Christianity Today*, June 1966, p. 11.

themselves to the city for Christian service. James Speer, a Brooklyn pastor, articulates this concept:

> The central city is not without Christian witness ... but in terms of effective witness there's as much dearth in the cities as there is in Zaire. It's a mistake for us to assume that people are really going to grasp the meaning of the gospel through television. Jesus commissioned people; he sent people. ... We really do assume that if we have a Christian radio station in a major city that that's getting the gospel out.[23]

However, the city suffers from benign neglect and little concern on the part of evangelical Christians. It is "almost as if God had abandoned the city or never had anything to do with it."[24]

The evangelical church must reassess its priority of ministries. According to Acts 1:8 the priority should be first, Jerusalem and Judea; second, Samaria; and third, the uttermost parts. The first priority is being addressed, and the foreign ministry is very effective. New effort is also being made to reach the newly recognized 17,000 unreached people groups around the world. However, it is precisely the success of the foreign mission effort that causes the dearth of urban ministry to stand out in stark contrast. It appears that "American Christians have tended to ignore or avoid ... urban evangelism."[25]

It is to be remembered that the Samaritans were also ignored and avoided by the Jews. Thomas Hopler, formerly a foreign missionary and now working in urban United States under the Africa Inland Mission, voices the frustration of many: "Why are so many personnel and millions of dollars invested overseas while little concern is expressed for the cities of our own country?"[26]

It is strange that the evangelical church is not ready to reach out to the urban mission field of America, especially when one realizes that it is in fact foreign missions. Although the Southern Baptists have the most extensive urban work in the United States, only 10 percent of their churches are in urban settings. One pastor explains that most Southern Baptists are rural people and that ghettos are as

23. Randy Balmer, "James A. Speer on Urban Ministry," *Voices*, Fall 1979, p. 10.
24. David L. McKenna, ed. *Our Twentieth Century Target—A City in the Urban Crisis* (Grand Rapids: Zondervan, 1969), p. 20.
25. Edward V. Hill, "Urban Evangelism: Christ as Credible," in *Urban Mission*, ed. Craig Ellison, p. 159.
26. Thomas Hopler, "Learning from Foreign Missions," in *Urban Mission*, ed. Craig Ellison, p. 175.

foreign to their people as any foreign country.[27] Jere Allen observes that of nearly 3000 Southern Baptist churches in changing communities (urban), 70 percent are declining in Sunday school attendance.[28]

The urban church has a unique opportunity to minister to some of America's most needy citizens. The city teems with every social disease imaginable. It seems that city life dehumanizes and warps lives. Transience, poverty, anonymity, fragmentation, and powerlessness can lead to a sense of despair. In fact, *National Geographic* magazine refers to South Bronx as the national capital of despair.[29] Urbanites are people with many problems and are regarded and often regard themselves as failures.

The greatest challenge before the urban church is to learn to minister to its total community. By so doing, it will become aware of the changing character of the community. One survey reveals that over one-half of all urban churches are in transitional communities and that 2,000 urban churches each year disband or merge.[30] Peter Wagner suggests that such churches are suffering from "ethnicitis," a terminal disease caused by inability to adapt to a changing community. If a church does not mirror the people in its community, it will ultimately die.

In conclusion, America's cities are an extensive and needy mission field. In the opinion of Kenneth M. Meyers, President of Trinity Evangelical Divinity School, "the need for missions in the city is perhaps as great as the missionary need overseas, and Evangelicals cannot lag behind but must be in the vanguard of this outreach."[31]

URBAN MINISTRIES

Facing urban America as a mission field can be confusing and bewildering. However, if the metropolitan area is considered in its several parts, the complexity is minimized. Suburban America's greatest need is for church planting. The larger segment of American society (45 percent) is concentrated around shopping centers; therefore, church planting mission organizations (see Figure 15.4) are giving priority to establishing local churches in the suburbs, which can in turn evangelize those complexes by means of normal in-house

27. Newton, p. 6.
28. Jere Allen, *The Church in the Changing Community,* p. 20.
29. Rick Gore, "Can We Live Better on Less?" *National Geographic,* Winter 1981, p. 57.
30. Jim Newton, "The Challenge of Change," *Missions USA,* January-February, 1982, p. 42.
31. Balmer, *Voice,* p. 6.

evangelistic programs. Effective, growing suburban churches, which are training congregations of active discipling Christians, are the key to efficient world evangelization. From this base should emerge the vision, manpower, and funds to minister to the spiritual needs of rural America, central city America, and even to the uttermost parts of the earth.[32]

Suburban church planting must include establishing ethnic churches that may well have congregations speaking in a language other than English, at least for some time to come. Ethnic suburban communities should provide excellent service opportunities for returned missionaries as well as internship experience for those directed to overseas ministry. For example, a tribe of hundreds and perhaps thousands of K'anjobal Indians of Guatemala are living in downtown Los Angeles. CAM (Central American Mission) International missionaries have discovered several Christians among them. Thriving ethnic churches should be the source of manpower for reaching the great number of emigres who have come and will continue to come to the United States. Similarly, well-established suburban black and Indian churches ought to be an important key to evangelizing black and Indian America.

Urban America is not only being evangelized by home missionaries but is also receiving missionaries from overseas. The Haitian church is sending missionaries to establish churches among Haitian emigres in Miami. Worldteam is one mission liaison between the Haitian and American Haitian communities. The Latin church is sending missionaries to work among American Hispanics. African missionaries are working among American blacks in Newark under the sponsorship of the Africa Inland Mission.

Central city, U.S.A., is the place where church and mission are called on to extend themselves in the most creative ways possible to reach an area where the highest percentage of lost Americans reside. Not all central city churches disbanded or fled to the suburbs. Some remained and work valiantly to reach the sea of humanity that surges with the pulse of the city. One church declares that it stays alive through their mission program. The church has started thirteen mission works including three Spanish works. New churches with innovative programs are also being established. Tom Maharis went to Brooklyn as a missionary-supported church planter. He is now pastor of the Manhattan Bible Church, which supports him as pastor. Some missionary activities in the inner city have a long and

32. Robert B. Reekie, "Paul the Urban Strategist," *Interlit*, March 1980, pp. 2, 18.

commendable record. Rescue missions began in 1872 when the McAuley Water Street Mission was founded in New York City to minister to drunken sailors and other alcoholics. Today most cities have at least one skid row mission. The ministry has greatly expanded over the years to include work among drug addicts, destitute families, homeless children, unwed mothers, the handicapped, prisoners, and the unemployed. The International Union of Gospel Missions, a fellowship representing 230 missions and 1,000 missionaries, suggests that the inner city is a vast mission frontier not reached for Christ. It is a field that calls for trained, creative, ambitious workers (see chapter 11).

Another early ministry is to the Jews, for Jewish missions are essentially urban. In 1885 the Chicago Hebrew Mission began its ministry of Jewish evangelism and continues to minister under its new name, the American Messianic Fellowship. Another fifty missions sponsoring 400 missionaries also minister in numerous cities. Yet, the Jew in his urban home is virtually unevangelized. Daniel Fuchs, director of the American Board of Missions to the Jews, suggests that part of the reason for the lack of Jewish evangelism is that there are many Jewish communities in the city in which there is no longer an evangelical church; therefore, it is not only necessary to evangelize the Jew but also to plant churches for his edification (see chapter 7).

Every kind of missionary service discussed in the preceding chapters is needed in the central city and more, because there are such great numbers of people pressed into so little space. Masses of people make the spiritual needs much more obvious. In the city, because sin is so visible, it appears to be more sinful, but in reality there is just more of it. The most difficult thing to understand about sin in the inner city is the urbanite's calloused attitude toward it and his unwillingness to help someone in trouble. There is a total lack of concerned community spirit. Everyone has learned to live in his own shell, created in the midst of an incessant bombardment of endless stimuli.

Missionaries who serve in the inner city must understand the city and the special world its people create. Dedication and commitment to service in the asphalt jungle is no less demanding than service in any faraway jungle. Ken Davis comments, "We urgently need pioneer missionary efforts in most of our metropolitan areas. . . . May it not be said that too little came too late or that we were so occupied with evangelizing the steaming jungles of Afro-Asia that we forgot the teeming asphalt jungles of Metro-America."[33]

There are also special kinds of missionary activity in the inner city because of the prevalence of certain kinds of evil. Teen Challenge was developed by Dave Wilkerson to minister to gang leaders and gang-bangers (members) in New York City. Gangs are created for personal protection and identity and function as an extended family. It is almost impossible to leave a gang, although most gang members will end up dead or in jail. Every city has its gangs. Chicago has 150 gangs with 5,000 members. The age of the members is usually 13 to 18, but may span the ages from 9 to 40. Most of the members are unemployed, poor, and unmarried. The gang is usually involved in drugs, guns, crime, and prostitution. Most members have or will have a police record.

Because of the high crime rate in the inner city, Duane Pederson founded the Children's Mission as a ministry of Prison Volunteers. The ministry is to the children of inmates, street kids, and disadvantaged youngsters who, without direction, will probably drift into crime and ultimately into prison. This preventive ministry provides clubs, camps, meals, tutoring, recreation, and spiritual encouragement to neglected and often abused children who are mostly from single parent homes. These youngsters daily face alcohol, drug abuse, and the prospect of being sold for child pornography and prostitution. Pederson's vision is to expand the ministry to fifty centers in ghetto areas in the next ten years.

Several other ministries to inner city youth also exist. Covenant House is a ministry to youth under 21 years of age, most of whom are runaways. In New York City alone there are 20,000 runaways under 16 years of age and thousands more between the ages of 16 and 21. What will these unemployable "throwaway kids" do in the city? They drift to the Minnesota Strip, a fifteen-block stretch of Eighth Avenue porno parlors, strip joints, pizza palaces, cheap bars, and fleabag hotels, and wander among the thousands of drifters, hookers, pimps, and johns until they join a stable of children whose bodies are rented by the hour. Over one-half of these teenaged prostitutes are boys. Most of them are afflicted with venereal diseases and tuberculosis and are hooked on drugs. A *Reader's Digest* article likened Times Square to a "scene straight out of hell."[34] The

---

33. Ken Davis, "The Challenge of the Cities," *Baptist Bulletin*, July-August, 1976, p. 9.
34. John G. Hubbell, "Father Ritter's Covenant," *Reader's Digest*, October 1980, p. 6.

founder of Covenant House, a Roman Catholic priest, demands of his 200 volunteer workers that they spend three hours daily in prayer.

New York City also has 36,000 homeless, who sleep in train and bus terminals, subways, or in cardboard boxes on the streets. The city provides 4,000 beds for the destitute and homeless. Studies reveal that one-half of the city's homeless are mentally disturbed. Spiritual and physical help for these "dregs of society" is available from the Salvation Army and rescue missions, but they cannot possibly reach the total community of two million box people.

Saint Paul's House is a hotline telephone ministry to Brooklynites who feel they have no one who cares. Those who call are counseled to help them find answers to their problems in Christ instead of joining the thousands who, in despair, commit suicide.

At least two organizations minister in the city by way of sound trucks. Open Air Campaigners and Pocket Testament League, using specially equipped trucks to amplify their message, work with local churches to do street evangelism. The local churches do the followup.

Finally, there is a need for high-rise evangelism. This work is difficult at best because many high-rise buildings are locked to nonresidents and at least one-half of the apartment dwellers go away on weekends. One strategy for high-rise evangelism is to establish house churches in the building. It may require that the missionary live in the building and start with his apartment as the first housechurch. Other flats can become house churches as their occupants are won to Christ.[35]

Serious problems face the urban missionary. Those problems include a firm commitment to accept urban America as a bona fide mission field. There are problems related to housing such as availability, cost, and location. If there are children, there are the problems of quality education and safety. The potential problem of personal racial bias and other problems must be addressed. The missionary must be flexible and find it easy to initiate new ideas and programs, for cultural heterogeneity demands diversity of approaches.[36] Several schools offer programs designed to prepare missionaries for urban minorities. (See Figure 15.5.)

Problems related to this ministry include transiency, unemploy-

35. Timothy Monsma, "Urban Explosion and Missions Strategy," *Evangelical Missions Quarterly*, January 1981, p. 7.
36. Roger Greenway, *Guidelines for Urban Church Planting* (Grand Rapids: Baker, 1976), pp. 16-17.

ment, fear, crime, vandalism, and anonymity of the people. The missionary faces concentrations of people who are poor and living with endless problems. He will also wrestle with the issue of how involved the ministry should be in the social and physical problems of the community. Should he establish a clinic-in-a-van to administer a program of preventative medicine as did the Conservative Baptist Home Mission (CBHM) in New York City? Or, as the CBHM, establish a counseling center with health and legal services such as the West Wholistic Family Center in Chicago?

CONCLUSION

The intensity of the spiritual needs of urban America needs to be urgently faced by the evangelical church. The question is asked, "What will it take before we realize that God means business when He tells us to go to Nineveh? For us modern Jonahs our Nineveh is the inner city." For far too many suburban Americans, the inner city is just a place to pass through on the way to work. Without question there is a need for suburban Americans to be reminded that they are, in fact, a part of the inner city and have a responsibility to help develop a strategy to reach the hostile in the central city. Yes, the whole evangelical church should be concerned for the metro areas and send the best missionaries the church can produce. Yet, according to Peter Stam, U.S. director of Africa Inland Mission's urban ministry, it is harder to recruit workers for the inner cities than for the interior of Africa and equally difficult to raise support for them.[37]

It would be helpful for evangelical periodicals to regularly address the needs of those in the city so that the Christian community at large can become aware of the suffering there. It is also necessary that the evangelical church develop a plan whereby urban Americans will be included in their evangelistic agenda. David Hesselgrave declares, "Any community of people without an accessible church—whether they reside in North America or South Africa—is a mission field."[38]

Finally, many have searched for the true meaning of the city and have concluded with Jacques Ellul that the city is the supreme work of man and as such represents man's ultimate rejection of God.[39] Let

---

37. *Pulse* (EMIS), October 17, 1984, p. 8.
38. David J. Hesselgrave, *Planting Churches Cross-Culturally* (Grand Rapids: Baker, 1980), p. 39.
39. Jacques Ellul, *The Meaning of the City* (Grand Rapids: Eerdmans, 1970), p. 154.

us have no traffic with the prophets of doom but rather evangelize the city as commanded by God.

MISSION BOARDS SERVING URBAN AREAS

Also listed are locations and mission emphases.

1. Africa Inland Mission (Newark, New Jersey: urban church planting among blacks)
2. American Missionary Fellowship (urban church planting)
3. Baptist Mid-Missions (urban church planting)
4. Children's Bible Fellowship (New York City: handicapped, camp, beach evangelism, inner city)
5. Children's Mission (Bible clubs, camps for urban children, see Prison Ministries)
6. Christians United Reaching Everyone (Cincinnati: urban youth)
7. Harlem Evangelistic Association (blacks)
8. Inner City Impact (Chicago: Humboldt Park, church planting; Puerto Rican, youth ministry)
9. Jews (see chapter 9)
10. Navigators (city community ministry)
11. Open Air Campaigner (urban evangelization)
12. Pocket Testament League (sound trucks in urban area)
13. St. Paul's House (New York City; telephone ministry)
14. Teen Challenge (New York City; addicts, camp)
15. Teen Haven of Christian Youth Services, Inc. (Philadelphia, Buffalo, Washington, D.C., Lancaster, Pa.)
16. Teens, Inc. (South Bend, Ind.; inner city youth, Camp Ray Bird)
17. United Missionary Fellowship (New York: urban church planting)
18. Whispering Hills Mission (Rochester, New York: inner city)
19. Word of Life Camp and Club (youth)
20. Young Life (urban youth)

Figure 15.4

SCHOOLS OFFERING SPECIAL STUDIES FOR URBAN MINISTRIES

1. Center for Urban Theological Studies (CUTS) Cooperative program:
   a. Westminster Seminary, Chestnut Hill, PA 19119
   b. Geneva College
2. Seminary Consortium for Urban Pastoral Education (SCUP)

Annual Congress on Urban Ministry, 30 W. Chicago Avenue, Chicago, IL 60610

3. Summer Institute for Urban Missions (SIUM) Simpson College, 801 Silver Avenue, San Francisco, CA 94134

Figure 15.5

16

Alaska

Alaska is a mission field because 90 percent of her 400,000 citizens are not born again nor could they hear the gospel from the existent small, struggling churches.[1] Once a foreign mission field, Alaska attained statehood in 1959, which made the evangelization of its natives and immigrants a priority of home missions. Alaska's location, geography, climate, and people influence missionary service far more than any other home mission field.

LOCATION

Located 500 miles northwest of the state of Oregon, America's "last frontier," which is the forty-ninth state's nickname, is accessible by air, sea, or a marathon 1,671-mile drive over the Alaska Highway, crossing Canada's British Columbia and the Yukon Territory. The terminus of the highway is Fairbanks, located in the central part of the state. As Alaska's second-largest city, boasting 34,000 people, it is only 100 miles from the Arctic Circle. In the mountain range to the south is the highest point in the United States—Mt. McKinley (20,320 feet). Because Alaska is remote it presents frontierlike conditions for missionary service.

Alaska's western neighbor, Russia, located only fifty-seven miles

---

1. John Gillespie, "The Forty-Ninth State," in *The Fields at Home*, ed. Peter Gunther (Chicago: Moody, 1963), p. 174.

away across the Bering Strait, discovered this land in 1741. It was from the U.S.S.R. that Secretary of State William Seward had the foresight to purchase in 1867 what was to become the country's largest oil producer. Not everyone was favorably impressed with this frigid and sparsely populated land, even at the bargain price of two cents per acre and a total cost of 7.2 million dollars. The disenchanted called it "Seward's Icebox." Even the Russians were happy to divest themselves of this barren land.

The United States military considers Alaska a strategic location for defense. During World War II nearly 40 percent of the populace was in the military services, but now only 33,000 military personnel are stationed there.

Some of the peoples are Slavic in origin, having migrated from eastern Russia and intermarried. The Russian Orthodox church became the national church and continues to be the largest religious body, with eighty-three churches and 10,000 members representing half the Christian community.[2] Religion, for the majority, is but a facade with very little meaning.

GEOGRAPHY

The geography of Alaska shapes the lives of the people and isolates them from one another. Through the years the natives have learned to cope with the conditions, but outsiders find the adaptation process extremely demanding. The land is massive, equaling one-fifth the land mass of the contiguous states. It stretches 1,200 miles north and south and 2,200 miles east and west. It is twice the size of Texas but ranks fiftieth in population; whereas Texas has fifty-three persons per square mile, Alaska has less than one person. Thirty-six percent of the populace is scattered in 200 isolated villages, often forty to sixty miles apart. Fishing villages found along the rugged coastline, which stretches for nearly as many miles as that of the lower forty-eight states, are connected with an often undependable ferry system. Remote mountain villages may be connected with ski trails or those trails left by snowmobiles. The many villages scattered along the Yukon and other rivers are accessible depending on the season, by boat, bush pilot, or snowmobile, for there are only 10,000 miles of roads, mostly connecting the five mainland cities— Anchorage, Fairbanks, Juneau, Sitka, and Ketchikan.

2. R. Pierce Beaver, ed., *The Native American Christian Community: A Directory of Indian, Aluet, and Eskimo Churches* (Monrovia, Calif.: MARC, 1979), p. 374.

The land may be divided into seven areas that stretch like bands laterally across the state. Each area is nearly isolated from the others geographically; therefore, the people and their life-styles vary widely. Even missions are often limited to working in certain areas. The southernmost band divides into two areas resembling the opposing sides of a handle bar mustache. To the east and following down the coast is the panhandle. This area includes Juneau (the capital), Sitka, and Ketchikan. It is home for 6,000 maritime Indians, the Tlingits, Haida, and Tsimshians. Gospel Missionary Union has planted three churches among the Indians and has developed several ministries among the 50,000 who inhabit the panhandle. (See Figure 16.1.) The panhandle is attached on the north end by means of the coastal range bordering the Gulf of Alaska.

A *National Geographic* writer describes the gulf as

> a wilderness on the edge of a wilderness, remote by water, remote by land, rimmed by ice fields, glaciers, and the second highest coastal mountains in the world. The people live in a few small towns and a scattering of cabins. . . . Like the rest of Alaska, the gulf is a harsh place to live . . . attracting young people who are disposed toward an absence of society.[3]

Nearly half of Alaska's population is to be found in Anchorage, the largest city, and in Valdez, the terminus of the 800-mile pipeline from the north slope. Ironically, the pipeline cost 1,000 times the original purchase price of the whole state. Baptist Mid-Missions, headquartered here, has established the Anchorage Baptist Bible Institute and also plants churches in the "bush." Solid Rock Ministries has a camp at Soldotna.

Area two is west of Anchorage and includes the peninsula and seventy Aleutian islands. It is home for 7,000 Aleuts among whom sixteen Slavic Gospel Association workers have been working since 1940. They have planted six churches.

Moving inland, area three encompasses the Alaska Basin, bordered on the north by the Alaska Range, which constitutes area four. Send International (formerly Central Alaska Mission), is headquartered in Glenallen and began work in 1936 in the basin. The mission maintains Alaska Bible College, a medical work, a radio station, KCAM, which blankets the area with the Good News, and does church planting.

3. Boyd Gibbons, "Risk and Reward on Alaska's Violent Gulf," *National Geographic,* February 1979, p. 237.

THE NATIVE AREAS OF ALASKA

Figure 16.1

The heartland of Alaska, area five, is dissected by several rivers that are dominated by the 2,000-mile Yukon River. The Athabascan Indians have built scattered, isolated villages along the rivers. The largest faith mission, Arctic Missions, has been evangelizing this area since 1951 and has 165 missionaries who work with six churches, the Arctic Bible Institute, a junior high school, a camp, a bookstore, and church planting ministries.

The last two areas are within the Arctic Circle. Area six includes the Brooks Range, which is essentially uninhabited except for scattered villages found in the mountain passes. Finally, the Arctic plains of the far north polar region are home for the Eskimos. They also live along the western coast. More than a third of North America's 60,000 Eskimos live in Alaska.[4] The term *Eskimo* means "eater of raw meat," reflecting the primitive conditions under which they may live. Most Alaskan Eskimos (22,000) live in settled villages, but those living in Greenland (23,000) and Siberia (12,000) may be nomadic. Pierce Beaver indicates that the Christian community numbers 20,000 Eskimos attending 138 churches. Over half of those belong to the Catholic church and 2,600 are Moravian; another 1,500 are Episcopalian, and 1,300 are United Presbyterian. Faith missions are represented by Send International, which has planted three churches attended by 118 members.

CLIMATE

The climate of Alaska varies from the temperate panhandle to the subzero (-80 degrees F.) temperatures of the high elevations, especially the northern end of the state lying above the Arctic Circle. At times the wind chill factor can reach 100 degrees (F.) below zero. The Eskimos have been especially endowed with a thick layer of flesh on the face and a short stubby body to cope with these temperatures, but they still have to be cautious.[5]

The long, hard winters are the most difficult for the missionaries in the bush. Most everyone heats with wood, because heating oil is expensive. Much time is required to prepare the substantial number of cords of wood needed for those months. It may be necessary to travel several miles to find dry wood. Before the freeze, the wood can be floated down the river, but later a dog sled or snowmobile will be used.

4. *Worldbook Encyclopedia,* 1970 ed., s.v. "Eskimo."
5. Ibid.

Another problem is maintaining a balanced diet. Game meats are available and some dry staples that have been flown in from the village store may be purchased. But fruits and vegetables are scarce.

Most areas of Alaska have a summer season during June, July, and August, when the average temperature ranges from 68 degrees to 76 degrees.

The coastal regions are plagued with dense fog, substantial rain, and calving glaciers. Violent storms are common fare. Such climactic conditions can be very depressing, but the fishermen hazard them because of the great wealth involved in the fishing industry.[6]

The missionary who contemplates working in Alaska will need to consider the special demands the climate can impose. Alaskan service may require strenuous physical labor, periods of isolation, and few supplies and conveniences. Bush ministry is for one who likes the life of an outdoorsman and is willing to work in a rural village of 100-300 people.

PEOPLE

The native population of Alaska, numbering 64,000 (16 percent of the state population) overwhelmingly lives in bush country, for only 8 percent are urban.[7] The natives are divided among three groups. The Eskimos number 28,800, the Indians number 28,200, and the Aleuts are 7,000. The Indians may be further subdivided into four groups: the Athabascans, 21,000; Tlingits, 4,500; Tsimshians, 850; and the Haida, 600.[8] The Aleuts are related to the Eskimos, but neither are Indian.

Urban Alaskans make up 64 percent of the populace. They earn 23 percent more than the average American, which reflects the higher cost of living. Oil revenues fill state coffers sufficiently so that in 1980 the state income tax was removed. During the decade of the 1970s the urban population grew by 34 percent. The construction industry is ever busy; however, the government is the largest employer. Tourism (100,000 annually), fishing, and manufacturing offer many jobs. Urban church planting needs to receive a higher priority by the faith missions. John Gillespie of Arctic Missions notes that faith missions work primarily with native people in the villages.[9]

6. Gibbons, p. 237.
7. Beaver, p. 373.
8. D'Arcy McNickle, *The Indian Tribes of the United States* (New York: Oxford U., 1970), p. 76.
9. Gillespie, p. 169.

MISSIONS ACTIVITY

Within fifty years of the discovery of Alaska, the Orthodox church began to evangelize the natives in 1792.[10] The Lutheran church sent missionaries in 1840, before Alaska was purchased. Six other denominations became active before the Gold Rush in 1898, when the population nearly doubled.[11]

Recognizing the overwhelming expanse of the state, the denominations entered into a comity of missions whereby they sought to avoid duplication of ministry. By this means each group worked in a different region that became known as the ministry of a particular church. Those entering to work in a particular area now must recognize this heritage.

Conditions in bush Alaska are rapidly changing. Today most of the larger villages have public elementary and secondary schools, provided by either the Bureau of Indian Affairs or Iditarod, the state-run system. This eliminates the problem natives face with sending their children to the city to attend high school. It also lessens the need for mission high schools and provides opportunity for national Christians to teach in the public school system.[12]

Transportation remains a major problem for bush missionaries. Roads are either nonexistent or very poor. River travel, which includes the cost of the boat, motor, and fuel, is expensive. Dog sleds and the huskies are very popular and are often entered in the state's annual dog sled race. The modern snowmobile, although expensive, is very popular. Most villages have airstrips, but bush pilots are not always reliable; therefore, Missionary Aviation Fellowship is a great help to missionaries.

A great need exists to train national pastors. Three of the five church-planting faith missions working in Alaska have established Bible schools for the training of the natives and whites. (See Figure 16.2.) Two of those began in the late 1960s. A survey in 1978 reveals that there are still only thirty-nine native pastors serving in 309 churches. The survey further indicates that the average age of those men is 63. The conclusion reached from this report was that "missions in Alaska have not been successful in producing native Christian leaders."[13]

10. Beaver, p. 32.
11. Ibid., p. 166.
12. Peter Deyneka, *Village Ministries* (Wheaton, Ill.: Slavic Gospel Association, 1980), p. 11.
13. *Interlit*, March 1978, p. 9.

Alcoholism is widespread in the Indian communities. No final explanation has been give to indicate why this is so. Perhaps joblessness, isolation, boredom, competition and a host of other reasons contribute. But without question, the only answer to the problem is the power to conquer through a vital relationship with Jesus Christ. Pierce Beaver indicates that only two counseling ministries exist in Alaska. The Salvation Army offers help in Anchorage and a Roman Catholic ministry exists in Fairbanks.[14]

Although improving, medical service in the bush is minimal. Resident doctors are at a minimum; therefore airlift to the nearest hospital makes the bush pilot a vital link in health care. Life expectancy is well below the national average with a heavy toll exacted by fighting, accident, flu and pneumonia, and a suicide rate ten times the national average. Many children are orphaned; therefore, the American Baptists established a children's home in Kodiak. The residents are 81 percent native.[15]

Communication media in Alaska have mushroomed with the advent of fourteen newspapers, twenty-two radio stations and sixteen television stations. Two of the radio stations are Christian broadcasters.

Nine denominational missions are presently working in Alaska[16] as well as five church-planting faith missions supported by five service organizations. Wycliffe Bible Translators is finishing up its work and will be closing out its Alaska field. The New Testament is available in Eskimo/Inupiaq from the American Bible Society. Although there are twenty living languages in Alaska, only the older natives use them; English is the medium of instruction in the schools. A mission brochure summarizes: "The old Indians speak only their native tongue. Middle-aged Indians are bilingual. The young people speak only English."[17]

Within the native community of 64,000 are 43,000 (71 percent) nominal Christians. The largest group is Orthodox (36 percent). The other two groups are Protestant (18 percent) and Catholic (17 percent). (See Figure 16.3.)

Presently there are over 374 faith missionaries working under eight boards. Thirty-nine churches serve a membership of under 1,000.

---

14. Beaver, p. 326.
15. Ibid., p. 333.
16. Ibid., p. 374.
17. *Southeastern Alaska* (Smithville, Mo.: Gospel Missionary Union, n.d.), n.p.

Send International reports that they have started a new ministry among the fastest growing minority group in Alaska—the Japanese, who remain isolated from the gospel.[18]

MISSION BOARDS SERVING ALASKA

Board	Missionaries	Churches
1. Artic Mission (1951)	165	11
Artic Bible Institute, Palmer		
2. Baptist Mid-Missions (1949)	49	14
Anchorage Baptist Bible Institute, Anchorage		
3. Gospel Missionary Union (1951)	28	5
Juneau		
4. Send International (1936)	101	3
Alaska Bible College, Glenallen		
5. Solid Rock Ministries, Inc.	11	unavailable
Soldotna		
6. Slavic Gospel Association (1939)	16	6
Anchorage		
7. Missionary Aviation Fellowship	2	unavailable
8. Wycliffe Bible Translators	2	unavailable
Total	374	39

Figure 16.2

CHURCH COMMUNIONS IN ALASKA

	Churches	Members	Community	Percentage
1. Orthodox	83	20,000	22,000	36
2. Protestant	120	10,000	11,000	18
3. Catholic	30	10,000	10,500	17
Totals	233	40,000	43,500	71

Figure 16.3

18. *Bridges to Help Alaskans* (Farmington, Mich.: Far Eastern Gospel Crusade, 1980), p. 8.

17

Hawaii

HAWAII AS A MISSION FIELD

Although the mention of Hawaii engenders for the tourist visions of sunshine, swimming, and relaxation in Eden-like conditions, there is another side of life for those who live on the islands. Continual reminders of man's depravity, of sickness, death, and destruction abound. Diamond Head, Hawaii's most famous landmark, now a review field, was once a volcano. Near the international airport is a military hospital, where terminally ill war victims live out their lives in broken bodies or minds.

Punch Bowl Crater is now a national cemetery. At Pearl Harbor stands the Arizona Memorial with its gun turrets jutting through the surface, reminding one of December 7, 1941, when Japanese planes attacked. But most Hawaiians, like the tourists, seek to forget about death and God. They have been very successful in doing so, for 70 percent of the people of Hawaii are unchurched. This is one of the highest percentages in the nation and far above the national average of 40 percent.[1] A 1973 survey revealed that the evangelical community numbered 14,000. By 1980 the number of Christians had grown to 20,000, but that is still only 2 percent of the state's population.

Among Hawaii's unchurched groups are the tourists, who are not reflected in the above statistics. For every citizen there are four

1. J. Russell Hale, *The Unchurched* (San Francisco: Harper and Row, 1980), p. 40.

tourists. Another large group is the military, who, along with their families and support personnel represent 14 percent of the populace. Yet another group is the 28,000 Waikiki employees, or "night people," whose work schedules preclude their attending church. Hawaii is a mission field, and it presents many unique problems for evangelization.

HISTORY

Although many mainlanders dream of vacationing in this Polynesian paradise of near-uniform seventy-five-degree temperature, their knowledge of the islands is limited to what the television camera has portrayed, which includes little more than surfing, sunbathing on Waikiki Beach, pineapples, feasting at luaus, the beautiful leis draped on travelers, the Hula dancers moving gracefully to the music of ukulele or Hawaiian steel guitar, and colorful muumuus (dresses) and aloha shirts.

Americans are only vaguely aware that many races live on the seven inhabited southeastern islands, which are only part of the Hawaiian archipelago of 122 islands scattered over 1,600 miles of the central Pacific Ocean. In 1778 Captain Cook first discovered these volcanic and coral projections, which at that time were peopled only by Polynesians. He named the home of these warring peoples the Sandwich Islands. (See Figure 17.1.)

By the turn of the century King Kamehameha had united the islands and initiated religious, political, cultural, and economic reforms. The economy depended mostly on exporting sandalwood and supplying the whaling ships that docked. But with the introduction of sugar cane (1835) and pineapple (1885), the economic base shifted. Plantation labor was provided by importing Chinese in the 1850s, other Polynesians, Japanese, and Portuguese in 1868, and Filipinos, Koreans, and Puerto Ricans in the 1900s.

At that time, when its military significance was recognized, Hawaii became a territory of the United States. Military bases were built for the various services and 60,000 personnel were stationed in the islands. Hawaii became a staging point for Pacific maneuvers and campaigns. During the Vietnam War it became a popular area for rest and relaxation for our combat troops. The tourist industry was also developed, and now nearly 4 million guests arrive annually.

Eighty percent of the residents live on Oahu Island, creating a density of 100 per square mile. Most live in the capital city of Honolulu. The second largest city is Hilo, the capital of the island of

Hawaii. In addition to those two cities, only seven others have a population of over 5,000. Three-fourths of the population of Hawaii is urban.

The Korean conflict in the 1950s proved the strategic importance of Hawaii's location as the hub of the Pacific. It is only five hours from California, seven hours from Japan and eleven hours from Australia. Following the war, Hawaii's economy exploded. In 1959 Hawaii was admitted as the fiftieth state. Each of the five larger islands became one of the state's five counties.

Further exposure came during the Vietnam era beginning in 1965. Thousands of soldiers and their families visited the islands. As the word spread, tourism became the number one source of basic income.

RELIGIOUS HISTORY

Originally the islanders were warring tribes without education and written language. They worshipped idols and practiced human sacrifice. King Kamehameha I subdued the tribes and outlawed the sacrifices. In 1820 missionaries came, and within 25 years 85 percent of the natives were evangelized. Churches were established, and missionaries began looking for other islands to evangelize.

Unfortunately, that success was not followed up with adequate training of national leadership. Sereno Edwards Bishop observed that "one of the errors of that generation of missionaries was the slowness in training competent native leadership to replace themselves."[2] Another weakness was that little was done to reach the ethnics who flooded into the islands. A 1973 study conducted by the Southern Baptists observed the lack of racially integrated churches and the shortage of "island-born" leadership.[3] Denominational churches seem to polarize around one racial group. They primarily attract haoles (Caucasians) and a few professional locals. There are now over 400 Protestant churches servicing 1 million residents, but according to Chester Dyer, a local Child Evangelism Fellowship director, there seems to be little evangelical fervor.[4] Perhaps 30 percent of the populace are evangelicals.

Hawaii does not lack religion. There are over 100 cultic churches including the Jehovah's Witnesses and the Mormon church, which

---

2. International Congress on World Evangelization, Status of Christianity Country Profile (Monrovia, Calif.: Mission Advanced Research Center, 1974), p. 2.
3. Ibid., p. 2.
4. Chester Dyer, Child Evangelism Fellowship of Hawaii, personal letter.

have established the Honolulu Stake, the Church College, and the Polynesian Cultural Center. Catholic churches number 70. Another 185 churches have been established by non-Christian faiths, including 100 Buddhist churches, the largest group in Honolulu. Confucianist and Taoist churches also exist.

MISSIONARY ACTIVITY

Modern missionary activity started in the decade Hawaii attained statehood, a century after the islands were first evangelized. Nearly a dozen agencies are involved in church planting.[5] Several Christian bookstores service the Christian community. Most campus ministries are represented on the several college campuses. There is one Christian radio station, KAIM. Two Christian colleges and one Bible institute concentrating on lay leadership training have been established, but there is no seminary.

Twenty pastors are listed in the Independent Fundamental Christian Fellowship roster. Several of those men are missionary pastors. Eleven men pastor churches that are self-supporting, and other churches are developing independent status.

Waikiki Beach is the challenging mission field of the Waikiki Beach Chaplaincy. Sixty-seven thousand people deplane daily in Honolulu, and most head for the beach. (See Figure 17.2.) Almost 100,000 people pass through Hawaii each day. Innovative programs are a must in seeking to evangelize even a few of those people.

Ethnic evangelism needs to be given a higher priority by missionary pastors and the evangelical churches. Although most evangelical churches are cosmopolitan in character, they still do not reflect the ethnicity of the population. As far as can be determined, nothing is being done to win the 7,000 national Hawaiian stock.

Although the majority of Hawaii's population lives on Oahu, four other islands are inhabited with people who have spiritual needs. Kaui, called the Garden Isle, has a population of 35,000. There is only one independent church, which is pastored by a local pastor. Molokai, the Friendly Isle, maintains 6,400 residents. That number includes the Hansen's Disease settlement. The Pacific Area Mission works on the island.

Maui, the Valley Isle, has 53,000 inhabitants. Pacific Area Mission is the only mission working with those people. Hawaii, the Big Island, and once the capital of the islands, now has 81,000

5. Celeste Pennington, "Waikiki," *Mission USA*, May/June 1981, p. 34.

people. It is famous for Hawaii Volcancoes National Park, which boasts two active volcanoes that periodically show off in a mild-mannered spilling of magma and fireworks. Baptist Mid-Missions has two works on this island. Missionary Dyer concludes that Hawaii is definitely a mission field today. There are only a few small groups who are truly evangelistic and evangelical in theology.[6]

UNIQUE PROBLEMS FOR MISSIONARY SERVICE

Several basic problems face the mainland missionary who would work in the Hawaiian Islands, especially on Oahu, "one of the most complex and difficult home mission fields."[7]

1. Although Hawaii is the fiftieth state, the culture of the people is clearly Asian (74 percent) and cosmopolitan. Everyone is a member of an ethnic minority in this interracial society. English is the primary language, but ancestral languages are heard. Attitudes about life in general and religion in particular are molded by Eastern beliefs. Church attendance is traditionally oriented to special occasions and not to weekly experience. Churches are often used for public functions of a nonreligious nature. The typical Hawaiian atmosphere seldom includes any thought of God or spiritual matters.

2. Even the beautiful weather can be a problem, especially to those who are accustomed to changing seasons. It can have a stultifying effect, which slowly lulls the unwary into a state of lethargy.

3. The tourist trade can have a demoralizing effect. Too much money (tourists spent 3.2 billion dollars in 1981 providing 30 percent of the economy), and the adherence to few morals are dehumanizing and degrading. For many tourists it is the great escape—a good time with no restraints. Although tolerated because each tourist spends about $200 per day, the tourist may be despised for ignoring mores considered important to the island peoples. The older locals are very unhappy about their youth imitating the tourists. The missionary finds his schedule interrupted by visitors who may wish to sightsee.

4. The military (accounting for 20 percent of the economy), although based there, are temporary residents and soon move on. It is easier to fill the church with these people, but they do not make it easier to reach those who are permanent residents.

6. Dyer, personal letter.
7. *World Survey* (New York: Interchurch, 1920), p. 133, n.a.

Life without spouse or family members can be lonely, boring, and demoralizing. Those who come for rest and relaxation sometimes leave behind a trail of attitudes and actions that linger a long time. Perhaps without realizing it, guests have left a feeling of distrust toward the Japanese locals who are a quarter of the populace. There is no spiritual ministry targeting the military.

In a similar vein, there is reaction to the extensive involvement of the U.S. government in local affairs. It is suggested that the government owns at least half the real estate. A high percentage of the populace works for the government. Pearl Harbor alone employs 10,000. After tourism and construction, the government is the third largest employer.

5. The cost of living is the highest in the nation except for Alaska. Hawaii is one of the most prosperous states with the highest per capita income. A single family home costs $118,000 compared with $85,000 in California. A problem to be faced is the departure of the pineapple industry to the Philippines in search of a cheaper labor market.

6. Interracial marriage between the local and the haole involves one in three families. It is generally accepted, but has led to tragic misunderstandings and failures. Such feelings are hard to overcome and sometimes lead to deep and bitter reactions. The missionary as a haole may become a target for the projection of those feelings.

7. The older generation obviously reacts to their youth rejecting the old customs and adopting new ways. The missionary is seen as a purveyor of new ideas and therefore suspect.

8. Although Hawaii is in many ways much like the Garden of Eden, not many older missionaries of many years of service are to be found there. This field has been likened to a graveyard for missionaries. Perhaps it would be in order to encourage mainlanders to realize that Hawaii is a needy, cross-cultural mission field and not just a playground. Successful service requires in-depth preparation, deep respect for local feelings and customs, and total commitment. William Hopper, pastor of the Honolulu Bible Church, confesses that having served on three mission fields, "Hawaii is the most difficult in terms of reaching people for Christ and getting decisions."[8]

9. Asian religions predominate, primarily Buddhism. However,

8. William Hopper, personal letter.

Catholicism and Mormonism are strong. Judaism is also practiced and some ancient Hawaiian heiaus (places of religious exercise) exist.

10. Finally, more emphasis must be placed on training locals for local ministries and on encouraging those whose permanent home is in the Islands to prepare to serve God in local ministries. The local church and the Christian community will need to respect and honor the leadership of local men. Hawaii is a mission field with unique problems and opportunities. The playboy mentality pervades life, including most of what parades as religion. Innovative ideas and zealous workers are needed to make Christ real in Hawaii for the second time. As a result of having been evangelized earlier, the state motto declares, "Ua mau ke ea o ka aina i ka pono," which means, "The life of the land is perpetuated in righteousness." May what was written in 1843 be made true again in the 1980s.

MISSION BOARDS SERVING HAWAII

1. Baptist Bible Fellowship (Oahu)
2. Baptist International Missions, Inc. (Oahu)
3. Baptist Mid-Missions (Hawaii)
4. Berean Mission (Oahu)
5. Child Evangelism Fellowship (Oahu)
6. Conservative Baptist Home Mission Fellowship (Oahu)
7. Independent Baptists (Oahu)
8. Pacific Area Mission (Oahu and Molokai)
9. United Missionary Fellowship (Oahu)
10. Waikiki Beach Chaplaincy (Oahu)

Figure 17.2

18

Mobile Americans

There are groups of people in the United States whose jobs keep them moving about the country. Their life-styles remove them from home, friends, community, and church. If those people are to be exposed to the gospel, it will probably be in their "ports of call," those places where they stop periodically. Seamen and truckers are two groups whose jobs keep them constantly on the move. Migrants are another group; however, their work is seasonal, for they move north with the maturing of the crops. Most migrants are Hispanic; therefore they are treated in chapter 5. Lumberjacks also move about the lumber camps. They are mostly French-speaking.

Americans love to travel. Opportunities for Christian ministry arise in times of emergency, despair, and loneliness. Even vacation centers become mission fields. Some missionaries have targeted those who gather at America's race tracks as a group in need of evangelization. There are groups in America whose unconventional life-styles make them unchurched. The gypsies are such a mobile group.

JOB-RELATED MOBILITY

SEAMEN

Four hundred fifty thousand seamen ply the seas of the world.

The United States is a regular port of call for many. Most merchant seamen have never heard the Good News and few know Christ as Savior. Time spent by these seamen on shore leave becomes an opportunity for alert Christians to engage seamen in conversation about spiritual matters.

There are over 100 ports in the United States. Ports like Baltimore, Houston, and San Francisco service between 4,000 and 5,000 ships annually. Crew members come from many different countries and speak a variety of languages.

Many are fluent in English; others are not. Another factor is that many have nothing to do.

Max Ward, field representative of the Seamen's International Christian Association (SICA),[1] says that merchant seamen are "some of the most neglected people in the world." (See Figure 18.1.) They need the gospel presented to them in a way that is meaningful. Home missionaries working with SICA are surely doing "foreign" mission work as they hand out tracts and Scripture portions in numerous languages.

SICA was founded in 1935 after pastor Tom Wright was challenged by a ferry boat captain with the searching question "Tell me, pastor, why is it all of the taverns and honkeytonks are interested in my men, and none of you fellows are?"[2] The mission he founded maintains workers in selected ports around the country and plans to staff every port as personnel are available.

TRUCKERS

Twenty million truckers maintain a vital lifeline of the country. The life of the trucker consists of living out of a suitcase, sleeping in motels, eating and refueling at truck stops, and ultimately arriving at a terminal. By law he can drive only so many hours and then must lay over. Such a life-style lends itself to drugs and alcohol, gambling, prostitutes, domestic problems, and a very high divorce rate, for he may be home only one day in six. There is little opportunity for these men to be reached by the ministry of the local church. In fact, the truck may become the driver's god, according to one trucker's chaplain.

In 1951 Transport for Christ (TFC) was established to minister to

1. Max Ward, "Some of the Most Neglected People in the World," *Interlit*, March 1981, p. 17.
2. Ward, "Neglected People," p. 17.

the specialized spiritual, emotional, and social needs peculiar to men in the trucking industry. Six mobile units ply the highways following a prescribed schedule for ministry that takes place primarily in truck terminals. TFC has combined a spiritual message with lectures on safety; thus, providing a multiple service for the trucking industry. Latimer Brooker, director of TFC, says that promoting safety through Christ is more than a motto; it is a ministry built on Proverbs 21:31: "Safety is of the Lord."

The ministry takes place appropriately in mobile chapels that are refurbished eighteen-wheelers. By means of pulpit and video screen the message is proclaimed to "people who live and work in a world seldom touched by routine church programs."[3]

Along the highways the mobile chapel also calls at truck stops, such as Jerry Brown's Truck Stop, northeast of Oklahoma City on Interstate 40. In such locations weary truckers can find a chaplain who knows the peculiar language of the trucking world and understands his special needs. Truckers are unique and often plagued with times of loneliness and depression.

TFC publishes for truckers a newspaper called the *Highway Evangelist,* which has a monthly circulation of 80,000. It also publishes tracts and annually distribute 20,000 Bibles, which have been given the title "Road Map of Life." The mission has divided the country into five regions and sponsors an annual gathering of Christian truckers. The ministry is now international.

In 1977 Jim Keys founded the Association of Christian Truckers as a charismatic counterpart of TFC. They claim dozens of chapters spread across the country. They sponsor truckers' jamborees and publish a newspaper called *Wheels Alive.* Their mobile chapel is likened to an electronic church.

Dan Robinson, a converted truck driver and mechanic, along with his wife, Shirley, travel the highways in their mobile home looking for truckers whose rigs have broken down. He carries his own tools, and while making free repairs, shares his testimony. The Robinsons are founders of Over the Road Evangelism, which now has two mobile units traveling the nation's highways and ministering to men of the trucking industry.

Truckin' for Jesus is another mission ministering to the world of eighteen-wheelers. The Citizen's Band Radio (CB) can be an opportunity to visit with a lonely trucker and tell the Good News. Other

3. David Wilkinson, "A World on 18 Wheels," *Missions USA,* March-April 1981, p. 72.

opportunities abound in the terminal, not only with the truckers but also with dockmen and terminal managers.

TRAVELERS

Millions of Americans travel each year on business and for pleasure. A growing number travel by air. In the course of a day, myriads of persons pass through air terminals. For some there are long layovers that can be tiring, frustrating, boring, and nerve wracking. Both young and old can find a large airport a frightening experience. In some instances the travel has been occasioned by a tragedy or some other traumatic experience. Sea-Tac Ministries was instituted in the Seattle-Tacoma International Airport in Seattle, Washington, to be of service to those who pass through the airport each day. Airport Chaplains is one of the divisions of Sea-Tac Ministries. The chaplains and volunteers minister to the spiritual needs of the travelers. This ministry should be expanded to include all major airports.

Numerous airline personnel work in the terminal serving the public. They, too, have spiritual needs. Four air terminals (Chicago's O'Hare, Greater Pittsburgh, Kennedy, Atlanta) have official chaplains, but they are of a cooperative nature, serving several religious groups. The Fellowship of Christian Airline Personnel is a group of believers in the airlines who want to give a positive witness on their job and to fellowship around the person of the Lord Jesus Christ. The ministry includes placing Christian books in conspicuous places for the personnel to borrow. An annual convention is held to encourage fellowship in the national ministry. A group of 200 has formed a prayer fellowship to pray for an effective testimony for Christ on the airlines.

For those who travel by taxi, Claude Frazier has established a ministry called Bible Taxi Ministry. It consists of placing Bible portions in taxi cabs for customers to read and take with them. The American Bible Society has prepared special Bible portions to be used. Unique aprons are prepared with three pockets to hold the portions. The aprons are tied to the driver's seat for display of the portions. Local churches are able to receive complete details for beginning this innovative and inexpensive ministry by writing to Bobby Sunderland, director of Mass Evangelism Department, of the Home Mission Board of the Southern Baptist Convention (SBC).

Although railroads are not as extensive as they once were, many people still travel by rail. The Railroad Evangelistic Association places Christian literature in depots and on the trains as permitted.

In the process of traveling, it is necessary at times to include an overnight in a motel or hotel. The Gideons place Bibles in these public residences. Another ministry to the residents of motels and hotels is that of a volunteer chaplain. Carl Hirt, director of the Chaplaincy Division of the Home Mission Board of the SBC, claims that "most motel managers recognize the minister's invaluable role and welcome his assistance."[4] Only a few major motel chains actively enlist clergymen as motel chaplains, but most of them will respond favorably when the idea is suggested. The ministry could include the personnel of the motel and their families.

VACATIONERS

Americans love to take vacations. Tourism is a multimillion-dollar industry. Seldom do those who are traveling on Sunday take time to find a church in which to worship. That is especially true of those on vacation. At least three organizations are concerned for the spiritual well-being of vacationing Americans. Drive-In Ministries of St. Petersburg, Florida, seeks to reach this vast segment of society through film evangelism. Two permanent facilities incorporate fixed platforms and screens that feature live music programs and films. The traveler looking for something to do during an evening can very easily come under the sound of the gospel.

Drive-In Ministries also maintains a mobile drive-in tractor trailer rig with a portable stage and screen that sets up in resort areas for a period of four weeks at a time. Another mobile unit sets up at festivals, air shows, motorcycle races and the like for one to seven days. A yacht ministry visits marinas with a film and live program to reach people where they are. Each concept operates under the umbrella of a local church in the area. Drive-In currently operates in twenty-two Midwest and Eastern states, Canada, and Mexico. An individual professing Christ receives personal follow-up, including enrollment in a Bible correspondence course.

Projections for future concepts include additional mobile units to a new creation exhibit that will travel from one shopping center parking lot to another. The exhibit will include a simulator shuttle orbiter (customized from a DC-3 fuselage) giving a simulated flight

---

4. Carl Hirt, *Volunteer Chaplaincy* (Atlanta: Division of Home Mission Board, Southern Baptist Convention, n.d.), p. 3.

into space. After visitors enter the unit, sights and sounds will simulate lift-off with G-forces, state-of-the-art digital and electronic equipment creating an authentic atmosphere of flight. TV monitors showing NASA's shots of outer space will depict the beauty of creation as the astronaut asks the question, "Why did God send His Son to planet earth to die? There must be a reason!" The astronaut will then give a biblical and logical invitation to receive Christ as Savior. The audience will then leave the shuttle and enter a debriefing van, where counselors can answer their questions.

The national parks of our country are beautiful and available for ministry. A Christian Ministry in the National Parks was established in 1951 and now operates in sixty national parks in twenty-three states. It is a unique Christian outreach that extends the mission and ministry of the church to the millions of people who live, work, and vacation in our national parks. Camping is very popular among those who are the outdoors type. Campsite Evangelism is a witness to family campers in areas open to the public for recreational purposes. The ministry involves tract distribution, evangelistic services, and a ministry to children. The ministry began in 1968 and now includes twenty campsites. Husband and wife teams are usually assigned to campgrounds. Campsite Evangelism is a home mission working in the states of Pennsylvania, Delaware, Maryland, Virginia, West Virginia, and Florida. The ministry will be expanded as personnel are available.

OTHERS

RACE TRACK PERSONNEL

All kinds of professional racing takes place in America and Americans gather at race tracks to participate in various ways. Horace W. Roberts recognized the spiritual needs of those who gather at the nation's race tracks and founded the Race Track Chaplaincy of America. There are twenty chaplains listed in the RTCA *Good News Paper* published by the mission. Sam Spence, executive director, indicates that it is the desire of the mission to place personnel, as available, on every race track facility to lead souls to a saving knowledge of Jesus Christ.

GYPSIES

Gypsies are an ancient group of people who originated in India. They number perhaps from 10 to 40 million and speak over thirty languages. They love to move about and have spread all over the world. Their history is full of banishments, torturings, and killings. Hitler exterminated 600,000 Gypsies in gas chambers.

No one knows how many there are in the United States, but estimates range from 100,000 to 1,000,000. Probably they number about 500,000.[5] Gypsies are now an urban people who are found in all fifty states. Because of their unconventional life-style they are functionally illiterate and cannot read or write their own language, Romany. Most of the women are palm readers and supply the bulk of the family income. The men work some of the time at jobs where they can be absent at will. Gypsies refer to themselves as *Rom*.

In recent years many of the Rom have become sedentary, but they are still essentially an insecure people. Fifteen thousand have settled in Los Angeles and 10,000 in Chicago. The largest Gypsy concentrations are to be found in New York, Virginia, Illinois, Texas, Massachusetts, and the Pacific Coast. Gypsies are difficult to win to Christ because they believe that the non-Gypsy is polluted or unclean; therefore, anything touched by the non-Gypsy is dirty. Gypsies are also very family oriented and live in a closed society. The family gives a Gypsy whatever sense of security he may have and helps make every decision. He is almost never alone except with another Rom.

Gypsies love to deceive non-Gypsies. They maintain several nicknames they use freely to escape detection by anyone in authority. They seek to exist "beyond the pale of public morality."[6] Gypsies do not want to become a functioning part of American society. They will not assimilate. They will not give up their unique identity or renounce their culture.[7]

A few Gypsies have found Christ as Savior. When they do, they usually leave the Gypsy culture, thus removing any continuing witness. Gypsy Smith is perhaps the most famous of several dozen Gypsy evangelists in Great Britain. Many were influenced by the Salvation Army.

The only Christian ministry among Gypsies thus far discovered is that of the Assemblies of God. They claim to have reached several thousands with the gospel and report 1,000 full-gospel Gypsies in the nation. Theodore Gannon, national director of the Division of Home

5. William Kephart, *Extraordinary Groups* (New York: St. Martin's, 1982), p. 5.
6. Ibid.
7. Ibid.

Missions, indicates that most of the evangelism being done among Gypsies is being done by the Gypsies themselves.

MISSION BOARDS SERVING MOBILE AMERICANS

SEAMEN

Seamen's International Christian Association (a list of records, tapes, cassettes, video cassettes, radio programs are available in English and other languages from J. E. F. Dresselhuis, Harbor Chaplain, 7449 Kerr Street, Vancouver, B.C. V5S 3E3)

TRUCKERS

1. MMAP (Mobile Missionary Assistants Program) in the Western United States
2. Over the Road Evangelism
3. SOWERS (Servants on Wheels Ever Ready)
4. Transport for Christ
5. Truckin' for Jesus

TRAVELERS

1. Bible Taxi Ministry
2. Fellowship of Christian Airline Personnel
3. Railroad Evangelistic Association
4. Sea-Tac Ministries Airport Chaplains is a division
5. Volunteer Chaplains in Motels and Hotels

VACATIONERS

1. A Christian Ministry in the National Parks
2. Campsite Evangelism
3. Drive-In Ministries

OTHERS

1. Gypsies: Assemblies of God Department of Home Missions
2. Race Track Chaplaincy

Figure 18.1

Epilogue

The original thesis presented in the Preface was "There are people groups in the United States who are beyond the sound of the gospel." Perhaps a better case was made for some groups than others, but one thing is certain—there are far more who cannot hear than we had imagined.

No longer can we plead ignorance. The truth is that the evidence presented in this volume is only the tip of the iceberg. May the reader be challenged to examine the various segments of his own community to determine which groups are not being evangelized.

If your local groups are all being evangelized, then expand your research to the nearest urban area. You'll not need to look further, for there are numerous people groups in each American city who cannot hear because of language or other cultural barriers.

What can you the reader do to help? Discover a people group that needs to be evangelized. Reread the chapter (and any other information available) that addresses that group, then discuss the need with your pastor or congregation. You might contact the mission organizations (listed at the end of chapters) to learn how to reach that group and invite an organization to present a seminar in your church on how to witness to the people group you want to reach. Then order tracts or Bible correspondence courses for distribution especially prepared with that group in mind.

If perchance the group speaks another language, contact a mission to learn of missionaries your church could sponsor to reach that community. One of your own church family could be challenged to consider this group for missionary service. The church could send that one to Bible college for training and then support his ministry.

Another effective outreach is through radio or television programs prepared for a particular people group. Special prayer cells could be organized to focus attention on the group's needs.

Discover whether or not your local church has a philosophy of missions. If not, make sure it does not discriminate against those in your community or county who will not hear the gospel without missionary assistance. If you do not have a philosophy of missions policy, write to this author for a free sample and advice on establishing such a policy.

If your church has an annual missionary conference, include a mission that concentrates on a neglected people group in your area. Furthermore, give priority to those foreign organizations that also service emigres in this country from their fields overseas. It is shocking that as of this writing only 40 of 600 foreign missions have such a policy.

If your church has no annual missionary conference, again this author would be happy to encourage and guide you in establishing such a program that will enlarge your vision of the whitened harvest fields everywhere.

May we all see this world as God sees it and do something about it.

Appendix 1

CHRISTIAN ORGANIZATIONS CITED

American Missionary Fellowship, P.O. Box 368, Villanova, PA 19085
Americans for Middle East Understanding, Inc., Room 771, 475
    Riverside Drive, New York, NY 10115
Assemblies of God Home Missions, 1445 Boonville, Springfield, MO
    65802
Association for Former Christian Scientists, 1550 South Anaheim
    Blvd., Anaheim, CA 92805
Association for North American Missions, 4372 Casa Brazilia Drive,
    Suite 200, St. Louis, MO 63137
Association of Christian Ministries to Internationals, P.O. Box 1775,
    Colorado Springs, CO 80901
Boys Brigade and Pioneer Girls, P.O. Box 788, Wheaton, IL 60187
Center for World Missions, 1605 East Elizabeth Street, Pasadena, CA
    91104
Chinese World Mission Center, 1605 East Elizabeth Street, Pasadena,
    CA 91104
Christian Deaf Fellowship, P.O. Box 563, Hampton, VA 23369
Christian Servicemen's Centers, P.O. Box 10308, Denver, CO 80210
Covenant House, 460 West 41st Street, New York, NY 10036
David C. Cook Foundation, Cook Square, Elgin, IL 60120
Evangelical China Office, 2118 Garfies Drive, Pasadena, CA 91104
Evangelical Ministries, Inc., 1716 Spruce Street, Philadelphia, PA
    19103

Evangelical Mission Information Service, P.O. Box 794, Wheaton, IL 60187

Fellowship of American Chinese Evangelicals, 262 Riskell Drive, Oakland, CA 94619

Hillwood Ministries, P.O. Box K, Toccoa, GA 30577

Home Mission Association of Evangelicals, P.O. Box 28, Wheaton, IL 60187

Independent Fundamental Christian Fellowship, Bethel Bible Church, 106 Pekelo Place, Wahiawa, HI 96786

Institute of Chinese Studies (see U.S. Center for World Missions)

International Union of Gospel Missions, P.O. Box 10780, Kansas City, MO 64142

Iranian Christians International, P.O. Box 2415, Ann Arbor, MI 48106

Kroc Foundation, Operation Cork, 8939 Villa, LaJolla Drive, Department FW, San Diego, CA 92037

Lausanne Committee for World Evangelism, P.O. Box 1100, Wheaton, IL 60187

Logos International Fellowship, P.O. Box 191, Plainfield, NJ 07060

Mission Advanced Research Center, 919 Huntington Drive, Monrovia, CA 91016

National Association of Homes for Children, 1500 City National Center, Charlotte, NC 28202

National Conference on Ministry to the Armed Forces, 1441 North Henderson Road, Arlington, VA 22203

Navigator's Communications Department, P.O. Box 20, Colorado Springs, CO 80901

New Tribes Mission, Sanford, FL 32771

Positive Action for Christ, Inc, P.O. Box 2583, Rocky Mount, NC 27801

Scripture Gift Mission, 32-300 Steelcase Road, West, Makham, Ontario, Canada L3R 2W2

U.S. Center for World Mission, 1605 East Elizabeth Street, Pasadena, CA 91104

Westside Wholistic Family Center, 5437-39 West Division Street, Chicago, IL 60651

The William Carey Library, 305 1/2 Pasadena Avenue, South Pasadena, CA 91030

Wycliffe Bible Translators Academic Publications, 7500 West Camp Wisdom Road, Dallas, TX 75211

Appendix 2

About Face (Fellowship of American Chinese Evangelicals). 262 Riskell Drive, Oakland, CA 94619

Available Ministries (American Missionary Fellowship). P.O. Box 368, Villanova, PA 19085

CAP News (Christian Apologetics Project). P.O. Box 105, Absecon, NJ 08201

Challenge (Conservative Baptist Home Mission Society). 25 West 560 Geneva Road, Wheaton, IL 60187

EMISary (EMIS). P.O. Box 794, Wheaton, IL 60187

Evangelical Mission Quarterly (EMIS). P.O. Box 794, Wheaton, IL 60187

Evangelical Newsletter (Evangelical Ministries, Inc.). 1716 Spruce Street, Philadelphia, PA 19103

Evangelizing Today's Child (Child Evangelism Fellowship). P.O. Box 348, Warrenton, MO 63383

Expect (Evangelistic Association of New England). 88 Tremont Street, Boston, MA 02108

Forward (Far Eastern Gospel Crusade). P.O. Box 513, Farmington, MI 48024

Global Church Growth Bulletin. P.O. Box 66, Santa Clara, CA 95052

Gospel Message (Gospel Missionary Union). 10000 North Oak, Kansas City, MO 64155

Handbook of Jewish Mission Agencies (American Board of Missions to the Jews). 460 Sylvan Avenue, Englewood CLiffs, NJ 07632

Home Missions (Assemblies of God Home Missions) 1445 Boonville, Springfield, MO 65802

Interlit (David C. Cook Foundation). Cook Square, Elgin, IL 60120

Jesus N.Y. (Jews for Jesus). 60 Haight Street, San Francisco, CA 94102

Jubilee (Prison Fellowship). P.O. Box 40562, Washington, DC 20016

Missionary News Service (EMIS). P.O. Box 794, Wheaton, IL 60187

Missiongrams (Berean Mission). 3536 Russell Blvd., St. Louis, MO 63104

Missions USA (Home Mission Board, Southern Baptist Convention). 1340 Spring Street, N.W., Atlanta, GA 30367

Mojdeh (Iranian Christians International). P.O. Box 2415, Ann Arbor, MI 48106

Perspective (Institute of International Studies). 1539 East Howard Street, Pasadena, CA 91104

PULSE (EMIS). P.O. Box 794, Wheaton, IL 60187

Roundtable (Association of North American Missions). P.O. Box 13619, St. Louis, MO 63137

Saints Alive in Jesus (Saints Alive in Jesus). Edward Decker, P.O. Box 348, Marlow, OK 73055

The Shantyman (Shantyman's Christian Association of North America). Glen Duff, R.F.D. 2, Houlton, ME 04730

Silent Evangel (Christian Deaf Fellowship). P.O. Box 563, Hampton, VA 23369

Sojourners (Sojourners). 1309 2nd Street, N.W., Washington, DC 10005

Spiritual Counterfeits Project Newsletter (Spiritual Counterfeits Project). P.O. Box 2418, Berkeley, CA 94702

Together in Prayer (Gospel Recordings). 122 Glendale Blvd., Los Angeles, CA 90026

Utah Evangel (Utah Missions, Inc.). P.O. Box 348, Marlow, OK 73055

Voices (Trinity Evangelical Divinity School). 2065 Half Day Road, Deerfield, IL 60015

Volunteer (Association of Christian Prison Workers). P.O. Box 2110, Orange, CA 92669

Worldwide News (Pocket Testament League). P.O. Box 368, Lincoln Park, NJ 07035

Youthletter (Evangelical Ministries, Inc.). 1716 Spruce Street, Philadelphia, PA 19103

Zwemer Institute Prayer Bulletin, Zwemer Institute Newsletter (U.S. Center for World Missions). 1605 East Elizabeth Street, Pasadena, CA 91104

Appendix 3

LIST OF MISSIONS WORKING IN THE UNITED STATES

Asterisk (*) indicates those foreign missions with a home missions department.

(Editor's note: The author has made an effort to present a complete table of data. Because of the unavailability of data in certain cases, a number of entries have been left blank. Also, the reader should be aware that information regarding personnel is constantly changing, but a general idea as to the size of a given mission can be derived by noting its staff size.)

Missions	Fields	Founded	Staff
*A Christian Ministry in the National Parks 222½ E. 49th Street, New York, NY 10017	National Parks	1951	4
Agape House Ministries P.O. Box 1967, Upland, CA 91786	Japanese students	1979	2
Agape Force, Inc. P.O. Box 386, Lindale, TX 75771	Evangelism, drug centers	1970	120
Amazing Grace Mission 4361 Mountview Dr. Chattanooga, TN 37411		1983	2
*Ambassadors for Christ, Inc. P.O. Box A.F.C., Paradise, PA 17562	Chinese	1963	
Ambassadors for Christ P.O. Box 447, Pine Lake, GA 30072	Youth		
American Association for Jewish Evangelism 5860 N. Lincoln Avenue, Chicago, IL 60659	Jews	1944	14
American Board of Missions to the Jews, Inc. P.O. Box 2000, Orangeburg, NY 10962	Jews	1894	71
American-European Bethel Mission P.O. Box 30562, Santa Barbara, CA 93105	European		3

Organization	Focus	Year	Number
American Indian Bible Mission, Inc. P.O. Box 230, Farmington, NM 87401	American Indians		
American Indian Crusade, Inc. P.O. Box 1575, Glendale, AZ 85301	Camps, literature		
American Ministries International Rapid City, SD 57701			
*American Messianic Fellowship 7448 N. Damen Avenue, Chicago, IL 60645	Jews, Muslims	1885	12
American Ministries International P.O. Box 3718, W. Sedona, AZ 86304	Indians		
American Mission to the Deaf P.O. Box 245, State Line, PA 17263	Deaf		
American Mission for Opening Churches P.O. Box 130, 6419 E. Lake Road, Olcott, NY 14126	Opening churches	1943	40
American Missionary Fellowship, Inc. P.O. Box 368, 672 Conestoga Road Villanova, PA 19085	French, migrants, blacks, Hispanics	1817	147
American Remnant Mission 1820 Pine St., Suite 8, Walnut Creek, CA 94596	Evangelism		

Missions	Fields	Founded	Staff
American Rescue Workers 2827 Frankford Avenue, Philadelphia PA 19134	Rehabilitation of alcoholics, transients, children		
America's Keswick Whiting, NJ 08759	Conference, alcoholics	1897	3
Anti-Christ Information Center P.O. Box 1076, Alta Loma, CA 91701	Catholics		
Appalachian Bible Fellowship, Inc. Bradley, WV 25818	Education, Bible conference, camping	1950	60
Arctic Missions, Inc. P.O. Box 512, Gresham, OR 97030	Bible Institute, camping, Indians, Eskimos		165
*Association of Baptists for World Evangelization, Inc. P.O. Box 5,000, 1720 Springdale Road, Cherry Hill, NJ 08034	Jewish, minorities, church planting	1939	22
Association of Christian Prison Workers P.O. Box 2110, Orange, CA 92669	Prisons		
Association of Christian Truckers P.O. Box 208, Halifax, PA 17032	Truckers	1977	6

Organization	Ministry		
Awana Youth Association 3201 Tollview Drive, Rolling Meadows, IL 60008	Bible clubs	1950	56
Bancroft Gospel Ministry Route 1, Kingsport, TN 37660	Camps, schools		
Baptist Friends of Israel 830 Layton Road, Route 1 Clarks Summit, PA 18411	Jews		25
*Baptist International Missions, Inc. P.O. Box 9215, Chattanooga, TN 37412	Deaf, Indians, church planting, migrants		223
*Baptist Mid-Missions 4205 Chester Avenue, Cleveland, OH 44103	Blacks, Indians, Jews, migrants, Hispanics	1920	320
Baptist Mission to Forgotten People P.O. Box 37042, Jacksonville, FL 32236	Military, refugees, boys	1980	7
*Berean Mission, Inc. 3536 Russell Blvd., St. Louis, MO 63104	Hispanics, Indians		28
Bethany Children's Home Bethany, KY 41313	Children		
Beth Emmanuel Fellowship P.O. Box 831, San Francisco, CA 94101	Jews		3

Missions	Fields	Founded	Staff
Beth Yeshua 117 S. 21st Avenue, Hollywood, FL 33020	Jews		4
*Bethany Fellowship Mission, Inc. 6820 Auto Club Road, Minneapolis, MN 55438	Publishing House, industry, church planting, education		12
Bethel Bible Camp Route 1, P.O. Box 655, Columbia, SC 29023	Camping, conference, blacks		
Bethel Bible Village, Inc. P.O. Box 500, Hixson, TN 37343	Group child care	1954	
Bible Baptist Shepherd 1105 S. Miller, Farmington, NM 87401	Indians		12
*Bible Christian Union 418 Chestnut Street, Lebanon, PA 17042	Jews		115
Bible Club Mission, Inc. RD 1, P.O. Box 134, Marquette, NE 68854	Youth		
*Bible Club Movement, Inc. 237 Fairfield Avenue, Upper Darby, PA 19082	Children, handicapped	1936	256

Organization	Work	Year	Number
Bible Memory Association, Int'l P.O. Box 12,000, 1298 Pennsylvania, St. Louis, MO 63112	Literature, camps	1943	40
Bible Mission to American Indians, Inc. P.O. Box 244K, RD 4, Dallas, PA 18612	Correspondence courses		6
Bible Mission of Southwest Virginia, Inc. P.O. Box 390, Wise, VA 24293	Camp, school visitation	1939	11
Bible Tracts, Inc. P.O. Box 508, Waterloo, IA 50704	Tracts	1938	5
Bible Visuals P.O. Box C, Akron, PA 17501	Jews		
Bible to Youth Crusade RD 1, P.O. Box 144, Mt. Union, PA 17066	Youth		
Biblical Research Society 4005 Verdugo Road, Los Angeles, CA 90065	Research		2
Bill Rice Ranch Route 2, Murfreesboro, TN 37130	Deaf, camping, church planting	1950	20
Black Evangelistic Enterprises P.O. Box 4539, Dallas, TX 75208	Blacks, church planting		31

Missions	Fields	Founded	Staff
Brethren Home Missions Council, Inc. P.O. Box 587, Winona Lake, IN 46590	Indians, Jews	1940	71
Buffalo Hebrew Christian Mission, Inc. P.O. Box 1675, 28 Crestwood Avenue Buffalo, NY 14216	Jews	1947	7
Calvary Missionary Fellowship 5440 E. Lee Street, Phoenix, AZ 85712	Automobile, transportation, construction, printing		4
CAM International 8625 La Prada Drive, Dallas, TX 75228	Spanish		32
Campsite Evangelism, Inc. P.O. Box 1826, 1185 Christian Street, Harrisburg, PA 17105	Campgrounds, prisons	1968	36
Campus Crusade for Christ, Inc. P.O. Box 1576, San Bernardino, CA 92402	College campuses, prisons, military	1951	3,000
Campus Light of Life Fellowship, Inc. P.O. Box 4253, Sather Gate Station, Berkeley, CA 94704	College campuses	1973	
Campus Living Association P.O. Box 1, Whipple, OH 45788	Programs/Christian schools	1968	8

Organization	Focus	Year	Number
Carver Bible Institute and College P.O. Box 4335, Atlanta, GA 30302	Blacks	1943	20
Catskill Messianic Fellowship P.O. Box 621, Liberty, NY 12754	Jews		3
Cedine Bible Mission, Inc. RD 1, P.O. Box 239, Spring City, TN 37381	Camping, youth, blacks	1946	35
Central Bible Mission 1825 Myrtle, Detroit, MI 48208	Church planting		
Chapel Crusades, Inc. Winona Lake, IN 46590	Evangelism		
Chicago Gospel Mission, Inc. 1125 W. Madison Street, Chicago, IL 60607	Urban		
Chief, Inc. 1432 N. 70th Street, Suite C, Phoenix, AZ 85006	Literature publishers		
*Child Evangelism Fellowship P.O. Box 348, Warrenton, MO 63383	Children	1937	600

Missions	Fields	Founded	Staff
*Children's Bible Fellowship of New York, Inc. 88 Southern Parkway, Box 92 Plainview, NY 11803	Handicapped, camps, blacks, inner city, beach evangelism	1942	50
Children's Bible Hour P.O. Box 1, Grand Rapids, MI 49501	Radio	1942	5
Children's Bible Mission, Inc. 1628 Gary Road, P.O. Box 44 Lakeland, FL 33802	Camps, correspondence courses, clubs, etc.	1935	87
Children's Haven, Inc. P.O. Box 152, E. Douglas, MA 01516	Bible clubs, radio, camp	1943	8
*Chinese Christian Mission P.O. Box 617, 951 Petaluma Blvd., S. Petaluma, CA 94952	Chinese, discipleship	1961	14
*Chinese for Christ, Inc. 922 N. Edgemont Street, Box 29126 Los Angeles, CA 90029	Chinese students		
*Chinese Gospel Crusade, Inc. P.O. Box 42-595, Miami, FL 33142	Chinese	1959	

Name and Address	Focus	Year	Number
Christ for the Lumberjack RFD 1, P.O. Box 107, Athens, ME 04912	Lumberjacks	1961	2
Christ for the Nations, Inc. P.O. Box 24910, Dallas, TX 75224	Bible school, church building assistance		
Christian Jew Foundation P.O. Box 345, San Antonio, TX 78292	Jews	1951	26
*Christian's Mission 275 State Street, Box 106 Hackensack, NJ 07602	Catholics, Spanish	1891	
Christian Apologetics Project P.O. Box 105, Absecon, NJ 08201	Tracts		
Christian Apologetics: Research and Information Service P.O. Box 1783, Santa Ana, CA 92702	Seminars, research, evangelism	1975	43
Christian Approach to the Jews 1907 Chestnut Street, Philadelphia, PA 19103	Jews		2
Christian Bible Mission 917 Humbolt Street, SE Grand Rapids, MI 49507	Church planting		
Christian Destiny, Inc. P.O. Box 100, Wheaton, IL 60187	Literature, radio	1963	

Missions	Fields	Founded	Staff
Christian Encounter Ministries P.O. Box 2188, N. Babylon, NY 11703	Prisoners		2
Christian Evangelical Association P.O. Box 528, Port Angeles, WA 98362	Evangelism		
Christian Fellowship for the Blind P.O. Box 26, 1124 Fair Oaks South Pasadena, CA 91030	Literature, Braille	1949	16
Christian Indian Ministries P.O. Box 4221, Dallas, TX 75208	Indians		
Christian Jail Workers, Inc. P.O. Box 4009, Los Angeles, CA 90057	Prisons	1926	400
Christian Jew Foundation P.O. Box 345, San Antonio, TX 78292	Jews		1
Christian League for the Handicapped P.O. Box 98, Highway 67 & County F Walworth, WI 53184	Handicapped		
Christian Military Fellowship P.O. Box 36440, Denver, CO 80236	Military		

Organization	Audience	Year	Number
Christian Mission for the Deaf P.O. Box 1254, Flint, MI 48501	Deaf, Africans		2
Christian Prison Ministries P.O. Box 1587, Orlando, FL 32802	Video cassette, prisons		
Christian Prison Volunteers P.O. Box 80, San Juan Capistrano, CA 92693	Prisons, inner city children	1969	
Christian Service Brigade P.O. Box 150, Wheaton, IL 60187	Boys		
Christian Service Centers Crockett and Broadway San Antonio, TX 78298	Servicemen		
Christians United Reaching Everyone 2308 Moerlein Avenue Cincinnati, OH 45219	Blacks	1971	
Church Bible Studies 191 Mayhew Way, Walnut Creek, CA 94596	Tapes		
Cleveland Hebrew Mission P.O. Box 21100, 14518 Cedar Road University Heights, OH 44122	Jews	1904	10

Missions	Fields	Founded	Staff
Clyde Dupin Reachout Ministries, Inc. P.O. Box 565, Kernersville, NC 27284	Evangelism		
Conservative Baptist Home Mission Society P.O. Box 828, Wheaton, IL 60187	Mormons, church planting, blacks, Spanish, military		199
Conversion Center, Inc. Drawer V, 18 W. Eagle Road Havertown, PA 19083	Catholics		
Conversion Center West P.O. Box 23786, San Jose, CA 95153	Catholics		
Cornerstone Ministry 4751 Highway 280, S. Birmingham, AL 35243	Evangelism		
Crew of the Good Ship Grace 2400 Hyperion Avenue Los Angeles, CA 90027	Radio		
Cult Exodus for Christ P.O. Box 4033, Covina, CA 91723	Cults	1978	4
Cumberland Mountain Mission P.O. Box 667, Martin, KY 41649	Church planting	1978	4

Organization	Focus	Year	
Cutshin Bible Mission, Inc. Route 1, P.O. Box 408 Yeaddiss, KY 41777	Medical	1936	6
Deaf Missions RR 2, P.O. Box 26, Council Bluffs, IA 51501	Deaf	1971	
Death Unto Life Ministries	Evangelism, church planting, blacks		
Dessie Scott Children's Home P.O. Box 54, Pine Ridge, KY 41360	Children	1941	
Detroit's Afro-American Mission 7826 Melrose Avenue, Detroit, MI 48211	Inner city, urban, education		4
Diaconian Society, The P.O. Box 11437, Chicago, IL 60611	Evangelism		
Dial-A-Story P.O. Box 316, Oak Forrest, IL 60452	Telephone		
Discipleship, Inc. 5105 7th Avenue, Brooklyn, NY 11220	Evangelism		
Drive-In Ministries P.O. Box 12345, St. Petersburg, FL 33733	Evangelism	1957	16

Missions	Fields	Founded	Staff
Eastern Independence Church Mission, Inc. P.O. Box 45, South River, NJ 08882	Church planting		
Edwin Denby Memorial Children's Home 20775 Pembroke Avenue, Detroit, MI 46219	Children		25
Eliada Homes, Inc. P.O. Box 6337, Asheville, NC 28806	Children	1906	9
Emmanuel Bible Fellowship Barboursville, KY 40906	Camp, church planting, school visitation	1945	
Emmanuel Gospel Center P.O. Box 18245, Boston, MA 02118	Church planting, summer evangelism, Spanish	1938	13
Encounter Ministries P.O. Box 1266, Holmes Beach, FL 33509	Evangelism		
*Evangelical Baptist Missions P.O. Box 2225, Kokomo, IN 46902	Arabic-speaking, Muslims		18
Evangelical Home Missions Association P.O. Box 242, Wheaton, IL 60187	Church planting		

*Evangelism Mission, Inc. P.O. Box 9477, Chattanooga, TN 37412	Catholics, Jews, literature, church planting		81
Evangelistic Association of New England 88 Tremont Street, Boston, MA 02108	Service agency		
Evangelistic Faith Mission, Inc. P.O. Box 609, Bedford, IN 47421	Radio, education, medical	1905	24
Evangelization Society of Philadelphia 5415 Rising Sun Avenue Philadelphia, PA 19120	Jews	1911	6
Exodus International P.O. Box 2121 San Rafael, CA 94912		1976	36
Faith Gospel Witness Dwarf, KY 41739	Church planting		4
Faith Life Center 1391 Dorchester, MA 02122	Inner city		
Faith Missions 604 W. Bank Street, Winston-Salem, NC 27101	Church planting		4
Faith Mountain Mission of Kentucky Guage, KY 41329	Church planting		

Missions	Fields	Founded	Staff
Faith Ventures, Inc. Route 3, P.O. Box 130, Clarksville, GA 30523	Literature	1978	2
Family Altar Broadcast, Inc. P.O. Box 150, Waterloo, IA 50704	Evangelism		
Fellowship of Baptists for Home Missions P.O. Box 455, 137 Winckles Street Elyria, OH 44036	Blacks, Jews, Indians, Hispanics, youth	1941	288
Fellowship of Christian Airline Personnel 225 McBride Road, Fayetteville, GA 30214	Airline personnel	1973	57
Fellowship of Iranian Christians P.O. Box 1201, Bellflower, CA 90706	Iranians	1979	
Fellowship of ISA P.O. Box 1206, Minneapolis, MN 55440	Muslims		
Fisherman's Wharf, Inc. P.O. Box 391, 2058 Sheridan Rd. N. Chicago, IL 60064	Military	1971	3
Flagstaff Mission to the Navajos P.O. Box AA, 6 W. Cherry Flagstaff, AZ 86002	Indians	1952	32

Organization	Focus	Year	Number
Florida Chaplain Service 626 Ashberry Lane Altamonte Springs, FL 32701	Chaplains, military		
Follow-Up Ministries, Inc. P.O. Box 6183, Hayward, CA 94540	Literature		
Forever Generation, The P.O. Box 6636, Greenville, SC 29606	Students		
Forgotten Man Mission, Inc. 3940 Fruitridge, NW, Grand Rapids, MI 49504	Alcoholics		18
Friends of Alcoholics Foa Road, Pocohantas, MS 39072	Alcoholics		13
Friends of Israel Gospel Ministry, Inc. P.O. Box 123, W. Collingswood, NJ 08107	Jews	1938	24
Friendship Ministries, Inc. P.O. Box 9885, Colorado Springs, CO 80932	Mexicans, youth		
Frontier School of the Bible P.O. Box 217, LaGrange, WY 82221	Rural, frontier people	1967	16
Frontline P.O. Box 1100, La Canada, Fultridge, CA 91011	Cults, Jews, Mormons	1980	1

Missions	Fields	Founded	Staff
Fundamental Baptist Home Missions P.O. Box 12842, Gastonia, NC 91011	Church planting	1982	2
Galilean Baptist Missions 3120 Leonard Street, N.E. Grand Rapids, MI 49507	Koreans		2
Genesis Ministries Hershey, PA 17033	Evangelism		
Go-Ye Fellowship P.O. Box 26405, Los Angeles, CA 90026	Jails, children	1944	2
Go Ye Mission, Inc. P.O. Box 534, Tahlequah, OK 74464	Prison, church planting, evangelism, education	1943	82
God's Helping Hands, Inc. Route 1, P.O. Box 179-1 Bloomingdale, MI 49026	Children, chalk, puppets	1980	2
God's News Behind the News 6550 Margo Avenue, S. St. Petersburg, FL 33707	Evangelism		
Golden Key Prison Ministry RD 1, P.O. Box 287, Newark Valley, NY 13811	Prisons	1977	5

Organization	Ministry	Year	No.
Good News Mission 1063 S. Highland Street, Arlington, VA 22204	Prisons, Bible correspondence courses	1961	72
Good News Mission to the Navajo Indians, Inc. P.O. Box 66, Houck, AZ 86505	Indians	1939	4
Goodwill Home and Rescue Mission 79 University Avenue, Newark, NJ 07102	Rescue missions		
Gospel Association for the Blind, Inc. 4705 N. Federal Highway Boca Raton, FL 33432	Correspondence courses in Braille	1947	
*Gospel Missionary Union Drawer C, Smithville, MO 64089	Eskimos, Indians		28
Gospel Outreach P.O. Box 7078, Philadelphia, PA 19149	Catholics	1975	4
*Gospel Projects, Inc. P.O. Box 551, Lansdale, PA 19446	Evangelism		
*Gospel Recordings 122 Glendale Blvd., Los Angeles, CA 90026	Cassettes, recordings		
Grace Children's Home Henderson, NE 68371	Children		

Missions	Fields	Founded	Staff
Grace and Truth Evangelistic Association Star Rt., P.O. Box 23, South Gibson, PA 18842	Camp, youth	1965	
*Greater Europe Mission P.O. Box 668, Wheaton, IL 60187	Spanish	1949	
Hear O Israel P.O. Box 2784, Birmingham, AL 35202	Jews		3
Hebrew Christian Fellowship, Inc. P.O. Box 777, 1033 Twining Road Dresher, PA 19025	Jews	1944	11
Hebrew Christian Witness P.O. Box 2, San Bernardino, CA 92407	Jews	1955	4
Heir Force for Christ P.O. Box 4849, Baltimore, MD 21211	Evangelism		
Helps International Ministries P.O. Box 836, Harlem, GA 30814	Builders	1976	20
Hephzibah House 508 School St., Winona Lake, IN 46590	Rehabilitation for girls	1971	

Organization	Description	Year	No.
Hi-Way Bi-Way Christian Crusade 1425 Neal Drive, P.O. Box 427 Rossville, GA 30741	Youth, literature		4
Hiawatha Baptist Missions 1526 Plainfield, NE, Grand Rapids, MI 49505	Church planting, Spanish	1968	191
High Flight Foundation 5010 Edison Avenue Colorado Springs, CO 80900	Travelers		
*High School Evangelism Fellowship, Inc. 46 W. Clinton Avenue, P.O. Box 780 Tenafly, NJ 07670	High schools	1944	6
His Mansion P.O. Box G, Hillsboro, NH 03244	Rehabilitation		
Home Sweet Home 300 Mission Drive Bloomington, IL 61701	Home for needy, runaways	1917	
Hope Aglow Ministries, Inc. P.O. Box 3057, Lynchburg, VA 24503	Film	1970	10
*Hope Bible Mission P.O. Box 161, RD 1, Morristown, NJ 07960	Jews, youth, correspondence courses		

Missions	Fields	Founded	Staff
Hope Hospital Chaplain 1800 W. Charleston Blvd. Las Vegas, NV 89102	Chaplains, hospitals		
Hospital Chaplain's Ministry 780 E. Gilbert Street San Bernardino, CA 92404	Hospitals, chaplains		
Hospital Chaplains Ministry of America P.O. Box 3567, Fullerton, CA 92634	Hospitals		100
Illinois Bible Church Mission 2214 S. Laramie Avenue, Cicero, IL 60650	Church planting	1952	12
Independent Baptist Indian Mission P.O. Box QQ, Bapchule, AZ 85221	Indians		
Independent Bible Mission 149 Lamoreaux Drive Comstock Park, MI 49321	Church planting		25
Independent Bible Mission of Michigan, Inc. P.O. Box 7421, Grand Rapids, MI 49510	Church planting		
Inner City Impact 2704 W. North Avenue, Chicago, IL 60647	Hispanics, blacks	1972	6

Organization	Focus	Year	Number
International Board of Jewish Missions, Inc. P.O. Box 3307, Chattanooga, TN 37404	Jews	1949	37
*International Christian Fellowship 213 Naperville Street, Wheaton, IL 60187	Muslims	(1982)	12
International Friendship Evangelism, Inc. 862 Ostrom Avenue, Syracuse, NY 13210	International students	1972	2
International Messianic Outreach 2055 E. Lake Road, NE, Atlanta, GA 30307	Jews	1974	4
*International Missions P.O. Box 323, Wayne, NJ 07470	International students		6
International Prison Ministry P.O. Box 63, Dallas, TX 75221	Prisons		
International Students P.O. Box C, Colorado Springs, CO 80906	International students	1953	150
Inter-Varsity Christian Fellowship 233 Langdon Street, Madison, WI 53703	Campuses, blacks	1941	400
Iranian Christians International P.O. Box 2415, Ann Arbor, MI 48105-2415	Iranians, evangelism	1980	2
Israel's Evangelistic Missions 14001 W. 11 Mile Road, Oak Park, MI 48237	Jews	1960	5

Missions	Fields	Founded	Staff
*Israel's Hope, Inc. 2107 E. 9th Street, Brooklyn, NY 11223	Jews, Catholics, prisons	1938	3
Israel's Remnant 22,000 Avon, Oak Park, MI 48237	Jews		4
Israel's Remnant Messianic Center 120 Wyman Street, Lynn, MA 01905	Jews		1
Jews for Jesus 60 Haight Street, San Francisco, CA 94102	Jews	1973	60
Joy Ranch, Inc. P.O. Box 727, Hillsville, VA 24343	Children	1961	
Kansas City Youth For Christ 4715 Rainbow Blvd. Shawnee Mission, KS 66205	Youth	1943	2
Kentucky Mountain Evangelical Fellowship, Inc. P.O. Box 850, Martin, KY 41649	Church planting		
Kentucky Mountain Mission, Inc. P.O. Box 548, Beattyville, KY 41311	Church planting, camp	1938	25

Keswick Colony of Mercy Keswick Grove, Whiting, NJ 08759	Alcoholic rehabilitation	1897	3
King's Garden, Inc. 19303 Fremont Avenue, N., Seattle, WA 98133	Conference, education		
Latin Evangelical Outreach 813 Hanford Road, Fairless Hills, PA 19030	Spanish, radio	1981	
Laurel Gospel Center Manchester, KY 40962			4
Lay Evangelism, Inc. P.O. Box 3063, Marion, IN 46952	Laymen		
Lazy Mountain Children's Home, Inc. P.O. Box 815, Palmer, AK 99645	Children		
Lederer Foundation 6204 Park Heights Avenue, Baltimore, MD 21215		1973	2
Light Bearers Association of America 415 W. Madison Street, Chicago, IL 60607	Chaplains, jails, nursing homes		6
Living Word Ministries, Inc. 1316 Lindwood Lane, Winter Park, IL 32792	Military	1978	4
Los Angeles Hebrew Mission P.O. Box 26387, Los Angeles, CA 90026	Jews		4

Missions	Fields	Founded	Staff
Los Angeles Messianic Witness 14159 Weddington Street, Van Nuys, CA 91401	Jews		1
Lydia Home Association 4300 W. Irving Park Road, Chicago, IL 60641	Children		
Mailbox Club, Inc. 404 Eager Road, Valdosta, GA 31601	Correspondence courses	1965	6
Main Rural Mission P.O. Box 483, Bradford, ME 04410	Rural		
Manhattan Bible Church 401 W. 205th Street, New York, NY 10034	Inner city		
Message to Israel, Inc. P.O. Box 718, Lebanon, PA 17043	Jews, Russian radio	1937	86
Messengers of the New Covenant P.O. Box 152, 242 Shunpike Road Springfield, NJ 07081	Jews		4
Messianic Fellowship Center 613 S. 48th Street, Philadelphia, PA 19143	Jews		2
Messianic Jewish Alliance 3814 W. Lawrence Avenue, Chicago, IL 60625	Jews		1

Organization	Focus	Year	No.
Messianic Jewish Center 1132 N. Negley Avenue, Philadelphia, PA 15206	Jews		4
Messianic Jewish Movement Int'l P.O. Box 30313, Bethesda, MD 20814	Jewish literature	1963	5
Messianic Witness of Kansas City Overland Park, KS 66207	Jews	1943	2
Mexican Gospel Mission, Inc. P.O. Box 2402, 2925 W. Park, Phoenix, AZ 85002	Cubans, Hispanics	1931	16
Mid-America Mission, Inc. P.O. Box 220, Highway 62 E., Green Forest, AK 72638	Jails, camps, church planting, correspondence courses, conference	1958	26
Midwest Hebrew Mission 1349 Midway Parkway, St. Paul, MN 55108	Jews		2
Midwest Messianic Center 13056 Olive Street Road St. Louis, MO 63141	Jews		7
Migrant Missionary Fellowship 508 NE 8th Avenue, Deerfield Beach, FL 33441	Migrants, prison	1957	4

Missions	Fields	Founded	Staff
Miracle Hill Children's Home P.O. Box 492, Greenville, SC 29602	Children	1958	10
Mission Outreach Society 109 S. Main Street, Upperlevel, Box 227 Oregon, WI 53575	Counseling, camp		5
Mission to the Catholics Int'l P.O. Box 19280, San Diego, CA 92119	Catholics		10
Mission to the Deaf, Inc. P.O. Box 1031, San Jose, CA 95108	Deaf		
Missions to the Military P.O. Box 6, Norfolk, VA 23501	Military	1958	21
Mission to Mormons P.O. Box 322, Roy, UT 84067	Mormons		
Missionary Gospel Fellowship 200 W. Main, Drawer W, Turlock, CA 95380	Migrants, internationals, prison, inner city, blacks		75
Missionary Tech Team 25 FRJ Drive, Longview, TX 75602	Building, technical		

Organization	Ministry	Year	Number
Missions Outreach, Inc. P.O. Box 73, Bethany, MO 64424	Eskimos, Indians		20
National Jewish Mission P.O. Box 718, Lebanon, PA 17042	Jews		1
Navajo Bible School and Mission P.O. Box F, Window Rock, AZ 86575	Radio, school	1938	34
Navajo Gospel Crusade, Inc. 24826 County Road L, Cortez, CO 81321	Church planting, Bible school	1955	25
Navajo Gospel Mission P.O. Box 2803, 3901 E. Elpaso Drive Flagstaff, AZ 86003	Indians		39
Navajo Missions, Inc. P.O. Box 1230, 2103 W. Main Street Farmington, NM 87401	Indians		30
*Navigators, Inc. P.O. Box 1659, Colorado Springs, CO 80901	Military, campuses	1931	139
New England Fellowship 48 High St., Danvers, MA 01923	Church planting		
New Horizons Youth Ministries, Inc. 2720 44th Street, Grand Rapids, MI 49508	Youth		10

Missions	Fields	Founded	Staff
New Life 1929 Cahaba Road, S., Birmingham, AL 35223	Youth		
New Life Centers, Inc. Limerick, ME 04048	Military		
New Life Fellowship, Inc. Plumtree, NC 28664	Youth, camps, conferences		
New Life, Inc. P.O. Box 11303, Knoxville, TN 37901	In home discipleship	1969	10
New Testament Baptist Missions, Inc. Missions Building, Ravencliff, WV 25913	Church planting		
*New Testament Missionary Union 514 Banner Avenue, Winston-Salem, NC 27107	Hispanics	1902	
North American Jewish Ministries of the Christian and Missionary Alliance P.O. Box C, Nyack, NY 10960	Jews		4
North Arkansas Gospel Mission Hasty, AR 72640	Education, correspondence courses, church planting, camping	1947	7

Organization	Focus	Year	Number
Northwest Baptist Mission P.O. Box 2386, Grand Junction, CO 81502	Mormon, church planting	1967	15
Northwest Independent Church Extension P.O. Box 234, 22905 56th West Mountlake Terrace, WA 98043	Church planting		129
Northwest Mountain Mission P.O. Box 863, McCall, ID 83638	Church planting		
Nurses Christian Fellowship 223 Langdon Street, Madison, WI 53707	Nurses		
Nursing Home Ministries P.O. Box 68237, Portland, OR 97268	Retirement homes	1975	
Oak Hills Fellowship, Inc. Route 3, Bemidji, MN 56601	Church planting	1926	13
Oakley Kimble Gospel Tape Ministry 564 Harrison Ave., S. Plainfield, NJ 07080	Tape ministry	1972	2
Ohio Messianic Fellowship 632 Jefferson Avenue, Cincinnati, OH 45215	Jews		
Overseas Christian Servicemen's Centers P.O. Box 10308, Denver, CO 80210	Military	1955	8

Missions	Fields	Founded	Staff
Oneida Baptist Institute Oneida, KY 40972	Children	1900	
Open Air Campaigners P.O. Box 469, 1028 College Avenue, Wheaton, IL 60187	Evangelism		17
Open Door Ministries, Inc. 1044 Pershall Road, St. Louis, MO 63137	Blacks, literature		16
Operation Concern P.O. Box 594, Boynton Beach, FL 33435	Migrants		
Operation Out-Reach P.O. Box 1597, North Platte, NE 69101	Camp, internship for rural ministries		
Outreach to Troubled Teens P.O. Box 973, Wilmington, DE 19899	Youth		
Over the Road Evangelism, Inc. P.O. Box 5623, Clearwater, FL 33518	Truckers		4
*Overseas Missionary Fellowship 404 S. Church Street, Robesonia, PA 19551	Refugees, literature, children		9
Pacific Area Mission P.O. Box 729, Paia, Maui, HI 96779	Church planting, education		

Name / Address	Description	Year	Number
Pacific Garden Mission 646 S. State Street, Chicago, IL 60605	Rescue mission, radio		
Pals for Christ, Inc. P.O. Box 203, Bethphage, LI, NY 11714	Prison, Bible correspondence		
Peace for Israel, Inc. 7222 Taft Street, Hollywood, FL 33024	Jews		
Personal Ministries P.O. Box 167, New Lenox, IL 60451	Evangelism		
Pilgrim Fellowship, Inc. 1212 Arch Street, Philadelphia, PA 19107	Bible Visuals		3
Pioneer Ministries P.O. Box 788, Wheaton, IL 60187	Girls	1939	65
*Pocket Testament League 117 Main Street, Box 368, Lincoln Park, NJ 07035	Inner city, correspondence courses, literature	1908	15
Portable Recording Ministries 581 Windcrest Drive, Holland, MI 49423	Recordings		
Positive Action for Christ (Proteens) P.O. Box 1948, 833 Falls Road, Rocky Mount, NC 27801	Youth	1972	2

Missions	Fields	Founded	Staff
Prison Fellowship P.O. Box 40562, Washington, DC 20016	Prisons	1976	100
*Prison Mission Association P.O. Box 3397, Riverside, CA 92519	Prisons, Bible correspondence courses		15
Probe Ministries Int'l 12011 Coit Road, Suite 107 Dallas, TX 75251	Campuses	1973	29
P.S. Ministries c/o Campus Crusade for Christ Arrowhead Springs, San Bernardino, CA 92414	Simplified Bible study materials		
Race Track Chaplaincy P.O. Box 18998, Ft. Worth, TX 76118	Race tracks	1972	20
Railroad Evangelistic Association 2250 N. Pennsylvania, Indianapolis, IN 46205	Railroad personnel		
R.B.M. Ministries 5325 West F Avenue, Kalamazoo, MI 49009	Youth, camp, released	1935	30
Reach Out Evangelistic Association P.O. Box 469, Whittier, CA 90608			

Organization	Ministry	Founded	Number
Real Life Ministries P.O. Box 284, Taylors, SC 29687	Colleges		
Rock Bottom Evangelistic Association P.O. Box 1717, Turlock, CA 95380	Prison		
Rock of Israel P.O. Box I, Tarzana, CA 91359	Jews		4
Rocky Mountain Bible Mission, Inc. P.O. Box 5111, 1541 S. 3rd West Missoula, MT 59806	Church planting		24
Rural American Missionary Society P.O. Box 1061, Crab Orchard, WV 25827	Rural		
Rural Bible Crusade 133 S. Central, Marshfield, WI 54449	Rural		
Rural Bible Crusade P.O. Box 1286, Salina, KS 67401	Youth, correspondence	1937	4
Rural Evangel Mission, Inc. P.O. Box 7, Bulan, KY 41722	Rural		
Rural Home Missionary Association, Inc. P.O. Box 300, 309 N. Main Street, Morton, IL 61550	Church planting	1943	25

Missions	Fields	Founded	Staff
St. Paul's House 335 W. 51st Street, New York, NY 10019	Telephone hot line		2
Salvation Army 120 W. 14th Street, New York, NY 10011	Prison, correspondence courses	1865	
Sanders Bible Mission P.O. Box 105, Sanders, AZ 86512	Indians	1952	3
San Francisco Careers Class, Inc. P.O. Box 14611, San Francisco, CA 94114	Evangelism		
Saints Alive in Jesus P.O. Box 1076, Issaquah, WA 98027	Mormons		
Scripture Memory Mountain Mission P.O. Box 25, Emmalena, KY 41740	Camp, youth, school visitation	1932	34
Scripture Press Ministries P.O. Box 513, One Pennsylvania Avenue Glen Ellyn, IL 60137	Literature		
Seaman's International Christian Association 7500 Howe Road P.O. Box 144, Wonder Lake, IL 60097	Seamen	1935	

Sea-Tac Ministries Seattle-Tacoma Airport Room 213, Seattle, WA 98158	Chaplains in airports		
Send International P.O. Box 513, Farmington, MI 48024	Chinese, Eskimos, Indians	1947	101
Servicemen for Christ Baptist Mission 1015½ Washington Street, Junction City, KS 66441	Servicemen		
Servicemen's New Life Center P.O. Box 89, 508 Hall Street, Killeen, TX 76514	Servicemen		4
Shalom Scripture Studies P.O. Box 6363, Orange, CA 92667	Jews, education	1974	1
Shepherd's Home P.O. Box 111, Union Grove, WI 53132	Handicapped		
Shofar 4104 Spruce St., Philadelphia, PA 19104	Jews		1
*Slavic Gospel Association, Inc. P.O. Box 1122, 139 N. Washington, Wheaton, IL 60187	Russians, Eskimos, Indians		6

Missions	Fields	Founded	Staff
Solid Rock Ministries P.O. Box 489, Soldotna, AK 99669	Camp		11
Source of Light Ministries, Inc. P.O. Box 8, Highway 441, S., Madison, GA 30650	Correspondence courses	1954	50
South East Asia Fellowship c/o U.S. Center for World Missions 1605 Elizabeth Street, Pasadena, CA 91104	International students		
South Side Witness to Israel 2645 E. 75th Street, Room 208 Chicago, IL 60649	Jews		2
Southern Bible Institute 830 S. Buckner Blvd., Dallas, TX 75215	Blacks		
Southern Highland Evangel Route 1, P.O. Box 115, Pounding Mill, VA 24637	Camp, church planting, school visitation	1930	35
Southwest Bible Church Mission P.O. Box, Phoenix, AZ	Church planting		
Southwest Indian Missionary Association 4239 N. 16th Drive, Phoenix, AZ 85015	Indians, Spanish	1957	15

33

Sowers P.O. Box 1914 North Brunswick, NJ 08902	Truckers
*Spanish World Gospel Mission, Inc. P.O. Box 524, Winona Lake, IN 46590	Hispanics
Spiritual Counterfeit Projects P.O. Box 4308, Berkeley, CA 94704	Cults, research, evangelism
Steer, Inc. P.O. Box 1236, 120 E. Turnpike, Bismark, ND 58502	Livestock, crop projects
Success with Youth Publications P.O. Box 27028, Temple, AZ 85282	Youth
Tarrant County Baptist Association c/o Chaplain Bobby Cox 300 W. Belknap, Ft. Worth, TX 76102	Chaplain, jails
Taxi Evangelism Doctor's Park, Building 4, Asheville, NC 18801	Evangelism
Teen Challenge, Inc. 444 Clinton Avenue, Brooklyn, NY 11238	Drug addicts
Teen Crusade, Inc. 2160 Forest Park Road, Muskegon, MI 49441	Teens

Missions	Fields	Founded	Staff
Teen Haven Christian Youth Services, Inc. 1811 Willow Street Pike, Lancaster, PA 17602	Inner city, camp		
Teens, Inc. P.O. Box 322, 724 W. Washington Ave. South Bend, IN 46624	Inner city, camp	1965	5
Telephone Evangelism P.O. Box 26405, Los Angeles, CA 90026	Telephone		
Tennessee Mountain Mission P.O. Box 455, Dayton, TN 37321	Youth, camp		4
Theological Students Fellowship 233 Langdon Street, Madison, WI 53703	Publishers	1974	
Tom Skinner Associates 19 S. Harrison, SE., E. Orange, NJ 07018	Blacks		
Trans America Crusade P.O. Box 579, Downey, CA 90241	Internationals	1970	
Transport for Christ International P.O. Box 1562, Akron, OH 44309	Truckers	1951	8
Truckin' For Jesus 1900 Eighth Avenue, SE, Minot, ND 58701	Truckers		

Organization	Focus	Year	Number
Twin Cities Baptist Messianic Witness 1758 Ford Parkway, St. Paul, MN 55716	Jews		
*UFM International P.O. Box 306, 306 Bala Ave. Bala-Cynwyd, PA 19004	Spanish		4
United Gospel Outreach 7225-27 S. Main Street, Los Angeles, CA 90003	Evangelism		
United Indian Mission 2920 N. Third St., P.O. Box U Flagstaff, AZ 86002	Indians, Spanish		80
*United Missionary Fellowship 3636 Auburn Blvd., Sacramento, CA 95821	Mormons	1908	40
Utah Bible Mission P.O. Box 7111, Salt Lake City, UT 84107	Mormons		8
Utah Missions, Inc. P.O. Box 348, Marlow, OK 73055	Mormons	1951	2
Victory for America P.O. Box 611 Fairdale, WV 35839	Jails, drugs	1984	2
Village Missions 10121 Grandview Road, Kansas City, MO 64137	Church planting, publishers	1948	450

Missions	Fields	Founded	Staff
Visitation Evangelism Training, Inc. 219 Seventh Avenue, Altoona, PA 16602	Training, visitation	1968	2
Voice of Calvary Ministries 1655 St. Charles Street, Jackson, MS 39209	Blacks, radio		65
Waikiki Beach Chaplaincy Box 15488, Honolulu, HI 96816	Beach ministry	1970	3
Walk Through the Bible Ministry 230 Peachtree Street, NW, #2100 Atlanta, GA 30303	Evangelism, discipleship, tapes		
Watchman Fellowship, Inc. P.O. Box 768, Columbus, GA 31908	Evangelism		
WEC/Muslim Ministries P.O. Box A, Washington, PA 19034	Muslims		
*WEF Ministries 116 N. Bellevue Avenue, P.O. Box 307 Langhorne, PA 19047	Muslims, church planting		4
Western Indian Ministries, Inc. P.O. Box F, Window Rock, AZ 86515	Indians, radio, education	1937	43

Organization	Focus	Year	Number
Whispering Hills Mission RD 2, McCardy Road, Dansville, NY 14437	Inner city, camp, family counseling	1973	6
Witness, Inc. P.O. Box 597, Clayton, CA 94517	Jehovah's Witnesses, telephone		
Word of Life Schroon Lake, NY 12870	Youth, Bible clubs, camp	1938	40
World Evangelism, Inc. P.O. Box 700, San Diego, CA 92138	Evangelism		
*World Gospel Mission P.O. Box 948, Marion, IN 46952	Indians		17
World Home Bible League 16801 Van Dam Road, S. Holland, IL 60473	Correspondence courses, Bible distributors		
World Impact, Inc. 2001 S. Vermont Avenue, Los Angeles, CA 90007	Ghettos, inner city		109
World Messianic Fellowship, Inc. Box 449, 57 Edmond Street, Lynbrook, NY 11563	Jews, publishers	1908	2
World Missionary Outreach Ministries, Inc. P.O. Box 3397, Chattanooga, TN 37404	Jews	1976	7

Missions	Fields	Founded	Staff
World Opportunities Inc. P.O. Box 548, Hollywood, CA 90028	Evangelism	1961	9
*World Radio Missionary Fellowship P.O. Box 3000, Opa-Locka, FL 33055	Spanish		33
*WorldTeam P.O. Box 343078, Coral Gables, FL 33134	Hispanics, Haitians, Jamaicans		4
Worldwide Discipleship Association Suite 315, 1001 Virginia Avenue Atlanta, GA 30354	Prisons, campuses, discipleship		76
World-Wide Missionary Crusader 4606 Avenue, N., Lubbock, TX 79404	Printing	1943	5
World-Wide Missions 1593 E. Colorado Blvd., Box G Pasadena, CA 91109	Evangelism	1957	13
*Wycliffe Bible Translators International, Inc. 19891 Beach Blvd. Huntington Beach, CA 92648	Translation	1935	60
Yoke Fellows International Prison Ministry 230 College Avenue, Richmond, VA 47374	Prisons	1955	

		1938
Young Life 720 W. Monument Street Colorado Springs, CO 80901	Youth	
Youth Evangelism Association P.O. Box 506, Bath, NY 14810	Bible clubs, rallies	
Youth For Christ, USA 360 S. Main Place, Carol Stream, IL 60187	Youth	1,050
Youth Guidance, Inc. RD 1, Sewickley, PA 15143	Troubled children	14
Youth Specialties, Inc. 861 Sixth Avenue, Suite 411 San Diego, CA 92101	Youth	—

Total 12,154

60% Return	12,000
50% (Estimate)	8,000
Estimated total	20,000

Those totals do not include the following:

1. International Union of Gospel Missions   1,000
2. Christian Camping International   4,000
3. Denominational missions:

Home Mission Board, Southern Baptist Convention 3,700
Assemblies of God 300

4. Foreign missions with home department

Selected Bibliography

Aherne, Pat. "Priority of Christian Investment," *Brown Gold*. March 1981, n.p.

Alford, Harold. *The Proud Peoples*. New York: New American Library, 1973.

Anderson, Lorna. *You and Your Refugee Neighbor*. Pasadena: William Carey Library, 1980.

Arden, Harvey. "Wanderers from Vung Tou: Troubled Odyssey of Vietnamese Fishermen." *National Geographic*, September 1981, pp. 378-94.

Arroyo, Antonio M. Stevens. *Prophets Denied Honor*. Maryknoll: Orbis, 1980.

Banks, William L. *The Black Church in the United States*. New York: Macmillan, 1969.

Beaver, R. Pierce, ed. *The Native American Christian Community: A Directory of Indian, Aleut, and Eskimo Churches*. Monrovia, Calif.: MARC, 1979.

——————. *Pioneers in Missions*. Grand Rapids: Eerdmans, 1966.

Benson, Jim. *Worldwide News*. Lincoln Park, N.J.: Pocket Testament League, 1982.

Bentley, William H. *National Black Evangelical Association: Reflections on the Evolution of a Concept of Ministry*. Rev. ed. Chicago: William Bentley, 1978.

Bergman, Peter M., and Bergman, Mort N., comps. *A Chronological*

History of the Negro in America. New York: The New American Library, 1969.

Bjork, Don. "Reaching Newcomers to North America." Paper presented at the joint National Association of Evangelicals and Evangelical Foreign Mission Association Convention, Orlando, Florida, Spring 1979.

Bjornstad, James. "America's Spiritual, Sometimes Satanic, Smorgasbord." *Christianity Today,* October 1981, pp. 28-29.

Blackwell, John. *20th Century New Religions: Help or Hindrance.* New York: United Church of Christ, n.d.

Bodey, Richard Allen, ed. "Dr. Lloyd M. Perry on the Small Church." *Voices,* Fall 1980, p. 9.

Bouvier, Leon F., and Lee, Everett S. *Population Profiles, the Nation's Minorities.* Washington, Conn.: The Center for Information on America, n.d.

Brandon, William. *The American Heritage Book of Indians.* New York: Dell, 1961.

Brauer, Jerald C., ed. *Westminster Dictionary of Church History.* Philadelphia: Westminster, 1971.

Butler, Robert. *Why Survive? Being Old in America.* New York: Harper & Row, 1975.

Davis, James H. White, Woodie W. *Racial Transition in the Church.* Nashville: Abingdon, 1980.

Dayton, Edward R. "Reaching the Unreached." *That Everyone May Hear.* Monrovia, Calif.: MARC, 1979.

Dimont, Max I. *The Jews in America.* New York: Simon and Schuster, 1978.

Dolce, Philip C., ed. *Suburbia.* New York: Anchor, 1976.

Dologan, Thomas, and Scates, David. *The Navajos Are Coming to Jesus.* Pasadena, Calif.: William Carey Library, 1978.

Douglas, Truman. *Mission to America.* New York: Friendship, 1951.

Dwight, Henry Otis, ed. *The Blue Book of Missions for 1905.* New York: Funk and Wagnals, 1905.

Ellis, William S. "Los Angeles: City in Search of Itself." *National Geographic,* January 1980.

Ellison, Craig, ed. *The Urban Mission.* Grand Rapids: Eerdmans, 1974.

Ellul, Jacques. *The Meaning of the City.* Grand Rapids: Eerdmans, 1970.

Elsbree, Oliver W. *The Rise of the Missionary Spirit in America.* Philadelphia: Porcupine, 1980, reprint.

Enroth, Ronald. "Dimensions of Cult Conspiracy." *Christianity Today,* Fall 1981.

_____. *The Lure of the Cults.* Chappaqua, N.Y.: Christian Herald, 1979.

Farah, Caesar E. *Islam.* Woodbury, N.Y.: Barron's Educational Series, 1968.

Frenchak, David, and Keyes, Sharrel, eds. *Metro-Ministry: Ways and Means for the Urban Church.* Elgin, Ill.: David C. Cook, 1979.

Gallup, George, Jr., and Poling, David. *The Search for America's Faith.* Nashville: Abingdon, 1980.

Geruson, Richard T. and McGrath, Dennis. *Cities and Urbanization.* New York: Praeger, 1977.

Gibbons, Boyd. "Risk and Reward on Alaska's Violent Gulf." *National Geographic,* February 1979.

Goad, Kenneth H. "Shall We Destroy Foreign Missions?" Elyria, Ohio: Fellowship of Baptists for Home Missions, n.d.

Gore, Rick. "Can We Live Better on Less?" *National Geographic,* February 1981, pp. 55-72.

Greenway, Roger. *Guidelines for Urban Church Planting.* Grand Rapids: Baker, 1976.

Grimes, Barbara, ed. *Ethnologue.* Dallas: Academic, 1974.

Gunther, Peter J. *The Fields at Home.* Chicago: Moody, 1963.

Hale, J. Russell. *The Unchurched.* San Francisco: Harper & Row, 1980.

Harris, Hendon, M. *The Asiatic Fathers of America.* Taipei, Taiwan: Wen To, n.d.

Heimbach, Carol, ed. *The Logos Guide to Prison Ministries.* Plainfield, N.J.: Logos International Fellowship, n.d.

Hessellgrave, David J. *Planting Churches Cross-Culturally.* Grand Rapids: Baker, 1980.

Hill, Bob and Hill, Georgia, ed. "Launching Pad at Syracuse." *Evangelical Review,* 1981.

Hinkle, J. Herbert. *Soul Winning in Black Churches.* Grand Rapids: Baker, 1978.

Hirt, Carl. *Voluntary Chaplaincy.* Atlanta: Division of Home Mission Board, SBC, n.d.

Hollings, Ernest F. "The Rural Poor." *Current History,* Summer 1973.

Houston, Jack. "When Latinos Reach Latinos." *Moody Monthly,* July-August 1975, pp. 24-26.

Huisjen, Albert. *The Home Front of Jewish Missions.* Grand Rapids: Baker, 1962.

Hunt, Dave. *The Cult Explosion.* Irvine: Harvest House, 1980.

Hunt, Thomas C., and Maxson, Marilyn M. eds. *Religion and Morality in American Schooling.* Washington, D.C.: University Press of America, 1981.

Hunter, Edwin. *Small Town and Country Church*. Nashville: Abingdon-Cokesbury, 1975.

Jacquet, Constant, ed. *Yearbook of American and Canadian Churches*. Nashville: Abingdon-Cokesbury, 1975.

Johnson, Gregory. "The Hare Krishna in San Francisco." In *The New Religious Consciousness*, pp. 38-43. Edited by C. Glock and H. Bellah. Berkeley: U. of California, 1976.

Jones, Howard. "The Black Church in America." *Good News Broadcaster*, March 1972, p. 9.

Joyce, Raymond H. "Islam Is Here in North America." *Interlit*, December 1977.

Kane, J. Herbert. *A Concise History of the Christian World Mission*. Grand Rapids: Baker, 1978.

——————. *A Global View of Christian Missions*. Grand Rapids: Baker, 1971.

——————. *Understanding Christian Missions*. Grand Rapids: Baker, 1974.

Keller, John E. *Ministering to Alcoholics*. Minneapolis: Augsburg, 1966.

Kellerman, Joseph L. *Alcoholism: A Guide for the Clergy*. New York: National Council on Alcoholism, 1955.

Kephart, William. *Extraordinary Groups*. New York: St. Martin's, 1982.

Kuchersky, David. "Toward a Red Theology." *Christianity Today*, May 1975.

Latourette, Kenneth S. *The Twentieth Century Outside Europe*, 5 vols. Grand Rapids: Zondervan, 1969.

Lawrence, Edgar. *Ministering to the Silent Majority*. Springfield, Mo.: Gospel, 1978.

Light, Donald, Jr., and Keller, Suzanne. *Sociology*, 2d ed. New York: Alfred Knopf, 1979.

Lincoln, C. Eric. "Black Consciousness and the Black Church in America."

——————. *The Black Experience in Religion*. New York: Doubleday, 1974.

Martin, Walter. *The New Cults*. Santa Ana, Calif.: Vision House, 1980.

Martin, William. "Video Evangelism." *Washington Post*, June 1978.

Maust, John. "The Exploding Hispanic Minority: A Field in Our Backyard." *Christianity Today*, August 1980.

Mazzatenta, O. Louis. "New England's Little Portugal." *National Geographic*, January 1975, pp. 90-109.

McKenna, David L., ed. *Our Twentieth Century Target—A City in the Urban Crisis*. Grand Rapids: Zondervan, 1969.

McNickle, D'Arcy. *The Indian Tribes of the United States.* New York: Oxford U., 1970.

McWilliams, Carey. *Ill Fares the Land: Migrants and Migratory Labor in the United States.* Reprint ed. New York: Arno, 1976.

_____. *North from Mexico.* New York: Greenwood, 1968.

Melton, J. Gordon. *The Encyclopedia of American Religions,* 2 vols. Wilmington, N.C.: McGrath, 1978.

Miller, P. D. *The Imperative of Home Missions.* Richmond, Va.: Whittet and Shepperson, 1931.

Monsma, Timothy. "Urban Explosion and Missions Strategy." *Evangelical Missions Quarterly,* Winter 1981, pp. 5-12.

Montgomery, James H., and McGavran, Donald A. *The Discipling of a Nation.* Santa Clara, Calif.: Global Church Growth Bulletin, n.d.

Neusner, Jacob. *American Judaism.* New Jersey: Prentice-Hall, 1972.

Noss, John B. *Man's Religions.* New York: Macmillan, 1967.

Noyce, Gaylord B. *Survival and Mission for the City Church.* Philadelphia: Westminster, 1975.

Pace, Dale K. *A Christian's Guide to Effective Jail and Prison Ministries.* West Tappan, N.J.: Revell, 1976.

Pang, Wing Ning. "Build Up His Church for My Kinsman's Sake: A Study of the North American Chinese Church." Study presented at the North American Congress of Chinese Evangelicals, Pasadena, California, Summer 1980. Available from Chinese World Mission Center.

Pederson, Duane. *How to Establish a Jail and Prison Ministry.* Nashville: Thomas Nelson, 1979.

Pennington, Celeste. "Waikiki." *Missions USA,* May-June 1981, pp. 25-37.

Perkins, John. *A Quiet Revolution.* Waco, Tex.: Word, 1976.

Petersen, William. *Those Curious New Cults.* New Canaan, Conn.: Keats, 1975.

"Pliny's Letter to Trajan." Cited by Earl E. Cairns in *Christianity Through the Centuries,* 4th ed. Grand Rapids: Zondervan, 1961.

Powers, William. *Indians of the Southern Plains.* New York: Capricorn, 1972.

Prebish, Charles S. *American Buddhism.* North Scituate, Mass.: Duxbury, 1980.

Quebedeaux, Richard. *Those Worldly Evangelicals.* San Francisco: Harper & Row, 1980.

Rifkin, Jeremy and Howard, Ted. *The Emerging Order.* New York: G. P. Putnam and Sons, n.d.

Rosten, Leo, ed. *Religions of America.* New York: Simon and Schuster, 1975.

Schaff, Philip. *The American Church History Series,* 13 vols. New York: The Christian Literature Company, 1897.

Schnell, William J. *Thirty Years a Watch Tower Slave.* Grand Rapids: Baker, 1965.

Sheffer, George, Jr. "Young Life in Metropolis." *Christianity Today,* Summer 1966, pp. 11-13.

Smith, Griffen, Jr. "The Mexican People on the Move." *National Geographic,* June 1980.

Sowell, Thomas, ed. *American Ethnic Groups.* The Urban Institute, 1978.

Status of Christianity Country Profile—Hawaii. A special study prepared for the International Congress on World Evangelization, 1974.

Stacker, Harry. *A Home Missionary History of the Moravian Church in the United States and Canada.* Moravian Church, 1924.

Sweet, Warren W. *The Story of Religion in America.* Rev. ed. New York: Harper & Row, 1950.

Tenney, James S. "Singing from the Soul: Our Afro-American Heritage." *Christianity Today,* May 1979, pp. 15-19.

Tuma, Elias H. "The Palestinians in America." *LINK,* July-August 1981. Published by Americans for Middle East Understanding, Inc., p. 3

Van Baalen, Jan Karel. *The Chaos of Cults.* Grand Rapids: Eerdmans, 1958.

Waddell, J. and Watson, O. *The American Indian in Urban Society.* Boston: Little, Brown, and Co., 1971.

Wakstein, Allen M., ed. *The Urbanization of America: An Historical Anthology.* Boston: Houghton Mifflin, 1970.

Wang, Thomas. "Christian Witness to the Chinese People." *Thailand Report,* n.d.

Ward, Max. "Some of the Most Neglected People in the World." *Interlit,* March 1981, p. 17.

Washington, Joseph, Jr. *Black Sects and Cults.* New York: Doubleday, 1973.

Wilke, Harold H. *Creating the Caring Congregation: Guidelines for Ministering with the Handicapped.* Nashville: Abingdon, 1980.

Wilkerson, David. "A World on Eighteen Wheels." *Missions USA,* March-April 1981, p. 72.

Wilson, Samuel, ed. *Mission Handbook,* 12th ed. Monrovia, Calif.: MARC, 1979.

Winters, Ralph. "The Concept of a Third Era in Missions." *Evangelical Missions Quarterly,* April 1981.

Wooley, William. *Alcoholic Rehabilitation As Related to the Colony Approach.* Albany, N.Y.: The Ambrose, n.d.

The World of the American Indian. Washington: The National Geographic Society, 1980.

World Survey, 2 vols. New York: Interchurch, 1920.

Index of Subjects

Index of Persons

Moody Press, a ministry of the Moody Bible Institute, is designed for education, evangelization, and edification. If we may assist you in knowing more about Christ and the Christian life, please write us without obligation: Moody Press, c/o MLM, Chicago, Illinois 60610.